NOLO *and* USA TODAY

NOLO
YOUR LEGAL COMPANION

For more than 35 years, Nolo has been helping ordinary folks who want to answer their legal questions, create their own documents, or work with a lawyer more efficiently. Nolo.com provides quick information about wills, house buying, credit repair, starting a business—and just about anything else that's affected by the law. It's packed with free articles, legal updates, resources, and a complete catalog of Nolo books and software.

To find out about any important legal or other changes to this book's contents, sign up for our free update service at nolo.com/legalupdater or go to nolo.com/updates. And to make sure that you've got the most recent edition of this book, check Nolo's website or give us a call at 800-728-3555.

USA TODAY
The Nation's Newspaper

USA TODAY, the nation's largest circulation newspaper, was founded in 1982. It has nearly 3.9 million readers daily, making it the most widely read newspaper in the country.

USATODAY.com adds blogs, interactive graphics, games, travel resources, and trailblazing network journalism, allowing readers to comment on every story.

1ST EDITION

Easy Ways to
Lower YOUR
TAXES

Simple Strategies
Every Taxpayer Should Know

by USA TODAY Money Expert Sandra Block
and Attorney Stephen Fishman

First Edition	SEPTEMBER 2008
Editor	ILONA BRAY
Cover & Book Design	SUSAN PUTNEY
Proofreading	ROBERT WELLS
Index	SONGBIRD INDEXING
Printing	DELTA PRINTING SOLUTIONS, INC.

USA TODAY CONTRIBUTORS

Book Editor	BEN NUSSBAUM
Contributing Editors	JIM HENDERSON, FRED MONYAK, AND GERI TUCKER
Special thanks to	JULIE SNIDER

Fishman, Stephen.
    Easy ways to lower your taxes : simple strategies every taxpayer should know / by
Stephen Fishman. -- 1st ed.
        p. cm.
    Includes index.
    ISBN-13: 978-1-4133-0913-3 (pbk.)
    ISBN-10: 1-4133-0913-5 (pbk.)
    1. Income tax--Law and legislation--United States--Popular works. 2. Tax planning--
United States--Popular works. I. Title.
KF6297.F67 2008
343.7305'2--dc22

                                    2008018179

For information on bulk purchases or corporate premium sales, please contact Nolo's Sales
Department. For academic sales or textbook adoptions, ask for Academic Sales. Call 800-955-4775
or write to Nolo, 950 Parker Street, Berkeley, CA 94710.

About the Authors

Sandra Block is a personal finance columnist/reporter for USA TODAY's "Money" section. Her "Your Money" column appears every Tuesday in the newspaper and online at USATODAY.com. She joined USA TODAY as a markets reporter in 1995 and then moved to the personal finance team in 1996.

Prior to joining USA TODAY, Block also worked as a personal finance reporter for the *Akron Beacon Journal* in Akron, Ohio; held a Knight-Bagehot Fellowship at Columbia University in New York; and was a reporter for Dow Jones News Service in Washington, DC.

Stephen Fishman is a San Francisco-based attorney and tax expert who has been writing about the law for over 20 years. He is the author of many do-it-yourself law books, including *Deduct It! Lower Your Small Business Taxes, Home Business Tax Deductions, Every Landlord's Tax Deduction Guide*, and *Working for Yourself: Law & Taxes for Independent Contractors, Freelancers & Consultants*. All of his books are published by Nolo.

He is often quoted on tax-related issues by newspapers across the country, including the *Chicago Tribune, San Francisco Chronicle*, and *Cleveland Plain Dealer*.

Table of Contents

Your Companion in Winning the War on Taxes

We've all heard that death and taxes are inevitable. Well, death may be inevitable, but taxes aren't. With some planning, you can minimize the taxes you pay each year. Many people don't do even the most basic planning, and end up paying more to the IRS than they need to. You don't need to be one of these people—but the key is to start now, not on April 14.

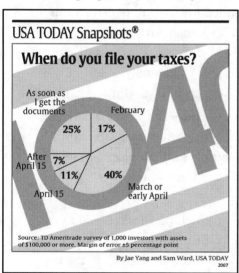

USA TODAY Snapshots®

When do you file your taxes?

As soon as I get the documents **25%**

February **17%**

After April 15 **7%**

April 15 **11%**

March or early April **40%**

Source: TD Ameritrade survey of 1,000 investors with assets of $100,000 or more. Margin of error ±5 percentage point

By Jae Yang and Sam Ward, USA TODAY
2007

We explain techniques for reducing taxes that every taxpayer should be familiar with. Nothing in here pushes questionable tactics like offshore bank accounts or convoluted tax shelters. We go over some basic (but often overlooked) strategies that are easy to use and are most likely to save you—the average taxpayer—money.

Let's take a quick look at our seven favorite tax-planning strategies, starting with the ones that could save you the most. You probably won't be able to use all seven in one year. That's fine. Just keep in mind that the more of these tips you put into practice each year, the less taxes you'll owe.

- **Maximize your tax-free income.** Certain types of income aren't subject to income tax at all. The single best way to avoid taxes is to earn as much tax-free income as possible. (See Chapter 2.)

- **Take advantage of tax credits.** Getting a tax credit is the next best thing to paying no taxes, because it reduces your taxes dollar for dollar—something a deduction doesn't do. Every year, the list of possible tax credits changes. Doing something as simple as adding insulation to your home can qualify you for a tax credit. (See Chapter 3.)

- **Defer the date when taxes are owed.** You'll have to pay tax on your taxable income sooner or later, but why not later? Deferring paying taxes to a future year is like getting a free loan from the government. There are many ways to do this, from postponing an employer bonus to investing in IRAs and other retirement accounts. (See Chapter 4.)

- **Deduct, deduct, deduct.** Perhaps the best-known way to reduce taxable income is to take tax deductions. The more deductions you have, the less tax you'll pay. We'll make sure you know all the possible deductions you're likely to qualify for, and act accordingly throughout the year. (See Chapter 5.)

- **Lower your tax rate on certain income.** How big a bite is being taken from your income? Federal tax rates can vary dramatically, from as low as 5% to as high as 35%. If you earn income from investments like stocks, bonds, mutual funds, and real estate, you may be able to take advantage of some of the lowest tax rates available (See Chapter 6.)

- **Shift income to others.** If you're in a high tax bracket, you can save a bundle by shifting your income to someone in a lower tax bracket—for example, your children. Recent changes in the tax law make this harder to do than in the past, but it's still a viable planning tool for many taxpayers. (See Chapter 7.)

- **Choose the best filing status and number of exemptions.** Few people give much thought to their tax filing status, but it can have a big effect on the taxes you pay. All individual taxpayers are entitled to tax exemptions. Those with dependent children or other dependents may be entitled to many. (See Chapter 8.)

CAUTION

This is not a how-to guide to filling out your tax forms. By the time you've got the forms in front of you, it will be too late to implement many of the tax-saving techniques you'll learn here. Instead, we cover strategies and tax-saving ideas to think about well in advance—so that you'll be among the few people looking satisfied on April 15.

Tax Basics Everyone Can Understand

To figure out which tax-saving strategies will work best for you, you'll need a basic understanding of how the income tax system works. Cheer up! This isn't as bad as it sounds. In fact, you may even find it fun to learn about taxes, particularly when you see how much money you can save with a little knowledge and planning.

What Can Tax Planning Do for You?

Tax planning means figuring out ways to minimize the taxes you have to pay each year. It's perfectly legal and makes sense for anyone who pays taxes.

This isn't tax evasion, which means cheating—for example, not reporting all your income to the IRS. Tax evasion is illegal, and people who are caught at it must pay all the taxes they owe, plus interest and penalties. Some even go to jail. Look at what happened to the winner of the first Survivor television series, Richard Hatch. He was sentenced to 51 months in federal prison for tax evasion after he failed to report his $1 million winnings to the IRS.

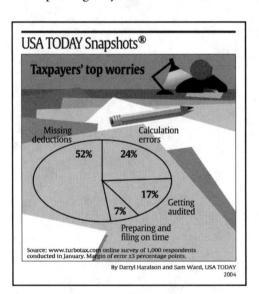

But you probably don't have $1 million to hide. In fact, you might be wondering whether tax planning isn't just for rich people who were looking for an excuse to sail to the Cayman Islands anyway. The answer is no. People with modest incomes can benefit from tax planning. And they often can do it themselves, without high-priced accountants and tax pros.

There are many easy-to-understand ways to lower your taxes you can implement yourself—for example, opening an IRA or hiring your children to work in your business. Others are more complex and may require the help of a tax professional, such as tax-free exchanges of business property. We'll focus on the ones that are easier to understand and let you know when you might need professional help.

Income Tax 101: How the System Works

First, a little background (we promise to keep it short). As the name implies, with income tax, you are paying tax on your income—for example, your salary from a job or the interest on your savings account. However, you don't have to pay income tax on all your income—not by a long shot. That's largely because not all income is considered "taxable income." The idea behind tax planning is to use all legal means available to keep your taxable income as low as possible.

To do this, you must go through a step-by-step calculation that will ultimately tell you how much you owe; it goes something like this.

- **Start with all your income.** First, you add up all the income you earn or receive each year, regardless of the source—salary, interest, net business income, investment income, and anything else. If you're married and file jointly (as the great majority of married couples do), include your spouse's income as well.

- **All Income – Exclusions = Gross Income.** Next, you get to exclude certain items from your income, to arrive at your gross income. (It's not called gross because it's disgusting; here, gross means the totality of your income, minus some important exclusions.) These exclusions include such things as gifts, life insurance proceeds, up to $500,000 in profits from the sale of your home if certain requirements are met, interest earned on municipal bonds, and other items. (Exclusions are covered in Chapter 2.)

- **Gross Income – Adjustments to Income = Adjusted Gross Income.** Hey, more subtractions! You get to adjust your income downward for things like contributions to deductible IRAs and self-employed retirement plans, contributions to health savings accounts, your health insurance payments if you're self-employed, moving expenses if you change jobs, and more. The resulting number is your adjusted gross income (AGI). (These adjustments are often called "above-the-line deductions," because they go before the line for AGI on your tax return.)

- **Adjusted Gross Income – Deductions and Exemptions = Taxable Income.** Now you can subtract out (1) any deductions you're claiming, and (2) your tax exemptions. The result is your taxable income. You'll choose between taking either a specified standard deduction or itemizing (listing) your deductions one by one. If you itemize, you can deduct expenses for such things as mortgage interest, state and local taxes, charitable contributions, and unreimbursed employee expenses (covered in Chapter 5). These are often called "below-the-line deductions" because they go after the AGI line on your tax return. Your exemptions consist of specified amounts you may deduct for yourself, your spouse, and your dependents (if any). (Exemptions are covered in Chapter 8.)

USA TODAY Snapshots®

Most taxpayers expect refund
More than half of taxpayers expect to get a refund after filing their 2007 taxes.

Getting a refund **53%**

Owing taxes **24%**

Breaking even **12%**

Not sure **11%**

Source: TransUnion's TrueCredit.com survey of 9,497 adults 18 and older conducted by Zogby International. Margin of error ±1 percentage point.

By Jae Yang and Veronica Salazar, USA TODAY 2008

- **Taxable Income × Tax Rates = Tax Liability.** By multiplying the amount of your taxable income by the tax rates set forth in IRS tax tables or schedules, you'll find out your tax liability. The tax rates vary according to the amount of your taxable income, from a low of 10% to a high of 35%. (These brackets are listed in Chapter 6.)

- **Tax Liability – Tax Credits = Tax Due.** Wait, you've got one last chance to lower your tax bill. You can subtract any tax credits you're entitled to, for such things as buying a hybrid car, paying for higher education or child care expenses, or making your home more energy efficient. (Tax credits are covered in Chapter 3.) The total remaining is the amount you owe the IRS.

EXAMPLE: Ron and Rachel are a married couple, with two young children, who file a joint income tax return. In 2008, Ron earned $70,000 in salary from his job, Rachel earned $20,000 from a part-time home business and they earned $5,000 in interest income. Their total itemized deductions are $12,000, which exceeds their $10,900 standard deduction, making it worthwhile for them to itemize. Here's how they compute their taxes:

Total Income	$ 95,000
Minus: Exclusions to Income	$ 95,000
Gross Income	$ 95,000
Minus: Adjustments to Income	$ 0
Adjusted Gross Income	$ 95,000
Adjusted Gross Income	$ 95,000
Minus: Itemized Deductions	− $ 12,000
Minus: Exemptions (4 × $3,500)	− $ 14,000
Taxable Income	$ 69,000
Tax Liability (25% tax bracket)	$ 9,938
Minus: Tax Credits	− $ 0
Tax Due	$ 9,938

Could Ron and Rachel have reduced their income tax by using one or more of the tax-planning strategies discussed in this book? C'mon, do you really need to ask? Here are just a few ways they could have reduced their tax:

- Deferred taxes. The couple could have deferred part of their income taxes to future years by opening an IRA and contributing the $10,000 maximum. Rachel could have put off collecting part of her business income until next year—$8,000 for example.
- Taken advantage of tax credits. The family could have purchased a hybrid car, and shaved thousands of dollars off their tax bill.
- Maximized tax deductions. Ron and Rachel could have increased their tax deductions by making a $1,000 contribution to their favorite charity.

Had they done these things, here's what Ron and Rachel's taxes would have looked like:

Total Income	$87,000	($95,000 – $8,000 of deferred income)
Gross Income	$87,000	
Gross Income	$87,000	
Minus: Adjustments to Income	$10,000	(IRA contribution)
Adjusted Gross Income	$77,000	
Adjusted Gross Income	$77,000	
Minus: Itemized Deductions	– $13,000	($1,000 more for charitable contribution)
Minus: Exemptions (4 × $3,500)	– $14,000	
Taxable Income	$50,000	
Tax Liability (15% tax bracket)	$6,698	
Minus: Tax Credits	– $2,000	(hybrid vehicle)
Tax Due	$4,698	

Too bad Ron and Rachel didn't buy and read this book. They could have paid $4,698 in taxes instead of $9,938.

How Low Can You Go?
Stopped by the AMT Stealth Tax

Before you start dreaming of reducing your tax bill to zero, realize that Congress tried to put a stop to that, with something called the Alternative Minimum Tax, or AMT. The AMT is designed to force taxpayers to pay a minimum amount of tax, even if they'd be required to pay less, or no tax at all, under the regular tax system. If you're required to pay the AMT, you pay it in addition to your regular income taxes.

But not everyone falls prey to the AMT. You're most likely to be subject to it if you have a high income (over $100,000 for singles and $150,000 for married couples) and have many exemptions and deductions that the AMT rules don't allow. You might owe the AMT if you:

- have lots of children—each one provides a $3,500 dependency exemption not allowed with the AMT

- live in a state with high income taxes, like New York or California

- have substantial miscellaneous itemized deductions, such as unreimbursed employee expenses or investment expenses

- have a very large medical expense deduction

- pay substantial interest on a home equity loan and didn't use the money to improve your home or buy or improve a second home, or

- receive stock options from your employer.

Unfortunately, if you are subject to the AMT, this book can't help you—it's a highly complicated system, and many of the tax-planning techniques we cover here simply won't work. The IRS has an AMT Assistant on its website (www.irs.gov) that you can use to see if you might be subject to the AMT.

Tax software like *TurboTax* can be a big help; but, if you're facing a substantial AMT liability you should see a tax pro. You might also wish to consult *The Alternative Minimum Tax*, by Harold S. Peckron (Sphinx Publishing).

Most States Have Income Taxes, Too

This book focuses on the federal income tax—the tax administered by the Internal Revenue Service (IRS). However, 43 states have their own income taxes. Many of these track federal law, so the tax-planning techniques covered in this book will probably help lower your state income taxes as well. Two states—Tennessee and New Hampshire—tax only dividend and interest income.

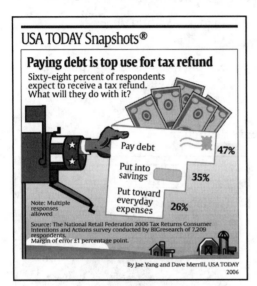

The seven states with no income tax are Alaska, Florida, Nevada, South Dakota, Texas, Washington, and Wyoming. Even if you owe state income taxes, they're likely to be much lower than your federal taxes (for a list of all state income tax rates, go to www.taxadmin.org/FTA/rate/ind_inc.html).

RESOURCE

For more information on state income taxes: Refer to your state tax department's website. A handy directory of links to these sites can be found at www.taxsites.com/state.html.

When to Start Tax Planning

People often wait until December to start thinking about ways to reduce their taxes for the year (if they think about it at all). This is too little, too late. If you really want to save some cash, start your tax planning no later than the beginning of the fourth quarter of the year—that is, October. But earlier in the year is usually better. For example, the best time to establish and contribute to tax-deferred accounts is at the beginning of the year, because you'll get a whole year's worth of tax-deferred income.

Start by making a simple projection of how much you'll owe in taxes this year without implementing any of the steps outlined in this book. (You'll need to estimate your income and expenses for the rest of the year based on how much you've earned and spent so far.) This can be done easily with tax preparation software such as *TurboTax*. There are also several online calculators you can use (www.hrblock.com/taxes, for example), but they don't provide as much information. If you like hard work, you can do it yourself with paper and pencil.

If you're happy with your projected tax bill, you don't need to do any more tax planning. But, if you want to reduce your taxes, keep reading.

The Best Tax Is No Tax: Income That's Tax Free

When you earn income, you usually have to pay income taxes. It doesn't matter where the income comes from—wages, bonuses, or benefits from a job; interest or dividends from investments; business or rental income; withdrawals from retirement accounts like IRAs and 401(k)s; or profits you earn by selling assets like real estate and stocks. There are exceptions, however.

Congress exempted certain types of income from taxes because it wanted to encourage people to engage in certain activities (many of which help stimulate the economy or contribute to the public good). Some of the most common ways to earn tax-free income are:

- selling your home
- saving money for your children's education
- investing in municipal bonds
- contributing to a health savings account
- receiving health insurance and certain other employee benefits from your employer
- spending some of your salary on out-of-pocket health costs instead of taking it in cash, or
- giving some investments to your children.

 TIP

The tax on retirement account earnings is only postponed. When you earn interest and other income on money in a 401(k), traditional IRA, SEP-IRA, or other retirement account, you don't have to pay tax on it right away. But, it's not tax free. Instead, the tax on these earnings is deferred until after you've retired and start withdrawing the money, at which time you have to pay taxes on it. (Roth IRAs and Roth 401(k)s work differently—withdrawals from those accounts are tax free.) Retirement accounts are covered in Chapter 4.

Almost anyone can earn at least some tax-free income. In fact, you're probably earning some already—for example, in fringe benefits like health insurance. For a person whose combined federal and state top tax rate is 40%, every dollar of tax-free income is equal to $1.67 in taxable income. That adds up to incredible savings—the trick is figuring out which types of tax-free income are available to you, and not letting them pass you by.

Timing Your Home Sale for Maximum Tax-Free Income

We're not suggesting you sell your home just to get a tax break. But if you do plan to sell, you may qualify for the largest tax break you'll ever get. If you meet certain requirements, you won't have to pay any tax on up to $250,000 of the gain from the sale of your principal home if you're single, or up to $500,000 if you're married and file a joint return. Even if you think you know all about this exclusion, keep reading to make sure you truly qualify and can make the most of it.

> EXAMPLE: Ed and Eve are married and file jointly. They bought their home in 1990 for $200,000. They sold it in 2008 for $600,000. Their gain (profit) on the sale is $400,000. If they qualify for the $500,000 exclusion, they don't have to pay any income tax on this gain. If they don't qualify, they have to pay a 15% long-term capital gains tax, or $60,000 (15% × $400,000 = $60,000).

You may do anything you want with the tax-free proceeds from the sale. If you buy another home, you can qualify for the exclusion in another two years if and when you sell that house. Indeed, you can use the exclusion any number of times over your lifetime as long as you satisfy the requirements discussed below.

Of course, the exclusion won't do you much good if you sell during a market that's gone flat, so that you don't earn any profit from your sale. And you can't write off losses on a home sale. But no matter what your local market is doing right now, U.S. real estate values have historically moved steadily upward. A time will probably come when you'll be able to take advantage of the exclusion.

Number one tax myth in the U.S.

Three out of ten taxpayers mistakenly believe that they can write off losses from a home sale, according to a survey by CCH (www.cch.com).

Forget the Old Law

The $250,000/$500,000 home sale exclusion came into effect in 1997. Before then, there were two different tax breaks for homeowners who sold their principal homes. One allowed homeowners to avoid (defer) any tax on their profits from a home sale if they purchased a new home within two years that cost as much as or more than their old home. Another law allowed taxpayers who were at least 55 years old to exclude one time, and one time only, up to $125,000 in profit when they sold their home. You can forget about these old laws. They are no longer in effect. If you meet the requirements discussed below, you may take advantage of the $250,000/$500,000 exclusion even if you previously used one or more of the old laws to avoid taxes on a home sale.

Can you show two years' ownership and use?

Here's the most important thing you need to know: To qualify for the $250,000/$500,000 home sale exclusion, you must own and occupy the home as your principal residence for *at least two years before you sell it.*

Your two years of ownership and use can occur anytime during the five years before you sell—and you don't have to be living in the home when you sell it.

One aspect of the exclusion that can be confusing is that ownership and use of the home don't need to overlap. As long as you have at least two years of ownership and two years of use during the five years before you sell the home, the ownership and use can occur at different times. This rule is most important for renters who end up purchasing their rental apartments or rental homes. The time that they lived in the home as a renter counts as "use," even though they didn't own the place at the time.

> **EXAMPLE:** Jackie rented the condo she lived in for five years—2001 through 2005. In 2006, she purchases the unit from her landlord and continues to live in it. In 2007, she gets a new job out of state and rents out the condo. In 2008, she sells it. Does Jackie qualify for the $250,000 exclusion? Yes. During the five years before the 2008 sale, she has two full years of ownership—2006 and 2007; and more than two years of use—2004 through 2006. Although she lived in the condo as a renter during 2004 and 2005, it still counts as use for purposes of the exclusion.

How do you make sure your home qualifies as your principal residence? It needs to have been the place where you (and your spouse, if you're claiming the $500,000 exclusion) live. You can have only one principal residence at a time. If you live in more than one place—for example, a condo in DC and a weekend home in Virginia—the property you use the majority of the time during the year will be your principal residence for that year. It doesn't matter whether your home is a house, apartment, condominium, townhouse, stock cooperative (a co-op apartment, for example), a mobile home affixed to land, or even a houseboat— they all can qualify for the exclusion.

Starting in 2009, a new law will limit the $250,000/$500,000 exclusion for homeowners who initially use their home for purposes other than their principal residence. For example, someone might originally own property as a rental or vacation home and then later convert it to a principal residence. In those circumstances, you must reduce pro rata the amount of profit you exclude from your income based on the number of years after 2008 you used the home as a rental, vacation home, or other "nonqualifying use."

> **EXAMPLE:** Jane buys a home on January 1, 2009 for $400,000, and uses it as rental property for two years. On January 1, 2008, she evicts her tenants and moves into the house, thereby converting it to her principal residence. On January 1, 2013, she moves out, and then sells the property for $700,000 on January 1, 2014. She has a $300,000 gain (profit) on the sale. Jane owned the house for a total of five years and used it as a rental property for two years before she converted it to her residence. Thus, two of the five years (40%) before the sale were a nonqualifying use, so 40% of her $300,000 gain ($120,000) does not qualify for the exclusion. This means that she must add $120,000 to her gross income for the year. Her remaining gain of $180,000 is less than the $250,000 exclusion, so it is excluded from her gross income.

A nonqualified use can occur only before the home was used as the taxpayer's principal residence. Time periods after the home was used as the principal residence do not constitute a nonqualified use. This is why Jane's nonqualifying use during 2013 does not reduce her exclusion. Similarly, converting your primary home into a vacation home won't reduce your exclusion when you sell as long as the house was your principal residence for two of the five years before the sale.

The most likely way for you to miss out on the benefits of this exclusion is to forget about the two-year requirement, and sell too early.

> **EXAMPLE:** Sean buys a houseboat in Seattle for $200,000 and uses it as his primary home for two full years—2004 and 2005. In 2006, he buys a house and uses it as his primary home instead. In 2008, he sells the houseboat for $300,000. Because the houseboat was his primary residence for two years, he qualifies for the $250,000 exclusion for single taxpayers and doesn't have to pay any income tax on his $100,000 profit from the sale. He then sells his house in 2009, earning a $50,000 profit. Because he took the exclusion for his houseboat in 2008, less than two years before he sold

the house, he doesn't qualify for the exclusion even though he used the house as his primary home for more than two full years. Had he waited another year to sell the house, he would have qualified.

The two-year rule is really quite generous, since most people live in their home at least that long before they sell it. By wisely using the exclusion, you can buy and sell many homes over the years and avoid any income taxes on your profits.

EXAMPLE: Nicole and Nick, a married couple who file jointly, bought their first house for $200,000 in 1998. They sold it for $300,000 in 2001 and avoided tax on the entire $100,000 profit using their $500,000 exclusion. They spent the money on a $400,000 house in 2001, which they sold for $600,000 in 2004. Again, they qualified for the $500,000 exclusion, so they owed no income tax on their $200,000 profit. They next bought an $800,000 house in 2004, which they sold for $1 million in 2006, owing no tax on their $250,000 profit. They purchased a $1 million house in 2006 that they sold in 2008 for $1.5 million—a neat $500,000 profit, all of which is tax free under the exclusion. From 1998 to 2008, Nicole and Nick earned a total profit of $1 million on the sales of their four homes, and didn't have to pay a penny in taxes on these profits.

How often do Americans sell their homes?

The average is every seven years.

Need to sell early? Partial exclusions

What if you have no choice but to sell your home at a time when you don't comply with all the requirements for the exclusion? Say, for example, you must sell before you've lived in the home for two years, or you've already used the exclusion for another home less than two years ago. Good news: You may still qualify for a partial exclusion if you have a good excuse for selling the property. Good excuses include:

- a change in your place of employment
- health problems that require you to move, or
- circumstances you didn't foresee when you bought the home that force you to sell it—for example, a death in the family, losing your job and qualifying for unemployment, not being able to afford the house anymore because of a change in employment or marital status, a natural disaster that destroys your house, or you or your spouse have twins or other multiple births.

A change in the place of employment is always a valid excuse if the location of the new job is at least 50 miles away from your old home. Moves of fewer than 50 miles may qualify depending on the circumstances.

Health problems are a valid excuse if a doctor recommends that you move—for example, you have asthma and your doctor tells you that living in Arizona would be better for you than Maine. The health problems can be yours, any co-owner of the property's, or a close family member's—for example, a spouse, child, or parent. Thus, for example, you can move if you need to be closer to an ill parent. If you want to use the health exception, be sure to get a letter from your doctor stating that the move is for health reasons and what they are. Keep the letter with your tax files.

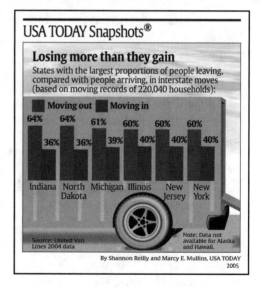

USA TODAY Snapshots®

Losing more than they gain

States with the largest proportions of people leaving, compared with people arriving, in interstate moves (based on moving records of 220,040 households):

■ Moving out ■ Moving in

	Indiana	North Dakota	Michigan	Illinois	New Jersey	New York
Moving out	64%	64%	61%	60%	60%	60%
Moving in	36%	36%	39%	40%	40%	40%

Source: United Van Lines 2004 data

Note: Data not available for Alaska and Hawaii.

By Shannon Reilly and Marcy E. Mullins, USA TODAY 2005

The amount of the exclusion will usually be based on the percentage of the two years that you met the requirements. For example, if you own and occupy a home for one year (50% of two years), you may exclude 50% of the regular maximum amount—up to $125,000 for a single taxpayer and $250,000 for married couples. You can figure the percentage using days or months.

> **TIP**
> **How will you back up your excuse?** No need to send anything to the IRS when you file your taxes. But if you've lived in the home for less than two years, you should keep good records in case you're audited. Useful documents include notice of a job transfer, a letter from your doctor, or birth certificates for the quadruplets.

$500,000 exclusion for married couples

If you're married and want to use the full $500,000 exclusion, you'll need to show that *all* of the following are true:

- you are legally married and file a joint return for the year
- *either* you or your spouse meets the ownership test
- *both* you and your spouse meet the use test, and
- during the two-year period ending on the date of the sale, neither you nor your spouse excluded gain from the sale of another home.

If either spouse does not satisfy all these requirements, the exclusion is figured separately for each spouse—meaning each can qualify for up to $250,000. When figuring out ownership and use, each spouse is treated as having owned the property during the period that either spouse owned the property.

> **EXAMPLE:** Emily and Jamie get married in June 2008 and become co-owners of a house that Emily had owned since 2002. They've been living together in the house since 2004. When they sell the home in June 2009, they both meet the ownership and use test, even though Jamie owned the home for only a year.

Starting in 2008, if your spouse dies and you sell your home, you qualify for the $500,000 exclusion if the sale occurs within two years after the date of death and all the other requirements were met immediately before the date of death. (That's a switch from a more stringent prior law, which, among other things, gave the surviving spouse less time to sell the house.)

How unmarried couples can use the exclusion

For joint owners who are not married, up to $250,000 of gain is tax free for each qualifying owner.

> EXAMPLE: Robin and Leslie bought a house together for $200,000. They lived in it for five years before selling it for $700,000. Dividing up their profits evenly, each earned $250,000 on the sale; and each may take a $250,000 exclusion. Neither of the two owes any tax on the deal.

How divorcing couples can use the exclusion

If you're divorcing and you own a house together that has gone up in value since you bought it, there are ways to get the full $500,000 exclusion, but you'll need to make sure you both own the house when you sell.

> EXAMPLE: Melinda and Mel were married for 20 years and owned a house together. Their divorce became final in 2007. They both moved out of the house and rented it out in December of that year. In 2008, they sold their house for a $400,000 profit and split the proceeds. They are each entitled to a $250,000 exclusion on their separate tax returns, so neither one needs to pay tax on their $200,000 individual gain.

If you're not yet divorced, avoid giving the house to one person in the course of the divorce. If that person later sells, they'll receive all the profit (as sole owner) and will have no way of bringing the ex-spouse into the picture to expand the exclusion beyond $250,000. If you can't afford to hang onto the house while going your separate ways, it would be better to sell the house while you're still married.

If your gain on the sale exceeds the exclusion

If you qualify for the $250,000 or $500,000 exclusion and your profit from the sale of your home is less than that amount, you're sitting pretty. You'll owe no income tax on the sale. Indeed, *you don't even have to report the sale on your income tax return.*

On the other hand, if your profit exceeds your exclusion amount, you'll have to list the excess as taxable income and pay tax on it. Remember—it's not the total amount of money you receive for the sale of your home, but the *amount of gain* on the sale that determines your tax bill.

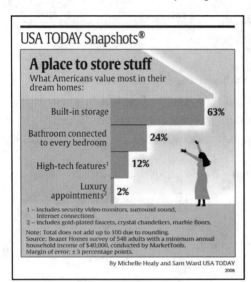

USA TODAY Snapshots®

A place to store stuff
What Americans value most in their dream homes:

Built-in storage **63%**

Bathroom connected to every bedroom **24%**

High-tech features[1] **12%**

Luxury appointments[2] **2%**

1 – includes security video monitors, surround sound, Internet connections
2 – includes gold-plated faucets, crystal chandeliers, marble floors.

Note: Total does not add up to 100 due to rounding.
Source: Beazer Homes survey of 548 adults with a minimum annual household income of $40,000, conducted by MarketTools.
Margin of error: ± 3 percentage points.

By Michelle Healy and Sam Ward USA TODAY 2008

If you owned the home for at least 12 months, you'll be taxed at the long-term capital gains rate, currently 15% for most people. (See Chapter 6 for more on capital gains and determining basis in property.)

EXAMPLE: Jim and Jennifer bought their home in 1980 for $100,000, including fees and other expenses. While they lived there, they spent $50,000 adding on a new bedroom and garage. That brings their tax basis (original costs plus improvements) to $150,000. Jim and Jennifer sold the house in 2008 for $800,000 (after expenses and commissions). Their gain on the sale is $650,000 (the purchase price minus their basis). They qualify for the $500,000 exclusion, but they still owe income tax on $150,000 of the sale proceeds.

Remember when we advised you not to sell your house just for the exclusion? Let's qualify that just a bit. If you're thinking of selling anyway and your potential profit on your home is nearing or above the applicable exclusion amount, then the sooner you sell the better (usually). You can turn around and buy a new home with all or part of the money and use the exclusion again in two or more years if you sell.

If you don't qualify for the exclusion

If you don't qualify for the home sale exclusion at all, you'll have to pay tax on all the gain from the sale of your home. If you owned the home for at least one year, you'll at least qualify for the long-term capital gains rate, which is currently 15% for most taxpayers. If you owned the property for less than one year, you'll have to pay tax at the short-term capital gains rate, which is the same rate as for ordinary income—up to 35%, depending on your tax bracket. Ouch.

If selling means a huge tax bill, you may want to think about possible alternatives. For example, you could convert the home into a rental property and either hold onto it or exchange it for another rental property (a somewhat complicated arrangement that we describe in detail in Chapter 4).

The Tax Advantages to Staying in One House

The single most effective way to avoid capital gains taxes on your home is, of course, to make it your permanent home. And there's another tax benefit to staying put: When you die, your home's value for tax purposes is "stepped up" to its fair market value. As a result, no tax would ever be paid, by you or your heirs, on the appreciation your home earned while you were alive.

EXAMPLE: Ernie and Edna purchased their home in 1950 for $50,000. In 2008, it is worth $1 million. If they sold the house in 2008, they'd have a $950,000 gain, far in excess of their $500,000 home sale exclusion. Instead, they continue to live in it. Assume they both die in 2010, leaving the home to their daughter Edwina. At their death, the home is worth $1.3 million—this becomes its value in Edwina's hands for tax purposes. If Edwina later sells the home, her taxable gain will be the amount she earns in excess of the home's $1.3 million tax basis.

Or you could sell the home in an installment sale, meaning the buyer pays you the purchase price over several years instead of all at once. You still have to pay tax on any profit you obtain over your applicable exclusion, but you pay only a little at a time as you receive your installment payments. (See Chapter 4 for more on installment sales.)

Limits on the exclusion if you've claimed a home office

Even if you qualify for the home sale exclusion, you'll owe some tax if you had an office in your home and took the home office deduction in prior years. That's because you were getting a depreciation deduction for the home office portion of your property—something you don't get for property used for personal purposes. You'll have to pay a 25% income tax on all the depreciation deductions you took after May 6, 1997 on the office.

> EXAMPLE: Carlos, a writer, used 10% of his home as a home office during 2001 through 2009. During that time he took $10,000 in depreciation deductions as part of his home office deduction. He sells his home in 2009 for a $200,000 profit. He qualifies for the $250,000 exclusion, so he doesn't have to pay any income tax on his profit. But he must pay a 25% tax on his home office depreciation deductions—$2,500.

Things don't work out nearly as well if you use a separate building, such as a free-standing garage, as an office (instead of using a space inside your home). The separate building is treated as a commercial property separate from your home. You'll need to allocate the gain on the sale of your property between the two properties, and the exclusion can be used only for the gain on the sale of your actual home.

EXAMPLE: Carlita, a writer, owns a three-bedroom house and uses a separate one-bedroom guest house on her property as her office. She sells the entire property for a $300,000 gain. She figures that the guest house accounts for 20% of the proceeds, so she must allocate $240,000 for the main house and $60,000 for the guest house. She may use the home sale exclusion for the gain on her principal house, but not for the guest house. Thus, she must pay income tax on the $60,000 gain from the guest house.

The Minor Advantage: Tax-Free Income for Children

It doesn't seem right, but children have to pay taxes on their income, just like everybody else. Fortunately, a certain amount of income earned or received by a child is tax free—just how much depends on the child's age.

Giving investments to your children

Parents, grandparents, and other relatives love to give children things like stocks, bonds, mutual funds, and savings accounts. This property generates investment income—interest, dividends, and profits from asset sales. It's called "unearned income," because the earner didn't actually have to work at a job or business to make the money.

Although your child doesn't have to pay tax upon receiving a gift, the child will be responsible for paying tax on any unearned income the property generates. How this investment income is taxed depends on the child's age—the rules change for children who turn 19 before the end of the tax year.

Children under 19 don't have to report or pay any tax on their first $900 of income for the year. Their minimum standard deduction is $900. That makes giving children income-producing investments a good strategy for creating a modest amount of tax-free income.

No Income Tax on Gifts

A person who receives a gift or inheritance never has to pay any income tax or gift tax on its value. However, the person who makes the gift must report gifts over a certain amount ($12,000 in 2008) and might eventually have to pay gift tax out of his or her estate. This potential gift tax concerns only the well-off: Someone would have to give away more than $1 million in money or property over a lifetime for his or her estate to be subject to any gift taxes. Moreover, there are ways to give away even more than $1 million without owing gift taxes. For more information on gifts, see *Plan Your Estate*, by Denis Clifford (Nolo).

If a child under 19 earns between $900 and $1,800 in investment income, the child becomes subject to the "kiddie tax." The child is taxed on this income at the child's tax rate, which is usually the lowest income tax rate (currently 10%). Any investment income over $1,800 is taxed at the parent's highest income tax rate, which can be as high as 35%.

There is no kiddie tax for children 19 years of age and older, with one very big exception: Children age 19 to 23 who are full-time students are treated the same as those under 19 years old if their earned income is less than half the support they receive from other sources.

Children over 19 who are not full-time students, or who provide over half their support from a job, are taxed like adults—all their income is taxed at their own income tax rates, not their parents' rates. If a child doesn't work, he or she will have the $900 standard deduction (just like children under 19) and won't have to pay any tax on that amount of income. Any income over $900 will be taxed at the child's own tax rates, which are usually lower than those of the parents.

(See Chapter 7 for a detailed discussion of transferring property to children.)

CAUTION

Do you really want to give your children investment property?
There can be significant drawbacks down the line. First of all, you
must give up ownership of the property. Even if you set up a custodial
account—most likely under the Uniform Gifto Minors Act (UGMA)
or Uniform Transfers to Minors Act (UTMA)—you can control the
funds as custodian only until the child reaches age 18 or 21 years of age,
depending on your state. After that, the child can use the account for
anything, whether it's college or a new BMW.

Also, the more money a child has in his or her name, the less financial
aid will be available. (See "Know Financial Aid Rules," below.)

Mommy, what's a 1040? Tax on children who work

Children who work may receive salaries, wages, tips, and other money
known as "earned income." This could be anything from babysitting
income to waitress salary and
tips. All earned income is taxed
at the child's tax rates, no matter
how old the child is. There's no
kiddie tax for earned income.

A child who works can
have a much larger standard
deduction than a child who
just has investment income.

> ### Who buys vacation homes?
>
> *The typical buyer in 2007 was 46 years
> old, had a household income of $99,100,
> and bought a place around 287 miles
> from their primary home. (Source:
> Realtor.com.)*

All taxpayers owe tax only on income above the standard deduction
amount, so a child can earn more tax-free income with earned income.
A working child gets a standard deduction that is the *larger* of:

- $900, or
- the amount of the child's earned income for the year plus $250
  (but this amount can't be more than the standard deduction for
  single adults—$5,450 in 2008).

EXAMPLE: Phillipa, a 17-year-old, earned $2,000 from babysitting during the year and $500 in interest income. Her standard deduction is limited to the greater of $900 or her earned income ($2,000) plus $250. Since $2,250 is larger than $900, her standard deduction is $2,250. Phillipa need only pay tax on $250 of her income ($2,500 minus $2,250 standard deduction = $250).

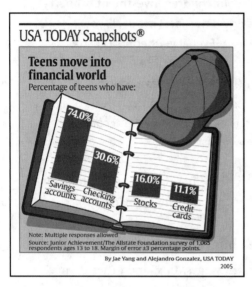

USA TODAY Snapshots®

Teens move into financial world
Percentage of teens who have:

74.0% Savings accounts
30.6% Checking accounts
16.0% Stocks
11.1% Credit cards

Note: Multiple responses allowed
Source: Junior Achievement/The Allstate Foundation survey of 1,065 respondents ages 13 to 18. Margin of error ±3 percentage points.
By Jae Yang and Alejandro Gonzalez, USA TODAY 2005

A child can have a standard deduction of as much as $5,450 in 2008 (the deduction for adult single taxpayers), provided the child had at least $5,200 in earned income from a job.

EXAMPLE: Burt, a 16-year-old, earned $6,000 from a summer job during 2008 and had $1,000 in investment income from some stocks his grandparents gave him. His standard deduction is $5,450 (the standard deduction for single adults, because his earned income plus $250 exceeds this amount). He must pay income tax on only $1,550 of his $7,000 total income.

TIP

It's not too early for your child to open an IRA. A child can get even more tax-free income by using salary or other earned income to open a traditional IRA and deduct the contributions. By putting in the maximum $5,000, the child could earn up to $10,450 per year tax free ($5,450 standard deduction + $5,000 IRA contribution = $10,450). Tax must be paid on the income the IRA earns only when the money is withdrawn.

If you have a business, whether full- or part-time, a great way to give your children earned income is to hire them as your employees (See Chapter 7 for details.)

Tax-Free Home Rental Income

A little-known tax rule allows homeowners to rent out their vacation homes or principal homes for a limited time and pay no tax on the rental income. That's right—tax-free money! It doesn't matter how much you earn.

To qualify for this tax-free treatment, during the year you must:

- rent out your home for 14 days or less, and
- personally use the home for *15 days or more*. Internal Revenue Code (I.R.C.) Sec. 280A(g).)

The home can be a vacation home, second home, or your principal home. This rule can provide you with a real windfall if you own a home in a desirable area where people are looking for short-term rentals.

> EXAMPLE 1: Senzo lives full-time in a condo on the beach in Hawaii. He leaves for a trip to Europe and rents out his condo for two weeks to some vacationers, earning $2,000. He doesn't have to pay income tax on this rental income.

> EXAMPLE 2: Yumiko rents her Florida beachfront condominium for 14 days during the summer for $3,000. She lives in the condo herself for two months during the year. She doesn't owe a penny of income tax on the rental income.

But don't get too ambitious about your tax savings. Because your home is considered your personal residence for tax purposes, you don't get to act like a business and deduct your operating expenses while it's rented out, nor depreciation. You don't file Schedule E as landlords do to report their income and expenses. However, you may continue to deduct your home mortgage interest and real estate taxes just like any other homeowner does.

Bonds, Roths, and Other Tax-Free Investment Income

Ordinarily, you have to pay tax on the income you earn on investments. For example, if your savings account earns $1,000 in interest, the bank sends you an end-of-year statement and you add that amount to your taxable income.

However, some types of investments are wholly or partly tax free—that is, you don't pay tax on the interest or income you receive from them. Bonds issued by state and local governments are the mainstay of tax-free investing (U.S. government bonds and notes have some tax-free attributes as well). However, muni bonds aren't the only tax-free game in town. Roth IRAs and Roth 401(k)s are the latest tax-free investment vehicles. And specialized accounts used to save money for a child's college education (discussed in the next section) can also be a major source of tax-free investment income.

Of course, the interest rates on these investments tend to be lower than on others, in recognition of their tax benefits. However, depending on your tax bracket, you may still come out ahead, as we'll describe below.

Tax-free bonds

Issuing bonds is one of the main ways that corporations and governments raise money. When you buy a bond, you are essentially lending money to the bond issuer. The issuer promises to send you regular interest payments at a specified interest rate (called the coupon rate) and to repay the face amount of the bond when it comes due. With some bonds, the interest you receive is wholly or partly tax free.

Municipal bonds. Municipal bonds are issued by state, city, and local governments, and by other government entities such as water and sewer districts or turnpike authorities. The interest on municipal bonds is usually exempt from not only federal tax, but also state and local tax if the bond purchaser lives in the state or locality where the bond was issued.

The moral: Buy muni bonds issued in your home state and locality if you want the maximum tax benefit.

If you decide to sell a municipal bond before it becomes due and are lucky enough to do so at a profit (called a capital gain), you must pay federal and state tax on your gain.

Because municipal bonds are tax free, they pay lower interest than bonds with taxable interest. But, depending on your top tax rate, municipal bonds can provide a greater after-tax return than taxable bonds. For example, if you're in the 28% tax bracket, a muni bond earning 4% interest would pay as much as a taxable bond earning 5.56% after taxes. The higher your tax bracket, the better your total return (yield) from a tax-free municipal bond. This makes muni bonds most attractive for wealthy people who pay high taxes.

For more information, see the website www.investinginbonds.com. It contains a calculator you can use to compare the returns from municipal bonds with those from taxable bonds.

U.S. government bonds, notes, and bills. The federal government in Washington, DC, needs to borrow money. To do this, it issues long-term Treasury bonds, and shorter-term Treasury bills ("T-bills") and notes. Interest income from T-bills, notes, and bonds is subject to federal income tax, but is exempt from all state and local income taxes. For more information, see the U.S. Treasury Web page at www.publicdebt.treas.gov.

Roth IRAs and Roth 401(k)s

Roth IRAs and Roth 401(k)s are different from other retirement accounts because all the profit you earn on them is tax free. You get no tax deduction when you deposit money in a Roth IRA or Roth 401(k), but, in return, you pay no taxes when you withdraw the money as long as you're at least 59½ and have owned the Roth for at least five years. Whether Roth accounts are better than traditional retirement accounts is not always clear. See Chapter 4 for more information on these retirement accounts.

CAUTION

Tax-free investments and regular retirement accounts don't mix. Do not place tax-free investments like municipal bonds in tax-deferred retirement accounts such as 401(k) plans and traditional IRAs. You must pay taxes at ordinary income rates when you withdraw money from these accounts after you retire, no matter where it came from originally. To avoid paying income tax on your tax-free investments, keep them in a taxable account, such as a brokerage account. (See Chapter 4.)

Saving for College, Tax Free

Paying for college has grown incredibly expensive—far outstripping the rate of inflation. According to predictions by the College Board, a student entering college in the year 2020 will pay more than $85,000 at a public university for a four-year education, and a whopping $225,000 at a private college.

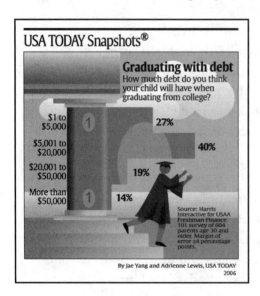

USA TODAY Snapshots®

Graduating with debt
How much debt do you think your child will have when graduating from college?

$1 to $5,000 — 27%
$5,001 to $20,000 — 40%
$20,001 to $50,000 — 19%
More than $50,000 — 14%

Source: Harris Interactive for USAA Freshman Finance 101 survey of 604 parents age 30 and older. Margin of error ±4 percentage points.

By Jae Yang and Adrienne Lewis, USA TODAY 2006

To help with the Herculean financial task of getting a kid through college, the government has created two types of tax-free accounts: Coverdell ESAs and 529 savings plans. Contributions to these accounts are not tax free, but the money in the accounts grows tax free, and withdrawals used for educational purposes are also tax free. The upshot is that, so long as the money is used for educational purposes, the income earned on it is tax free.

Coverdell ESAs and 529 savings plans each have their pros and cons. However, they are not an either-or proposition. You can contribute to both a 529 plan and an ESA for the same beneficiary in the same year.

You can also claim tax credits (including the Hope tax credit or the Lifetime Learning credit, discussed in Chapter 7) in the same year you take a tax-free distribution from a Coverdell ESA or 529 plan, as long as you don't try to claim the same expenses twice.

USA TODAY Snapshots®

Classroom pay

The average full-time public college faculty member earned $68,400 for nine months of teaching in 2006.

Average income, by academic rank:

Professor $91,400

Associate professor $66,300

Assistant professor $55,900

Instructor $40,100

Sources: American Association of University Professors, Census Bureau

By David Stuckey and Alejandro Gonzalez, USA TODAY 2006

Coverdell ESAs and 529 savings plans are not the only way to save for a child's college education. Other options include savings bonds, prepaid tuition plans, and custodial accounts. See "Best Ways to Save for College," below.

RESOURCE

The following websites contain a mountain of information on Coverdell ESAs and 529 plans:

- www.collegesavingsfoundation.org
- www.nasd.com, and
- www.savingforcollege.com.

Also, refer to IRS Publication 970, *Tax Benefits for Education*.

Best Ways to Save for College		
Plan type	Description	Pros
529 Plans	These state-sponsored plans allow you to invest for college tuition and other expenses.	You can save up to around $300,000 per child (the amount varies from state to state). Grandparents and other relatives can also contribute. In many states, you get a tax deduction when you contribute to your state's plan. And as long as the money is used for college, withdrawals are tax-free, so you don't pay tax on the growth.
Prepaid Tuition Plans	Let you buy tuition shares at state-funded colleges and universities, which are guaranteed to retain their value even if tuitions increase.	You won't lose your money if the stock market declines. Even if your child goes to a private or out-of-state college, the plan will pay out the average of in-state tuition rates.
Education Savings Accounts (ESAs); also called Coverdell ESAs or CESAs	Allow you to invest in mutual funds or other investments for your child's education. Withdrawals are tax-free as long as the money is used for education expenses.	You can design your own portfolio. Savings can be used for primary and secondary school tuition as well as college expenses.
Uniform Gifts to Minors and Uniform Transfers to Minors Accounts	These are established in your child's name, but you control the assets until the child is 18 or 21, depending on your state.	You determine how the money is invested, and it can be used for anything that benefits your child.
Roth Individual Retirement Account	You can always withdraw the amount of your original contributions without paying taxes or penalties. If you withdraw more than that to pay for college, you'll pay taxes on gains, but the 10% early withdrawal penalty will be waived.	You decide how to invest. Any money you don't use for college will continue to compound until you retire.

Cons	For more information
Some 529 plans carry large expenses and fees. Returns aren't guaranteed: If your investments perform poorly, you could lose money.	Check out www.collegesavings.org (by a nonprofit group; has a handy plan comparison tool); www.savingforcollege .com; and www.morningstar.com.
Most prepaid plans are limited to state residents. Not all states offer them.	See www.collegesavings.org.
Contributions are limited to $2,000 per year per beneficiary. A married couple must have adjusted gross income of less than $190,000 to contribute the full amount.	See www.savingforcollege.com/coverdell_ esas, IRS Publication 970, *Tax Benefits for Higher Education*, at www.irs.gov, and www.babycenter.com (click "Articles & Tools," then "Baby," then "Family Finances").
Your child controls the assets after reaching the age of majority. The money is considered the child's asset, which might reduce the amount of financial aid available.	
The maximum you can invest in a Roth this year is $5,000, or $6,000 if you're 50 or older. (2008 figures; annual income limits also apply.) Diverting money from a Roth will reduce the amount available for your retirement.	

Best Ways to Save for College, continued		
Plan type	Description	Pros
U.S. Savings Bonds	Interest from savings bonds used to pay for college might be tax-free.	Savings bonds are a risk-free investment.
401(k) Loan	Many employers allow workers to borrow from their 401(k) plan.	You pay interest on the loan to yourself, not a lender.
Home Equity Line of Credit or Loan	Many homeowners in hot real estate markets have a large amount of equity in their homes, providing a potential source of funds for college tuition.	Interest rates on home equity lines are low, and the interest is usually tax deductible.

Coverdell ESA: The education IRA

Coverdell ESAs (short for Education Savings Accounts, and formerly called Education IRAs) are much like Roth IRAs except that they're used only for education expenses. Here's how a Coverdell ESA works.

- You open an account with a bank, brokerage, or mutual fund company and name someone under age 18 as the beneficiary—this can be your child, grandchild, or anyone else.

- You can deposit up to $2,000 per year, until the child turns age 18.

- Contributions may be made only by people whose adjusted gross income for the year is less than $110,000 ($220,000 for individuals filing joint returns). If your income is between $95,000 and $110,000 (between $190,000 and $220,000 if filing a joint return), the $2,000 limit for each designated beneficiary is gradually reduced to zero.

- Your contributions are *not* tax deductible, but the funds in the account grow tax free.

- The money may be withdrawn at any time and is tax free to the child and parents as long as it's used for "qualified education

Cons	For more information
The tax break is limited to parents who meet income limits. Savings bonds must be in the parents' names, not the child's.	See www.savingsbonds.gov.
Borrowing from your 401(k) will limit the growth of your retirement savings. If you leave your job, you'll have to repay the balance to avoid taxes and early withdrawal penalties.	
Rates on home equity lines of credit are variable and will go higher if interest rates rise. If you fall behind on payments, you could lose your home.	

expenses," which include tuition, fees, books, supplies, and equipment to attend an accredited college or elementary or secondary school. This is a unique feature of the Coverdell ESA.

- If the money is used for noneducational purposes, the account earnings are taxed and there's a 10% penalty.

- After reaching age 18, the child takes over control of the account.

- The money in a Coverdell ESA must be spent by the child's 30th birthday. If any funds are left over, the child can choose between receiving the money (in which case the account earnings become taxable), naming another family member as beneficiary, or rolling the account over into a family member's Coverdell ESA.

EXAMPLE: Irving and Ida establish a Coverdell ESA at a brokerage firm for their 12-year-old daughter Irene. They put in $2,000 every year. They get no tax deduction for their contributions, but the money grows tax free. When Irene turns 18, she takes control of the account, by now worth $18,000. She withdraws the money to pay for tuition, room, and board at Dartyard University. Neither she nor her parents have to pay taxes on these withdrawals.

Know Financial Aid Rules

If you want your child to qualify for financial aid to help pay college expenses, pay careful attention to how you invest his or her college money.

Colleges and universities expect students to spend at least 35% of all assets in their name on their college expenses. The more money in a child's name—for example, in a custodial account—the less financial aid the child will qualify for.

It's better to keep as much money as possible in the parents' names, because only 5.6% of parents' assets are factored into the family's expected contribution. Assets in the parents' names include Coverdell ESA and 529 savings plans established for their children.

Money parents hold in retirement accounts is not considered at all in determining a child's eligibility for financial aid. So you should first fully fund your IRA and 401(k) before putting any money in an education account or giving gifts to your children. You can withdraw money from an IRA free of penalty each year to pay for a child's college education. For more information, see *IRAs, 401(k)s & Other Retirement Plans*, by Twila Slesnick and John C. Suttle (Nolo).

For more information on college financial aid, see the Department of Education's website at www.studentaid.ed.gov.

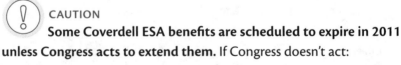

CAUTION
Some Coverdell ESA benefits are scheduled to expire in 2011 unless Congress acts to extend them. If Congress doesn't act:

- the annual ESA contribution limit will be reduced to $500 per year
- ESA withdrawals will not be tax free in any year in which a Hope tax credit or Lifetime Learning credit is claimed for the beneficiary, and
- elementary and secondary school expenses will no longer qualify for tax-free ESA withdrawals.

Most tax experts believe that Congress will step in to avoid these changes, but there's no guarantee. Even if some ESA withdrawals are taxed after 2010, the tax would be paid at the child-beneficiary's tax rate, which is usually low.

What If You Exceed the Coverdell ESA Income Limits?

If you exceed the income limits, you are not allowed to contribute to a Coverdell ESA. There's an easy way around this, however. Ask the child's grandparents or other relatives whose incomes are below the income ceiling to contribute to the ESA in their own names. You can simply repay them—it's perfectly legal.

529 savings plan

A popular option these days is the 529 savings plan (named after Section 529 of the tax code, and also called a Qualified Tuition Program or QTP for short). 529 savings plans are more complicated than Coverdell ESAs, but you can contribute more money to them. Do careful research before investing in one.

Unlike other tax-advantaged accounts, 529 plans are sponsored by state governments or state agencies. While you may open a 529 account in any state, there can be tax advantages to choosing a plan sponsored by the state where you live. For a directory of, and links to, all the state 529 plans, see www.collegesavings.org. And to compare fees and other plan attributes, go to www.morningstar.com (click on the "Personal Finance" button on the home page, and then on "529 Data").

Grandparents: Give to Child's 529 Plan, Check for Tax Benefits

Looking for something you can give your grandchildren this holiday season that can't be swallowed, won't be recalled, and doesn't contain excessive amounts of lead? Consider contributing to your grandchildren's 529 college savings plan.

Grandparents can set up their own 529 plan, naming the grandchild as a beneficiary, or contribute to an existing plan set up by the child's parents.

Even if the account isn't in your name, you might be eligible for a state tax break. Make sure you keep a copy of your canceled check for your state tax records. You can find the rules for your own state at www.collegesavings.org.

The biggest drawback to contributing to an existing account is that you relinquish control of the money. Bill Raynor, vice president of 529 plan sales for OppenheimerFunds, says he generally advises grandparents to set up a separate account and name themselves as owner, so they can retain control of the money. That's particularly important if you plan to make a large contribution to a 529 plan, he says. Otherwise, he says, your contribution "could become a red Porsche convertible instead of the kid's college fund."

In addition, keeping the account in your name means you'll be able to withdraw the money for emergencies, such as catastrophic medical expenses. You can withdraw money in your 529 account. at any time, for any reason. If the money isn't used for higher-education expenses, however, you'll owe income taxes and a 10% penalty on the earnings.

Contributions to a 529 savings plan are removed from your taxable estate, even if the account is in your name. That feature makes 529 savings plans a powerful estate-planning tool for wealthy grandparents who are concerned about inheritance taxes, Raynor says.

You can contribute up to $12,000 a year, per beneficiary, to 529 plans without filing a gift-tax return with the IRS. Better yet, you

Grandparents: Give to Child's 529 Plan, Check for Tax Benefits, cont'd

can "frontload" your 529 plans by contributing five years' worth of annual contributions in one year.

That means you can contribute up to $60,000 to a grandchild's 529 plan—or $120,000 if you're married—without filing a gift-tax return. If you have several grandchildren, you can set up multiple accounts and shelter hundreds of thousands of dollars from estate taxes, Raynor says. And if a couple of your grandkids eventually don't go to college, you can always change beneficiaries—as long as the accounts are in your name.

There's one major drawback to setting up a 529 plan—or several plans—in your name. If you need nursing home care in the future, your 529 plan could hurt your eligibility for Medicaid, a joint federal/state health insurance program for low-income people. Because you control the account, the government considers your 529 plan a "countable asset." That means you'll be required to use that money to pay for your long-term care expenses before you qualify for Medicaid. (Except if you live in Arkansas, which enacted a law exempting 529 plans from Medicaid eligibility.)

If you think you might need to apply for Medicaid in the future, consider contributing to an account in someone else's name, says Joe Hurley, founder of Savingforcollege.com. That way, the plan won't be considered a countable asset for purposes of Medicaid.

Yet even this strategy won't get you off the hook entirely. When you apply for Medicaid, the state will review your finances during the previous 60 months. Financial gifts made during this period, including contributions to a 529 savings plan, could hurt your eligibility for Medicaid benefits.

For more information, consult an elder-law attorney or a financial adviser who specializes in long-term care.

 "College 529 plan could make great gift for grandkids, but heed caveats," by Sandra Block, November 13, 2007.

> **CAUTION**
> **Weigh tax breaks against fees and investment choices.** Your state may provide a tax break for its own 529 savings plan, but offer only high-fee plans or limited investment options. As Gail Fialko, a financial planner in Fairfax, Virginia, told USA TODAY, "If you found a plan with better investment options and lower fees, you would certainly be better off" in the long run.

Here's how 529 savings plans work:

- You open a 529 account with the investment company. Anyone can open an account in any state.

- A 529 is a trust account—you're its owner and the child (or other person) is the beneficiary. The beneficiary doesn't gain control of the money until becoming an adult (usually at 18 or 21).

- You contribute as much as you like each year, until you hit the overall contribution limit set by your state (usually between $200,000 and $300,000, including investment earnings). You're allowed to make a one-time contribution equal to five years' worth of gift-tax exclusions—$60,000 at 2008 gift tax exclusion rates, $120,000 if both spouses make gifts. Otherwise, it's best to keep your contributions under the annual gift tax exclusion ($12,000, or $24,000 if both you and your spouse make contributions). (These numbers are for 2008.)

- Over half the states allow a tax deduction for state residents. If you live in a high-tax state like New York, this can save you some money. You get no federal tax deduction for contributions.

- The money in your 529 account grows tax free. Withdrawals are tax free if used for qualified educational expenses—tuition, fees, books, supplies, and equipment required for enrollment at an accredited college, university, or vocational school (but not for elementary or secondary school expenses)

- In most states, there is no age limit or time limit for when the money in a 529 plan must be used.

- If you withdraw money from a 529 plan and don't use it on an eligible college expense, you generally will be subject to income tax and an additional 10% federal tax penalty on the earnings from the account.

EXAMPLE: Armand and Ophelia are a married couple who live in New York. They open a 529 account for their daughter, Foreste, with a New York-sponsored 529 plan. Over ten years they deposit $100,000 in the plan. Their contributions are not deductible from their federal income taxes. However, they're able to deduct them from their New York state taxes. By the time Foreste is 18, the account has grown to $150,000. Foreste enters BigApple University and her parents withdraw $20,000 to pay her tuition, room, and board. The $20,000 withdrawal is tax free. The parents also withdraw $2,000 for Foreste's personal spending. This withdrawal is not tax free. Foreste must pay regular income tax on it, plus a 10% penalty.

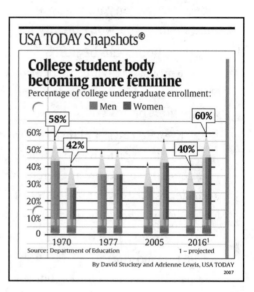

USA TODAY Snapshots®

College student body becoming more feminine

Percentage of college undergraduate enrollment:
■ Men ■ Women

Source: Department of Education
1 – projected

By David Stuckey and Adrienne Lewis, USA TODAY
2007

Other tax-free education options

There are several other ways you can obtain tax-free treatment for income you use to pay for education expenses.

U.S. savings bonds. The interest earned on U.S. savings bonds is not subject to state or local tax, but it usually is subject to federal income tax. However, certain bonds issued under the Education Savings Bond Program—Series EE and Series I—may be cashed in without paying any federal or other tax on the interest, if the money is used to pay tuition and fees to enroll yourself, your spouse, child, or other dependent at any accredited college, university, or vocational school.

You'll get less tax benefit if your income is high: With an adjusted gross income of over $130,650 (for married couples) or $82,100 (for individuals), you can't exclude the interest at all. If your AGI is a little lower—between $100,650 and $130,650 for married couples, or between $63,100 and $78,100 for individuals—you can exclude some interest, but in decreasing amounts the higher your income. (These figures are for 2008.) The bond must be issued in your name or in your spouse's name (or your and your spouse's names). If it's issued in your child's name, you won't qualify for this tax break.

Savings bonds can be purchased online or at most banks, credit unions, or savings institutions. For more information see: www.treasurydirect.gov/indiv/products/products.htm, and www.savingsbonds.gov.

529 prepaid tuition plans. This involves prepaying a child's tuition at a specific college or university. It locks in your tuition payments, because you deposit the money at current rates, then never have to pay more. Your deposits are not tax deductible, but plan earnings are tax-free as long as they're actually used to pay tuition.

What if your child doesn't end up going to the college or university you've prepaid tuition to? (Contrary to some parents' hopes, prepaying doesn't improve the child's chances of getting in.) You can usually transfer your money to another state school; if not, you'll have to have it refunded to you or change the plan beneficiary to another family member. Some plans refund only the amount of your original contribution, without any interest.

If your child ends up going to an out-of-state college or private school, you may be able to transfer your prepaid tuition to that school. However, depending on the state, you may not get the full value of your payments.

For more information, refer to: www.collegesavings.org and click on "Common Questions."

Custodial account. You can also open a custodial account for your child at a financial institution and use the money for college. But this has some serious drawbacks (see "Do you really want to give your children investment property?" above).

Speaking of Freebies, What About a No-Tuition College?

If your son or daughter is accepted at Yale this year, you probably won't have to borrow a dime to pay for that Ivy League education, thanks to Yale's expanded financial aid for middle- and upper-middle-income families.

But don't start learning the Whiffenpoof Song just yet. Only a fraction of extraordinary students manage to gain admission to Yale, which hasn't raised the size of its freshman class in 40 years, even as applications have soared. The same is true for other elite schools that have also liberalized their aid plans.

Generous new financial initiatives from Yale, Harvard, the University of Pennsylvania, and some other elite schools have drawn renewed attention to the plight of families struggling to afford college. But what if you can't get into one of these brutally selective schools? Though some other private colleges have taken modest steps to aid more families, they can't begin to match the Ivies' financial bounty. Most middle-class families, experts say, won't find any additional aid on the table, and some schools might feel compelled to reduce aid for low-income students.

Private schools are experimenting with other ways to attract low- and middle-income students, from freezing tuition to paying interest on loans taken out by parents.

School officials say they hope these initiatives will help students and their parents overcome the sticker shock associated with private-school tuition rates. But the initiatives are also key to the schools' survival, says David Warren, president of the National Association of Independent Colleges and Universities.

"There's a keen awareness of the issue of affordability and access to private colleges," he says. "They're not going to stay in business if they're unable to make their colleges affordable."

 "Private colleges try to stay affordable," by Sandra Block, February 5, 2008.

Tax-Free Scholarships and Fellowships

If your child is fortunate enough to win a scholarship (only one in 15 do), or a fellowship, the money is tax free if:

- the child is enrolled in a degree program at an accredited college or university, and
- the money is used to pay "qualified education expenses"— tuition and fees and course-related costs, such as books and supplies.

Scholarship or fellowship funds used to pay for other education expenses—for example, room and board—are taxable to the student. Also taxable is scholarship money a student earns by working at a college job ("work study" programs).

Health Savings Accounts: The Triple Tax Break

Health savings accounts (HSAs), which first became available in 2004, are

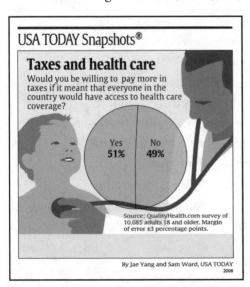

USA TODAY Snapshots®

Taxes and health care
Would you be willing to pay more in taxes if it meant that everyone in the country would have access to health care coverage?

Yes **51%** No **49%**

Source: QualityHealth.com survey of 10,685 adults 18 and older. Margin of error ±3 percentage points.

By Jae Yang and Sam Ward, USA TODAY 2008

a great way to avoid taxes on part of your income and pay for your and your family's health expenses. The HSA concept is very simple: Instead of relying on health insurance to pay small or routine medical expenses, you pay them yourself from a health savings account that you establish with a health insurance company, bank, or other financial institution. Your deposits entitle you to a tax deduction, and the interest you earn is tax-free, as well.

However, HSAs are available only in conjunction with health insurance policies with a high deductible, so you may use up the money in your HSA account faster than you'd expect. And to open one, you need to be under 65 and not covered by another health plan.

HSA nuts and bolts

To establish an HSA, you first need a bare-bones, high-deductible health plan that meets the HSA criteria (is "HSA qualified"). It can be a preferred provider organization (PPO), health maintenance organization (HMO), or traditional plan. If the coverage is for only for you, your plan must have a $1,100 minimum annual deductible. If it's for you and your family, $2,200 is the minimum deductible. (These are 2008 figures. In 2009, the minimum deductible will change to $1,150 for individuals and $2,300 for a family.)

USA TODAY Snapshots®

Kids who contribute value college more

Asked if students who help pay for college appreciate it more, those surveyed said they:

69% Strongly or somewhat agree

29% Strongly or somewhat disagree

Note: Responses do not total 100% because of rounding.

Source: Public Agenda for the National Center for Public Policy and Higher Education

By Cristina Abello and Karl Gelles, USA TODAY 2005

If you're setting up your own HSA, the following websites contain directories of insurers providing HSAs: www.hsainsider.com and www.hsafinder.com. The U.S. Treasury has an informative website at www.treas.gov/offices/public-affairs/hsa. You can also contact your present health insurer.

Once you have an HSA-qualified health insurance policy, you can open your HSA account. Your HSA account must be established with a trustee who keeps track of your deposits and withdrawals and reports your HSA deposits to the IRS.

The IRS places annual limits on how much you contribute to your HSA account (but no minimum). The maximum per year is $2,900 if you have individual coverage and $5,800 if you have family coverage (2008 figures; they're adjusted annually for inflation, and are scheduled to change to $3,000 for individuals and $5,950 for a family in 2009).

If you're between 55 and 64 years old, you can make optional, tax-free catch-up contributions. The limit on this is $900 per HSA in 2008; $1,000 per HSA in 2009.

> **CAUTION**
> **Avoid health plans with super-high deductibles.** If you choose a plan whose deductible is higher than the maximum amount you can put into your HSA account, you'll leave a gap. You'll then have to pay out-of-pocket if you spend all the money in your account, perhaps because you or a family member develops a chronic illness. Try to find a plan whose deductible is below the maximum HSA account contribution.

Compare account plans offered by several companies, looking especially at the fees charged to set up the account, as well as any other charges (some companies may charge an annual service fee, for example). Ask about special promotions and discounts. And find out how the account is invested.

Your employer may offer HSAs to its employees—an increasingly popular option. And, if you're lucky, your employer may even put a little money into your HSA account. If you change jobs, your HSA account is portable, because you own all the contributions and earnings. If you obtain a new policy, you can roll over your account to the new policy. Otherwise, you can continue to use your funds for medical expenses but you can't make new contributions until you get a new policy.

HSA tax benefits

HSAs combine three great tax benefits. First, you can deduct HSA contributions that you make with your personal funds, as a personal deduction on the first page of your IRS Form 1040. You deduct the amount from your gross income, just like a business deduction. This means you get the full deduction whether or not you itemize your personal deductions.

Second, you don't have to pay tax on the interest or other money you earn on your account. If you don't tap into the money, it will keep accumulating free of taxes. If you stay healthy, you may end up with a substantial amount in your account. Once you turn 65, you can withdraw this money without penalty, though you'll have to pay tax on it if you use it for something other than medical expenses.

Finally, if you or a family member needs health care, you can withdraw money from your HSA to pay your deductible or any other qualified medical expenses—and pay no federal tax on the withdrawals. And you'll be happy to find that "qualified medical expenses" are broadly defined to include many types not ordinarily covered by health insurance—for example, dental and optometric care.

USA TODAY Snapshots®

Common injuries children suffer

Top traumatic orthopedic injuries for which children are hospitalized:

Spinal 5.2%
Lower arm 14.7%
Upper arm 17%
Lower leg 21.5%
Thighbone 21.7%

Source: The American Academy of Orthopaedic Surgeons

By Shannon Reilly and Frank Pompa, USA TODAY
2004

If you withdraw funds from your HSA to use for something other than qualified medical expenses, you must pay the regular income tax on the withdrawal plus a 10% penalty.

No other account provides both front-end and back-end tax breaks. With IRAs, for example, you must pay tax either when you deposit or when you withdraw your money. This feature makes HSAs an extremely lucrative tax shelter—a kind of super IRA.

CAUTION

HSAs are not for everybody. If you or a member of your family has substantial medical expenses, you could be better off with traditional comprehensive health insurance. Otherwise, you'd likely end up spending all or most of your HSA contributions each year and earning little or no interest on your account (though you'll still get a deduction for your contributions). However, if your choice is an HSA or nothing, get an HSA.

Employee Fringe Benefits: Don't Miss These Tax Savings

Wouldn't it be great if employees could avoid paying taxes on at least part of their pay? In a way, they can. You don't pay any taxes on the value of tax-qualified fringe benefits your employer provides—no federal and state income tax, no Social Security and Medicare taxes, no nothing. The fringe benefits might include health insurance, medical expense reimbursements, dental insurance, education assistance, day care assistance, and transportation allowances.

If you're saying, "Big deal, I never expected to pay tax on those things anyway," realize that everything is negotiable. If you have a chance to increase your fringe benefits—even if it means lowering your salary—the tax advantages might be a good reason to go for it.

> **EXAMPLE:** Ralph needs health insurance for himself and his family. He can pay for it out of his own pocket (which will cost $6,000 per year) or he can enroll in his employer's, BigTech, group health insurance plan and BigTech will deduct $6,000 per year from his salary. Which option should he choose? The $6,000 salary reduction. The salary he receives is taxable income. Before Ralph can use it to buy health insurance or anything else, he must pay a combined state and federal tax of 41% on it—an annual tax of $2,460. In contrast, Ralph pays no tax on the $6,000 BigTech deducts from his salary. So Ralph effectively saves $2,460 in income taxes by having part of his salary converted into a tax-free employee fringe benefit.

No federal law requires employers to give employees any benefits, but most employers provide at least some benefits. Unfortunately, many employees fail to take full advantage of them—a lost opportunity for tax savings.

Which fringe benefits are tax-free

Only certain types of employee fringe benefits qualify for tax-free treatment. Here are some of the most common ones (all numbers are for 2008):

Health benefits. This includes health, dental, and vision insurance you receive from your employer, as well as uninsured health-related expenses your employer pays for. Although businesses aren't required to provide health benefits for employees (except in Hawaii and Massachusetts), most do.

Employers have many choices: They can purchase a group policy to cover all employees, or have each employee purchase his or her own policy and be reimbursed all or part of the cost. Employers can also fully or partly fund a health savings account (HSA) instead of providing traditional health insurance. Moreover, employers can require employees to pay part or even all of the premiums. Employers can also choose to pay for uninsured health-related expenses by providing their employees with health reimbursement accounts.

Long-term care insurance. If your employer buys you long-term care insurance, its premiums are not included in your taxable income. However, benefits you receive under the insurance may be partly taxable if they exceed IRS limits.

Group term life insurance. A company may provide up to $50,000 in group term life insurance to each employee tax free. If an employee is given more than $50,000 in coverage, the employee must pay tax on the excess. (Not a lot of tax; the rates are low.)

Disability insurance. If an employer buys you disability insurance, the premiums are excluded from your income. However, you must pay income tax on any disability benefits you receive under the policy, unless the payments are for the loss of a bodily function or limb (in which case they're tax free).

Educational assistance. Employers may pay employees up to $5,250 tax-free each year for educational expenses such as tuition, fees, and books.

Dependent care assistance. Employers can provide up to $5,000 in dependent care assistance to employees tax-free. Working parents also may be able to obtain a tax credit for child and dependent care. Unfortunately, you can't take both—you must choose either the assistance or the tax credit. Which is better? The one that saves you the most taxes, which depends on your overall child care expenses, household income, and tax filing status.

Transportation benefits. Employers may also pay up to $220 per month for employee parking or up to $115 per month for mass transit passes for those employees who don't drive to work.

Working condition fringe benefits. Working condition fringes are anything your employer provides or pays for that you need to do your job—for example, local and long-distance travel for business, business-related meals and entertainment, professional publications, and company cars used for business driving.

Other fringe benefits. Other tax-free employee fringe benefits include employee stock options, employee discounts (up to 20% off), moving expense reimbursements, meals provided for the employer's convenience, adoption assistance, achievement awards, and retirement planning help, employee gyms, and free services to employees. Other de minimis (minimal) benefits can also be provided, such as occasional office parties, picnics, or tickets for entertainment or sporting events.

> ⃝! **CAUTION**
> **Are you receiving a benefit that's not on this list?** You must pay tax on the fair market value of any benefits you receive that are not tax qualified—for example, a company car you use for personal driving.

Cutting back the fringe: Cafeteria plans and flexible spending accounts

An employer can pay for the tax-free benefits listed above or require its employees to pay for them. Having employees pay or share the cost is a growing trend, usually done through cafeteria plans and flexible spending accounts (FSAs).

A cafeteria plan (also called a "Section 125 Plan") allows employees to choose between receiving straight cash salary (which is taxable) or certain tax-qualified fringe benefits (which are tax free, and thus potentially more valuable). For example, you could choose between receiving health insurance coverage or an additional $5,000 in salary.

Depending on what your employer includes in its cafeteria plan, your choices might include:

- group health, dental, and vision insurance (but not medical savings accounts or long-term care insurance)
- prescription drug benefits
- long-term disability insurance
- adoption assistance
- dependent care assistance
- 401(k) plan contributions, and
- group term life insurance coverage.

Health benefits are, of course, the most important for most employees. Many cafeteria plans are used just for premiums for medical, dental, and other insurance. These are often called premium-only plans, or POPs.

Another way employees can pay or share in the cost of their medical expenses is through flexible spending accounts (FSAs). An FSA is like a savings account you fund from your salary. But, unlike your salary or money in a regular savings account, the money in your FSA is not taxed. Each year you decide how much you want to contribute to your account and your employer withholds the amount from your paychecks.

For example, if you elect to put $1,200 in your FSA and you're paid monthly, your employer will withhold $100 from each of your 12 paychecks during the year. The deducted amounts wouldn't be counted when your employer determines how much tax to withhold from your paycheck.

FSAs can be used by employees to pay for out-of-pocket medical and dental expenses. These expenses typically include co-payments and deductibles, as well as many expenses not covered by a health plan, such as eyeglasses and contact lenses, laser eye surgery, fertility treatments, chiropractic care, doctor-recommended weight loss programs, and prescription and nonprescription drugs. Separate FSAs can also be used to pay for day care.

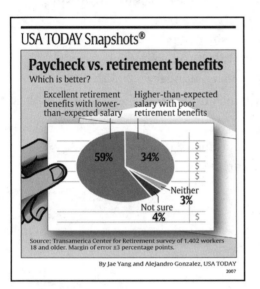

USA TODAY Snapshots®

Paycheck vs. retirement benefits
Which is better?

Excellent retirement benefits with lower-than-expected salary

Higher-than-expected salary with poor retirement benefits

59% 34%

Neither
3%
Not sure
4%

Source: Transamerica Center for Retirement survey of 1,402 workers 18 and older. Margin of error ±3 percentage points.

By Jae Yang and Alejandro Gonzalez, USA TODAY
2007

The IRS places no limit on how much money can be put in a regular FSA each year, but most employers impose their own annual limits. FSAs used for child and dependent care are limited by the IRS to $5,000 per year. You can change or revoke your salary reduction amount only if there is a change in your employment or family status that is specified by the plan—for example, if a divorce or death in the family reduces your health care expenses for the year.

FSAs have one serious drawback—they are use-it-or-lose-it accounts. Any money left unspent in an FSA at the end of the year is forfeited to your employer. Some plans provide for a grace period of up to 2½ months after the end of the plan year.

How Much to Deposit to Your FSA

To avoid forfeiting your money, planners recommend using conservative estimates, especially if you've never had an FSA before. Here's how to get the most from your health-care FSA:

- Add up your out-of-pocket costs for routine medical and dental treatment during the year. Include costs for teeth cleaning, vision exams, glasses, contact lenses, and contact lens solution.

- Estimate the cost of ongoing prescription medications not covered or only partially covered by your insurance, such as birth control pills.

- If you know you'll need elective surgery or other procedures, ask your dentist or doctor for a cost estimate. Use your plan information to figure out how much will be covered by insurance.

- Consider using an FSA to reduce your premiums. Choose a less expensive plan with a higher deductible, and use money from your FSA to pay the deductibles.

Too often, workers get caught up in the holiday bustle and forget about their FSAs, says Barbara Steinmetz of Steinmetz Financial Planning in Burlingame, California. Don't expect your plan to remind you to spend the money. "It's on your back to make sure you use it," she says. "This is really your money you're losing."

 "How to pay medical bills and save taxes; Flexible spending accounts do have a hitch: Use it or lose it," by Sandra Block, December 1, 2000.

EXAMPLE: Ralph (the BigTech employee in the earlier examples) elects to divert $200 of his monthly salary (or $2,400 a year) to his FSA. Because BigTech doesn't count these $200 monthly contributions as salary, Ralph saves $928 in taxes (the sum of a 25% federal income tax, 7.65% Social Security and Medicare tax, and 6% state income tax). By December, he's used $2,000 on doctor visits, but still has $400 to use or lose. Ralph quickly stocks up on aspirin and schedules a dental appointment, and succeeds in claiming his entire contribution.

Employee benefits for business owners

If you're a business owner—whether a sole proprietor, partner in a partnership, member of a limited liability company, or an over-2% shareholder in an S corporation—you don't qualify for any tax-free employee fringe benefits (except for working condition fringes). If your business provides you with any benefits, you'll have to pay tax on their fair market value.

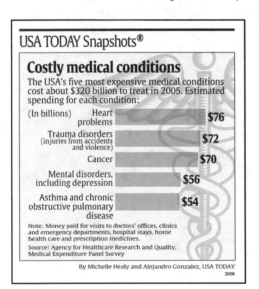

USA TODAY Snapshots®

Costly medical conditions

The USA's five most expensive medical conditions cost about $320 billion to treat in 2005. Estimated spending for each condition:

(In billions)

Heart problems	$76
Trauma disorders (injuries from accidents and violence)	$72
Cancer	$70
Mental disorders, including depression	$56
Asthma and chronic obstructive pulmonary disease	$54

Note: Money paid for visits to doctors' offices, clinics and emergency departments, hospital stays, home health care and prescription medicines.

Source: Agency for Healthcare Research and Quality, Medical Expenditure Panel Survey

By Michelle Healy and Alejandro Gonzalez, USA TODAY 2008

So what do you do about health insurance? Luckily, people with their own businesses may deduct 100% of the health insurance premiums they pay for themselves and their families (including dental and long-term care coverage) as a special personal income tax deduction. But this deduction is limited to the business's annual profit each year—no profit, no deduction.

If that doesn't work for you, you have a few other options.

First, you can incorporate your business (as a regular C corporation) and work as its employee. You'll then qualify for tax-free fringes just like any other employee. You'll also have to be treated like an employee for all tax and other purposes—for example, have income and employment taxes withheld from your pay, and possibly be covered by workers' compensation insurance.

If you're married, you could hire your spouse as your employee instead, and provide employee benefits. These benefits, such as health insurance, can cover you, your spouse, your children, and other dependents. For this to work, your spouse must be a real employee—that is, do real work—and be paid a reasonable salary on which taxes are withheld.

> EXAMPLE: Joe, a self-employed consultant, hires his wife, Martha, to work as his full-time office assistant. He pays her $25,000 per year and provides her with a health insurance policy covering both of them and their two children. The annual policy premiums are $6,000. Martha doesn't pay tax on the value of the insurance because it's a tax-qualified employee fringe benefit. Moreover, Joe may deduct the $6,000 as a business expense for his business, listing it on his Schedule C.

Social Security Benefits: Tax Free Until They're Not

Once you start receiving Social Security benefits, they're tax free— unless you earn too much income during the year. So before you decide to start collecting Social Security early (which you can do as soon as age 62), or accept a part-time or new job after you retire, do the calculations to figure out the tax impact.

To know whether you'll owe taxes, you first have to figure out your "combined income." Simply add one-half of the total Social Security you'll receive during the year to all your other expected income, including any tax-exempt interest (for example, interest from tax-exempt bonds).

You'll have to pay tax on part of your benefits if your combined income exceeds these thresholds:

- $32,000 if you're married and file a joint tax return, or
- $25,000 if you're single.

If both members of a married couple file their taxes separately, the threshold is reduced to zero—they always have to pay taxes on their benefits. The only exception is if they did not live together at any time during the year, in which case the $25,000 threshold applies.

How much of your Social Security benefits will be taxed depends on just how high your combined income is.

Individual filers. If you file a federal tax return as an individual and your combined income is between $25,000 and $34,000, you have to pay income tax on up to 50% of your Social Security benefits. If your income is above $34,000, up to 85% of your Social Security benefits will be taxed.

Joint filers. If you file a joint return, you have to pay taxes on up to 50% of your benefits if you and your spouse have a combined income between $32,000 and $44,000. If your income is more than $44,000, up to 85% of your Social Security benefits will be taxed.

> EXAMPLE: Betty and Bruno are a retired married couple who file jointly. Both work at part-time job, at which Betty earned $12,000 last year and Bruno earned $18,000. They also had $10,000 in investment income, including $5,000 in interest from tax-exempt municipal bonds. They received $20,000 in Social Security benefits during the year. Their combined income is $50,000 ($30,000 in wages + $10,000 investment income + (50% × $20,000 Social Security benefits) = $50,000.) Because this is more than the $44,000 ceiling, they must pay income tax on 85% of their Social Security benefits. Of course, they must also pay tax on the income from their part-time jobs.

Unmarried couples who file their taxes separately can earn more than married couples without being taxed on their Social Security benefits. Each will be entitled to earn $25,000 in combined income without paying tax on their benefits, for a total of $50,000. A married couple can get the same treatment if they live apart part of the year and file taxes separately.

If you earn enough for your benefits to be taxable, you could end up paying the highest income taxes in the country. Here's why: Every dollar you earn over the 85% threshold amount will result in 85 cents of your benefits being taxed, plus you'll have to pay tax on the extra income. So for every dollar you earn over the 85% threshold, you'll end up paying tax on $1.85. If you're in the 28% bracket, this works out to a 52% tax rate (28% × 1.85 = 0.518).

Calculating the exact amount of tax that must be paid on Social Security benefits can be quite complicated. IRS Publication 915, *Social Security and Equivalent Railroad Retirement Benefits*, contains detailed instructions and a worksheet.

If you plan to work after the normal retirement age, consider putting off claiming your Social Security benefits. If you wait until your full retirement age to claim Social Security retirement

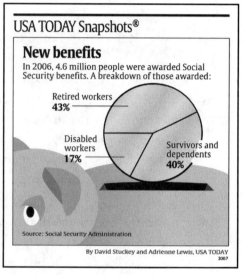

USA TODAY Snapshots®

New benefits

In 2006, 4.6 million people were awarded Social Security benefits. A breakdown of those awarded:

Retired workers **43%**

Disabled workers **17%**

Survivors and dependents **40%**

Source: Social Security Administration

By David Stuckey and Adrienne Lewis, USA TODAY 2007

benefits, your benefit amounts will be permanently higher than if you'd retired early. The benefit amount continues to increase by a certain percentage each year until you reach age 70. After age 70, there is no longer any increase, so plan on claiming your benefits regardless of the tax bite.

Once you start receiving Social Security benefits, to keep your income below the applicable threshold, or at least as low as possible, you should:

- put off taking money out of retirement accounts like traditional IRAs and 401(k)s. You don't have to take any money out until you reach age 70½.

- choose investments that don't generate a lot of taxable income during the year—for example, stocks that don't pay dividends, or tax-managed mutual funds that have low or no taxable distributions (see Chapter 2).

- put your retirement money into Roth IRAs and Roth 401(k)s. Your earnings are not subject to any tax if you hold the account for at least five years and are over 59.5 years old. If you have a traditional IRA, you can convert it into a Roth IRA.

- consider reducing your income by giving income-producing assets to your children or other relatives, or to charities (see Chapter 8).

How Not to Game the Social Security System

If you don't need Social Security to pay your living expenses, you might be tempted to use this option to make a little extra money. Under current rules, you could start taking Social Security benefits at 62 and put the money in a certificate of deposit or other low-risk investment. Later, you could repay the benefits, reapply (for Social Security), and keep all the interest you've earned.

One drawback to this strategy: You could owe taxes on your early-retirement benefits. If all your income comes from Social Security, your benefits usually aren't taxable. But if you stash all of your Social Security benefits in a CD, you'll probably need to rely on other income, such as withdrawals from your individual retirement accounts, to pay expenses. That income could trigger taxes on 50% to 85% of your benefits. That said, if you repay your benefits and reapply, you could be eligible for a deduction based on taxes you've already paid on the benefits.

H.K. "Bud" Hebeler, founder of the retirement-planning website Analyze Now (www.analyzenow.com), doesn't recommend this investment strategy because the government could change the rules. If Social Security decides to eliminate the option to reapply, he says, "You could really be stuck."

Reapplying for benefits, Hebeler says, is best suited for people who took early retirement, regret that decision, and want to increase their benefits.

 "Have your retirement cake early and eat it, too," by Sandra Block, February 22, 2008.

For more information on Social Security, refer to *Social Security, Medicare & Government Pensions: Get the Most Out of Your Retirement & Medical Benefits,* by Joseph L. Matthews and Dorothy Matthews Berman (Nolo).

Live and Work Abroad and Avoid U.S. Taxes

Ever dreamed of working in another country? Up to $87,600 (in 2008) of your earnings need not be counted as U.S. taxable income if all of the below are true:

- The income is earned income—salary, wages, or professional fees you were paid for your work—but not interest, dividends, or other money earned from foreign investments.

- You earned the income for performing services outside the U.S.— it's fine if you worked for a U.S. company abroad, but you can't have worked for the U.S. government.

- The income was for services you performed while either (1) you were physically outside the U.S. for at least 330 days (about 11 months) out of any 12 consecutive months, or (2) you were a resident of a foreign country for at least a full calendar year.

- Your tax home (the place of your principal place of employment) is in a foreign country.

If your employer pays for your foreign housing, you can also exclude part of the payments from your U.S. taxable income. You may only deduct housing costs that exceed $14,016 in 2008; and the maximum amount of the exclusion is $26,280.

> **Which foreign countries have the highest per capita income?**
>
> Luxembourg, Switzerland, Ireland, Norway, and the United Arab Emirates usually top the charts.

Of course, you'll probably have to pay income taxes in the country where you're working. However, if you qualify for the exclusion, you'll likely qualify for the foreign tax credit as well. (See Chapter 3.)

For more information, refer to IRS Publication 54, *Tax Guide for U.S. Citizens and Resident Aliens Abroad.*

Bonus Round: Other Types of Tax-Free Income

If you receive any of the following, you'll be glad to know that they're tax free:

- property received as a gift or inheritance
- life insurance proceeds received because of someone's death
- child support payments
- welfare benefits
- accident and health insurance proceeds
- veteran's benefits
- worker's compensation benefits for an occupational sickness or injury, and
- death gratuity benefits paid to survivors of deceased armed forces members for deaths occurring after September 10, 2001.

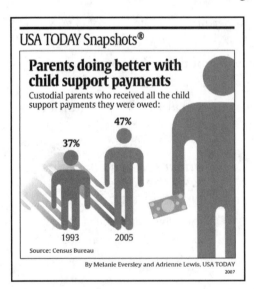

USA TODAY Snapshots®

Parents doing better with child support payments

Custodial parents who received all the child support payments they were owed:

47%

37%

1993   2005

Source: Census Bureau

By Melanie Eversley and Adrienne Lewis, USA TODAY
2007

For more information about gifts, inheritances, and life insurance, see *Plan Your Estate*, by Denis Clifford (Nolo). For more on all forms of tax-free income, see IRS Publication 525, *Taxable and Nontaxable Income*.

How to Win the Nobel Prize Tax Free

If you win the Nobel Prize, Pulitzer Prize, or a similar award that comes with a cash payment, you'll ordinarily need to pay income tax on the amount. The Nobel Prize comes with a cash award of 10 million Swedish kroner—about $1.3 million—so you could have a hefty tax bill. But there is a way to collect a Nobel tax free: Immediately donate the cash payment to a tax-exempt charity. As long as you don't use the award before it is transferred, you need not include it in your income. This tax rule applies not only to well-known awards like Nobels or Pulitzers, but to any prize awarded to you in recognition of your accomplishments in religious, charitable, scientific, artistic, educational, literary, or civic fields.

Dollar-for-Dollar Refunds: Tax Credits

t's not quite free money, but close: A tax credit lets you get directly reduce the amount of taxes you pay by the amount of your credit.

It's usually based on money you've already spent, such as for child care or a hybrid car. So if you have a $1,000 tax credit, you pay $1,000 less in taxes.

A tax credit is much better than a tax deduction, which only reduces your taxable income. If you're in the 28% income tax bracket, a $1,000 tax deduction saves you only $280 in taxes (28% × $1,000 = $280). A person in the 28% tax bracket would need $3,571 in tax deductions to save $1,000 in income taxes.

Credits Versus Deductions	
Credits	**Deductions**
Tax credits are subtracted directly from your tax liability. Credits reduce tax liability dollar for dollar.	Tax deductions are subtracted from your total income to compute your taxable income. Deductions reduce tax liability by the amount of the deduction times the tax rate.
$1,000 credit = $1,000 tax reduction	**$1,000 deduction × 28% tax rate = $280 tax reduction**

So, how do you get these wonderful tax credits? Congress hands them out as rewards to taxpayers who do things it wants to encourage. Take, for example, John and Jenny Jones. Their combined taxable income in 2007 and 2008 was $100,000 per year. They paid $20,000 in income taxes in 2007 but owed only $13,500 in 2008. Why the difference? Because In 2008, they received tax credits for having:

- given birth to their first child ($1,000 credit)
- purchased a hybrid car ($2,000 credit)
- added new insulation to their home ($500 credit)
- incurred child care expenses so that they could both work ($500 credit), and
- paid for night classes for John at the local college ($500 credit).

John and Jenny received a total of $4,500 in tax credits for these activities, which meant they owed $4,500 less in taxes that year.

Congress has taken a great liking to tax credits, and adds new ones all the time. Each tax credit is different, with its own eligibility rules and amounts. Most credits are based on the amount you spend, but some have specified maximum annual limits. Several credits have income limits and are reduced or not available to people whose income is on the high side.

You claim tax credits on the second page of your Form 1040. First, you figure out your taxes due without any credits, then you deduct from this amount the total of all your credits—a highly enjoyable bit of subtraction. You'll also need to include with your tax return a special form for each credit you claim—there are different forms for different credits.

A tax credit usually defrays only part of a covered expense, so there's no point in buying something you don't really need just to get a tax credit. For example, if your old car is running fine, the tax credit alone isn't a reason to buy a hybrid. But, if you need the item, or were looking for a reason to buy it anyway, the credit will help defray the cost.

Tax Credits Come and Go

Some tax credits have been around for years and are more or less permanent—the child care credit and low-income housing credit, for example. Others have been created more recently and are scheduled to phase out. Congress can, and often does, extend credits that have a phase-out date. The research and experimentation, work opportunity, welfare to work, and Indian tax credits have been extended for one year at a time for several years. But just in case, it's wise to act before the expiration date.

Below are tax credits with expiration dates:

Credit	Expiration Date
Hybrid car	December 31, 2010
Solar power for homes and businesses	December 31, 2008
Build energy efficient homes	December 31, 2008
Work opportunity	September 1, 2011

Hybrid Cars: New Wheels and a Tax Break, Too

High gas prices got you down? Hybrid cars, such as the popular Toyota Prius, are powered by both an internal combustion engine and a rechargeable battery, and get mileage of up to 60 miles per gallon or more. However, you'll pay more for a hybrid. To encourage people to purchase these cars and reduce the country's dependence on foreign oil, Congress allows a hybrid vehicle tax credit to anyone (well, almost anyone) who purchases a new hybrid vehicle between January 1, 2006, and December 31, 2010.

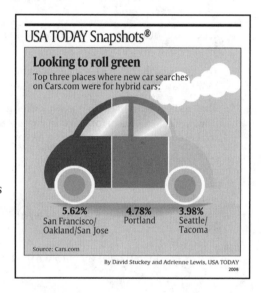

USA TODAY Snapshots®

Looking to roll green

Top three places where new car searches on Cars.com were for hybrid cars:

| 5.62% San Francisco/ Oakland/San Jose | 4.78% Portland | 3.98% Seattle/ Tacoma |

Source: Cars.com

By David Stuckey and Adrienne Lewis, USA TODAY 2008

To qualify for the credit, the hybrid you buy must be on the IRS's certified list of hybrids (see the IRS website at www.irs.gov). There are no tax credits available for leasing a hybrid car.

To complicate matters, Congress got a little stingy and said that once a hybrid manufacturer sells 60,000 vehicles, the credit will be phased out over the following 15 months for all hybrids produced by that company. That means you'll need to act quickly if you've got your eye on a popular hybrid model. (The Toyota Prius, the most popular hybrid, is no longer eligible for the tax credit.) To keep track, the manufacturers must give the IRS quarterly sales reports showing where they stand as to the 60,000-vehicle limit; and the IRS posts this information on its website. Be sure to check these reports before you buy a hybrid; otherwise, you could be disappointed to discover you'll get no tax credit.

Just how much is the tax credit worth? Good question. Unfortunately, the size of the credit is determined using a complex formula based on each hybrid vehicle's fuel efficiency, so different model hybrids qualify for different credit amounts. The credit consists of two parts: (1) a fuel economy amount that is based on the car's fuel consumption; and (2) a conservation credit based on the estimated lifetime fuel savings of the vehicle. The maximum allowable credits are listed in the chart below.

Type of Hybrid Vehicle	Maximum Tax Credit
Passenger cars and other hybrid vehicles weighing less than 8,500 pounds	$3,400
Trucks and other hybrid vehicles weighing 8,500–14,000 pounds	$3,000
Trucks and other hybrid vehicles weighing 14,001–26,000 pounds	$6,000
Trucks and other hybrid vehicles weighing more than 26,000 pounds	$12,000

The credit is scheduled to end on December 31, 2010. As a practical matter, however, it will end before that in cases where the manufacturer has already sold up to 60,000 vehicles of a certain model.

Tax Credits Are Available for Other Fuel-Efficient Vehicles

Tax credits are also available for fuel cell vehicles and alternative fuel vehicles.

Fuel cell vehicles are powered by one or more cells that convert chemical energy to electricity by combining oxygen with hydrogen fuel. The maximum allowable credit for fuel cell vehicles is $8,000, but greater credits are available for heavier vehicles.

Alternative fuel vehicles include those fueled by compressed natural gas, liquefied natural gas, liquefied petroleum gas, hydrogen, and any liquid that is at least 85% methanol. The maximum allowable credit for alternative fuel vehicles weighing less than 8,500 pounds is $5,000. But if you were hoping to get a credit for running your car on French fry oil—that is, biodiesel—you're out of luck. Only producers and sellers of biodeisel and ethanol fuel (refineries and gas stations primarily) can use the credit—not individuals.

Solar Power—Let the Sun Burn Up Your Tax Bill

If you install solar water-heating or electric power systems in your home, you can get a tax credit of:

- 30% of the cost of solar water-heating equipment, up to a $2,000 maximum each tax year, and

- 30% of the cost of solar panels and related equipment that generates photovoltaic electricity, up to a $2,000 maximum each tax year.

The solar equipment must be placed into service in your main home sometime between January 1, 2006 and December 31, 2008. You can't use the credit for heating a pool or hot tub. If you use your solar heating system to heat a pool or hot tub, you must allocate the costs of the system between your home use and the your hot tub or pool use. Only include the costs allocable to your home when you figure out the amount of your deduction.

So, is it time for you to go solar? Maybe … maybe not. The cost of a solar water heater typically ranges from $3,500 to $6,000, which means a 30% tax credit saves you anywhere from $1,050 to $1,800. That is a big chunk of the expense. With heating bills going through the roof in many parts of the country, your investment could pay off quickly.

Solar panels to produce electricity for home use are a different story. Home solar panel electricity systems are expensive—they range from $16,000 to $64,000, depending on the size of the home. A $2,000 maximum credit won't defray much of that cost. However, several states have much more generous tax incentives. For example, California provides tax rebates equal to approximately 35% of the cost of installing solar panels, while New Jersey offers a tax rebate of approximately 60%. You can find out whether your state offers any tax incentives by checking the Database of State Incentives for Renewable Energy at www.dsireusa.org.

Before deciding to go solar, try to figure out how long it will take you to recoup your investment. You'll have to look at your cost (after federal and state tax credits and rebates) and your estimated utility savings.

In some cases, it could take as many as 20 years to recoup the cost; in other cases, just a few years. For help running the numbers, use the solar estimator at www.findsolar.com.

Tax Joy From Your Bundles of Joy

As any parent knows, having kids adds whole new layers of expenses to your life, from child care to sippy cups. Two different tax credits can help you offset these:

- a child tax credit of $1,000 per child, and
- a child and dependent care tax credit of up to $2,100.

If you qualify, you can get both credits in the same year, and you can still get the tax exemption for children and other dependents (see Chapter 8). Another tax credit helps people who adopt children.

All these credits, however, are subject to limitations that can reduce or eliminate the benefit, depending on your circumstances.

Which children qualify you for tax credits?

Both the child tax credit and the child and dependent care tax credit are available only if you have what the IRS calls a "qualifying child." That's one for whom you can claim a dependency exemption. Your son, daughter, stepchild, adopted child, foster child, brother, sister, stepbrother, stepsister, or a descendant of any of them might all qualify—for example, your grandchild, niece, or nephew.

You may claim the child tax credit for any qualifying child under age 17. For the child and dependent care tax credit, however, the child must be under age 13. If a child turns 17 or 13 during the year, you'll need to cut the credit down to match the part of the year the child was under the age limit.

Who can use the child tax credit

Before you get too excited about how much money Junior is going to save you, read on. The child tax credit was created for low- and middle-income taxpayers. The amount of credit you can take each year goes down as your income approaches a threshold amount. Here's how it works.

Everyone with a qualifying child starts out the tax year entitled to a $1,000 credit per child for the tax year, regardless of how much you actually spend on the child. If you have two qualifying children you'll start with a $2,000 credit, and so forth. The credit or credits are gradually phased out for taxpayers whose incomes rise up to and above the annual threshold amount specified for the year. The income threshold is $110,000 for a married couple filing jointly, $55,000 for a married couple filing separately, and $75,000 for a single person, head of household, or widower.

The phaseout works like this: For each $1,000 that your modified adjusted gross income (MAGI) exceeds the income threshold level, the total child tax credit for a family (not the amount per child) is reduced by $50. If you make too much money, you won't get any credit at all. For example, a married couple filing jointly with one qualifying child gets no child tax credit if their MAGI exceeds $130,000. The $1,000 credit they started the tax year with would be whittled down to zero by a total of 20 $50 reductions.

USA TODAY Snapshots®

Grocery shopping for the kids

Most important factors moms consider:

Taste **21%**

Child's preference **22%**

Price **17%**

Nutritional content **27%**

Source: Ronzoni Smart Taste survey of 1,000 mothers or female guardians of children ages 5-17 conducted by Synovate. Margin of error ±3 percentage points.

By Michelle Healy and Veronica Salazar, USA TODAY 2008

If the great composer Bach were alive today and living in the United States, he'd be entitled to a $20,000 child tax credit, because he had 20 children (with two wives, thankfully). But what if Bach owed only $9,000 in income taxes for the year? What happens to the remaining $11,000 in tax credits? Luckily, depending on his income, Bach could get all or part of the excess child credit amount paid to him by the IRS as a refund. Taxpayers in this situation are entitled to a refund equal to 15% of their earned income over a threshold amount ($12,050 in

2008). If, for example, Bach's earned income was $82,050 in 2008, he'd be entitled to a refund of $10,500 (15% × $70,000 = $10,500).

To claim this refund, Bach (or you) will need to fill out and submit an extra form (IRS Form 8812). The IRS will then send you either the unused portion of your child tax credit or 15% of your taxable earned income over an annually adjusted amount, whichever is smaller. How much will that actually gain you? You'll need to run the numbers to find out, but families with lots of kids usually benefit the most.

Who can use the child and dependent care tax credit

Unlike the child tax credit (which you get simply by having a qualifying child), you can use the child and dependent care credit only if your reason for spending money for child care is to allow you (and your spouse, if you're married) to work. Although there's no income ceiling on this credit, people with higher incomes get a smaller credit than those with more modest incomes.

You qualify for the credit if:

- You have a qualifying child or other dependent under the age of 13, or you have a child over 13 who is totally and permanently disabled.
- You incur child care expenses so that you and your spouse, if any, can earn income.
- You and your spouse file a joint tax return (if you're married).
- You and your spouse, if any, both work either full- or part-time, unless you or your spouse is a full-time student or disabled. (Looking for work counts as being employed.)

The amount of the credit is based on a percentage of the child care expenses you pay on the days that you or your spouse work, with an annual limit of $3,000 for one child and $6,000 for two or more. The percentage ranges from 20% to 35% of expenses, depending on your income. Taxpayers with an adjusted gross income (AGI) of over $43,000 use the 20% amount. Those with an AGI under $15,000 use the 35% amount. Those with AGIs between $15,000 and $43,000 use a percentage based on a sliding scale.

EXAMPLE: Lazaro and Aletha, who both work, had two qualifying children and $10,000 in child care expenses. Their AGI was $100,000, so they used the 20% percentage to figure their credit. Even though they had $10,000 in child care expenses, they can take only 20% of $6,000, because $6,000 is the annual ceiling for people with two or more children. They are entitled to a $1,200 credit for the year (20% × $6,000 = $1,200).

If you're lucky enough to have an employer that reimburses you for child care expenses, you must deduct the reimbursed amount from the amount you use to calculate your credit.

Obviously, you need to keep track of everything you spend on child care during the year and hang onto receipts, bank records, and cancelled checks. Child care expenses include expenses both in and outside your home, such as:

- babysitting
- day care center
- nursery school, and
- day camp (but not if the child sleeps overnight at the camp).

The costs of sending a child to school in the first grade or beyond are not included. Nor can you hire your spouse, child, or other dependent as a day care provider. If your child turns 13 during the year, you can only include those expenses you incur before the child's 13th birthday.

To claim the credit, you'll have to list on your tax return the name, address, and Social Security or Employer Identification number of the people you pay for dependent care, so be sure to get this information.

USA TODAY Snapshots®

Who's minding the tots?
Regular primary child-care arrangements for 2-year-olds, 2003-04:

No non-parental care
Relative 19%
Center-based 16%
Non-relative 15%
Multiple[1] 1%
F

1 – Multiple arrangements are when an equal amount of time is spent in two or more arrangements. Percentages do not add up to 100% Because of rounding.

Source: U.S. Department of Education

By Tracey Wong Briggs and Frank Pompa, USA TODAY
2006

Who can use the adoption tax credit

People who adopt a child are entitled to a tax credit of 100% of their adoption expenses up to a maximum of $11,650 per child (2008).

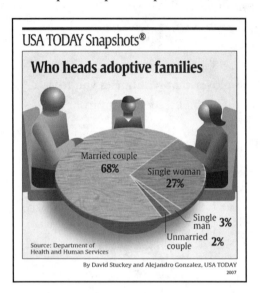

USA TODAY Snapshots®

Who heads adoptive families

Married couple **68%**

Single woman **27%**

Single man **3%**

Unmarried couple **2%**

Source: Department of Health and Human Services

By David Stuckey and Alejandro Gonzalez, USA TODAY 2007

Any reasonable and necessary expenses for the adoption may be counted—for example, adoption agency fees, attorney fees, court costs, and traveling expenses (including meals and lodging).

There is an income limit on the credit and the credit is gradually phased out for taxpayers whose MAGI exceeds the annual ceiling. In 2008, the ceiling was $174,130, at which point the credit phaseout started, and anyone with a MAGI over $214,729 got no credit at all.

Get Educated and Get a Tax Break

Congress figures that well-educated taxpayers will make more money and pay more taxes, so it has created two tax credits for higher-education expenses. Yet millions of families leave money on the table every year by overlooking these valuable tax breaks, including:

- the Hope tax credit, and
- the Lifetime Learning credit.

You can't take both credits in the same year for the same person. However, both credits can be claimed on the same return for different students. For example, you could take a Hope credit for your child who's enrolled in college and take the Lifetime Learning credit based on your own enrollment in a work-related course.

If the total expenses involved are $7,500 or less, it's usually better to use the Hope credit if you have a choice. If your expenses are above that amount, it's better to use the Lifetime Learning credit, because it's larger for expenses over the threshold amount.

TIP

For more information about education tax credits, see IRS Publication 970, *Tax Benefits for Education*.

Hope tax credit

The Hope tax credit is designed to help low- and middle-income taxpayers pay tuition for the first two years of higher education. You can claim the credit for tuition and related fees you pay an accredited college, university, vocational school, or other educational institution eligible to participate in the federal student aid program.

The payments must be made on behalf of an eligible student, who could be any dependent child or children, your spouse, you, or any other dependents for whom you claim tax exemptions. The student must be in the first or second year of school, attending school at least half-time, and enrolled in the program to obtain a degree or other credential. Like the three child-tax credits discussed above, the Hope tax credit is subject to an income threshold—if you earn over a certain amount, say goodbye to the credit.

USA TODAY Snapshots®

High cost of learning

Total back-to-college spending in 2007: (in billions)

Textbooks — $15.6

Electronics or computer-related equipment — $12.8

Dorm or apartment furnishings — $5.4

School supplies — $3.1

Shoes — $3.0

Source: National Retail Federation

By David Stuckey and Karl Gelles, USA TODAY
2007

The amount of the credit is the sum of:

- 100% of the first $1,200 of education expenses you pay for the eligible student, plus
- 50% of the next $1,200 of education expenses you pay for that student.

Choosing a Student Loan? Think Federal, First

Student loans are often categorized as good debt, because a college education is considered a sensible long-term investment. But it's important to understand that not all student loans are alike. Federally guaranteed student loans, known as Stafford loans, have fixed interest rates, now 6.8%, and flexible repayment terms. Any full-time college student, regardless of family income, can take out a Stafford loan.

Private student loans, which are often offered by the same lenders that provide federal loans, are more expensive. Interest rates are variable, so there's no limit on how high they can go. And repayment terms aren't as flexible as they are for federal loans.

Yet despite these drawbacks, private student loan borrowing has soared in the past decade. In 2007, private loans accounted for 29% of all loans taken out by undergraduates, according to a report by the College Board.

The amount of federal money that students can borrow is limited, and those limits haven't kept up with increases in college costs. As a result, some students who attend high-cost schools rely on private loans to pay for expenses not covered by their federal loans.

But that doesn't entirely explain the growth in private loans. An analysis by the American Council on Education found that one in five undergraduates with private loans didn't first take full advantage of federal loans.

So why do borrowers take out higher-cost loans? Marketing probably plays a role. Many lenders advertise private loans on television and over the Internet. The U.S. Public Interest Research Group, a consumer advocacy group, has charged that some of these ads are misleading and entice borrowers to take out unnecessarily high-risk, high-cost loans.

In addition, recent cuts in government subsidies have made federal loans less profitable for lenders. Consequently, lenders may become even more aggressive in marketing their private loans,

Choosing a Student Loan? Think Federal, First, cont'd

says Stephen Burd, senior research fellow for the New America Foundation, a policy institute.

Ads for private loans often point out that borrowers don't have to start repaying the loans until six months after graduation. But what they fail to mention is that this feature isn't unique to private loans. Repayments on federal student loans, too, are deferred until six months after graduation.

Many ads for private loans also claim that loan applicants can get their money in less than a week. By contrast, Stafford loan borrowers must fill out a Free Application for Federal Student Aid, which is eight pages long and contains more than 100 questions.

But while the FAFSA takes time, it's time well spent. Congress recently added some important benefits to the federal student loan program. Under a $20 billion financial aid bill, Stafford loan borrowers will never have to spend more than 15% of their discretionary income on loan payments.

The law also gradually reduces interest rates over the next four years for new federally subsidized Stafford loans, which are available to borrowers who can show financial need. The government pays the interest on subsidized Stafford loans while the borrower is in school.

In addition, borrowers who work in certain public-service jobs for at least ten years will be eligible to have the balance of their student loans forgiven. But this relief will be available only to borrowers with federal loans.

"There seems to be no reason for students to take out private loans without exhausting their federal eligibility first," Burd notes. "Federal loans are much cheaper and have many more protections."

 "Students often overlook federal loans that are great deals," by Sandra Block, October 30, 2007.

That adds up to a maximum credit per eligible student of $1,800, assuming you paid at least $2,400 in education expenses.

However, that maximum is gradually reduced if your modified adjusted gross income (MAGI) is between $48,000 and $58,000 ($96,000 and $116,000 if you file a joint return). The credit will completely slip from your grasp if your MAGI reaches $58,000 or more ($116,000 or more if you file a joint return). See IRS Publication 970, *Tax Benefits for Education*, for details on how the credit is reduced.

> EXAMPLE: Jon and Tanisha are married and file a joint tax return. For 2008, they claim an exemption for their dependent daughter on their tax return. Their MAGI is $70,000. Their daughter is in her sophomore (second) year at the local university. Jon and Tanisha pay tuition and related fees of $4,300 in 2008. They can claim the full $1,800 Hope credit. This is 100% of the first $1,200 of their education expenses, plus 50% of the next $1,200.

Remember, you can get the Hope credit only for the first and second years a student attends college. After that, you get no credit for that student. Thus, Jon and Tanisha from the above example will get no Hope credit for their daughter for her junior (third) and later years at college.

When you figure the amount of the credit, you can include what you spend for tuition and any other related school fees (for example, student activity fees). You can't take into account personal expenses such as room and board, insurance, medical expenses (including student health fees), or transportation, even if you pay the school for them. The college or university will send each enrolled student an IRS Form 1098-T by January 31 of each year showing how much tuition and related fees were paid for the prior year.

You can pay the education expenses in cash or borrow money to pay them. It doesn't matter for purposes of the credit. Also, you or your dependent can pay the expenses—for example, you can include the amount of a student loan your child takes out to help pay for tuition.

Lifetime Learning credit

The Lifetime Learning credit comes with many of the same rules and restrictions as the Hope credit. However, it is far more flexible, because:

- the student does not have to be in the first or second year of school
- it can be used for nondegree education to acquire or improve job skills (for example, a continuing education course), and
- the student need not be enrolled at least half-time—it can be used for a single course.

If you qualify, your credit amount will be 20% of the first $10,000 of postsecondary tuition and fees paid during the year for any and all eligible students in your family, for a maximum credit of $2,000 per tax return. (This differs from the Hope credit, which is figured per student.) The credit is phased out and then eliminated at the same income levels as the Hope credit.

You can take this credit not only for a dependent child (or children), but for yourself or your spouse (if you file jointly). And it can be taken any number of times.

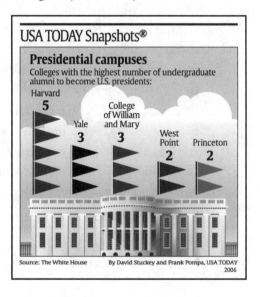

USA TODAY Snapshots®

Presidential campuses

Colleges with the highest number of undergraduate alumni to become U.S. presidents:

Harvard **5**
Yale **3**
College of William and Mary **3**
West Point **2**
Princeton **2**

Source: The White House   By David Stuckey and Frank Pompa, USA TODAY
2006

EXAMPLE: Arturo and Jane are a jointly filing married couple with a MAGI of $100,000. They spend $5,000 on tuition so that their dependent son Biff can attend his fourth year at the local state college. Arturo, an attorney, also spends $1,000 on continuing legal education for himself. They have $6,000 in total education expenses that qualify for the Lifetime Learning credit. Their credit is $1,200 (20% × $6,000 = $1,200).

Choosing Education Tax Credits

To help you play your credits wisely, consider both when you can use them and how many children you have in college or other post-secondary school. As Sandra Block explains (using 2008 tax figures):

The Hope credit is available only for the first two years of your child's undergraduate education. The lifetime learning credit can be taken in any year to offset the cost of college education or classes to improve job skills. You can't take both credits at the same time for the same child, so during the first two years, you need to determine which one delivers the bigger tax break. The maximum lifetime learning credit each year is 20% of the first $10,000 you spend on college expenses, up to $2,000. To get the maximum, you have to shell out at least $10,000. If your college costs are considerably lower than that, the Hope may be the better deal.

You can claim a Hope credit for each eligible student. If you have twins who were college freshmen last year, you may be eligible for up to $3,600 in credits. For the lifetime learning credit, though, the maximum applies to all eligible students in the family. No matter how many kids you have in college, the most you can claim in a year is $2,000.

 "Learning about education deductions can pay off at tax time," Sandra Block, February 21, 2006.

Is Saving for Retirement a Challenge? Here's a Boost

There's a retirement tax credit that's designed to benefit people with modest incomes who save for their retirement. You qualify for the credit if:

- you were born before January 2, 1988
- you're not a full-time student

- no one else (such as your parents) claims an exemption for you on their tax return, and
- your adjusted gross income (in 2008) is not more than:
  - $53,000 if you're married and filing jointly
  - $39,750 if you're a head of household (with qualifying person), or
  - $26,500 if you're either single, married filing separately, or a qualifying widow(er) with a dependent child.

To get the credit, you must invest in a traditional or Roth IRA, 401(k) plan, SIMPLE IRA, or employee SEP. The actual amount of the credit depends on the amount of your contributions and your income level. The most a single person can get is $1,000, if the person makes a $2,000 contribution and has an AGI below $15,000. The most a married couple filing jointly can receive is $2,000, if they each make a $2,000 contribution and their joint AGI is less than $30,000. People with higher incomes receive much less.

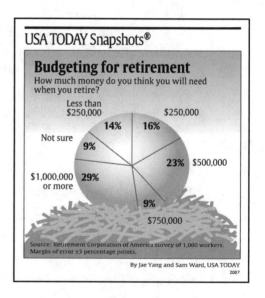

USA TODAY Snapshots®

Budgeting for retirement
How much money do you think you will need when you retire?

Less than $250,000: 14%
$250,000: 16%
$500,000: 23%
$750,000: 9%
$1,000,000 or more: 29%
Not sure: 9%

Source: Retirement Corporation of America survey of 1,000 workers. Margin of error ±3 percentage points.

By Jae Yang and Sam Ward, USA TODAY 2007

This credit does not affect or reduce the tax deduction and deferral benefits of investing in traditional IRAs and tax-deferred retirement plans. (See Chapter 4.)

Own a Business? Tax Breaks for Good Corporate Citizens

A number of tax credits are available just to business owners. To get one, your business must do something that Congress likes or views as socially beneficial. Broadly speaking, the main categories include:

- helping the disadvantaged or disabled
- improving the environment
- helping your employees, or
- investing in research and development.

You may qualify for more than one credit at the same time. However, there is an overall limit on the total business credits you can take in a year, based on your tax liability. If you exceed the limit, you can take the credits in future years or apply them to previous years' taxes—within limits.

> **CAUTION**
> **Many business credits are quite specialized and can be used only by specific types of businesses.** They all tend to be complicated, so you may want a tax pro to handle the details. We discuss some of the more commonly used ones below. For more information about all available business tax credits, see IRS Publication 334, *Tax Guide for Small Business.*

Business credits for helping the disadvantaged or disabled

Several tax credits are available if your business helps someone who is disadvantaged or disabled. Here are some ways to make the most of these credits.

Hire people. A great way to help someone who is low-income or disabled is to give that person a job. Several tax credits are intended to encourage this.

Work opportunity credit. You can take a credit of up to $2,400 for the first year you hire anyone from targeted groups that have a particularly high unemployment rate or other special employment needs—for example, welfare and food stamp recipients, low-income ex-felons, disabled people, and high-risk young people. You can use the credit even if you hire only one person—the amount of the credit is based on the amount of wages you pay. You can also get a $1,200 credit for giving disadvantaged youths summer jobs.

Empowerment zone employment credit. You can take a credit of up to $15,000 ($3,000 per employee) if you hire someone to work in a federal "empowerment zone"—an area designated as economically disadvantaged.

Indian employment credit. You can get a credit of up to $20,000 ($4,000 per employee) for hiring Indian tribe members who live and work on a reservation.

For more information on these credits, see IRS Publication 954, *Tax Incentives for Distressed Communities.*

Make your business accessible. The disabled access tax credit is designed to help small businesses defray the costs of complying with the Americans with Disabilities Act, or ADA. (The ADA prohibits private employers with 15 or more employees from discriminating against people with disabilities in the full and equal enjoyment of goods, services, and facilities offered by any "place of public accommodation"—and includes businesses open to the public.) The credit may be used by any business with either:

- $1 million or less in gross receipts for the preceding tax year, or
- 30 or fewer full-time employees during the preceding tax year.

The credit can be used to cover a variety of expenses, including the cost to remove barriers that prevent a business from being accessible to disabled people. However, the credit may be used only for buildings constructed before November 5, 1990. The credit may also be used for equipment acquisitions and services such as sign language interpreters.

The amount of the tax credit is equal to 50% of your disabled access expenses in a year that are over $250 but below $10,250. Thus, the maximum credit is $5,000.

Credit for improving the environment

This is the largest group of business credits—for businesses that take a hand in improving the environment. Most of these credits are highly specialized and can be used by only a few types of businesses (probably not including yours). For example, there is a low-sulfur diesel fuel production credit for oil refineries and a reforestation credit for timber companies. (All you oil-refinery-owning readers, stand up and cheer.)

Solar power. One credit you may be able to use is the solar power credit. Businesses can get a credit of up to 30% of the cost of buying and installing solar equipment to generate electricity to heat or cool (or provide hot water for use in) a structure, or to provide solar process heat. Unlike the solar credit for homeowners, there's no dollar limit on this credit.

Energy-efficient new homes. If you're a contractor who builds homes, you can get a credit of up to $2,000 for building an energy-efficient home that is sold anytime before the end of 2008. The credit is available for all new homes, including manufactured homes, built after August 8, 2005. To meet the energy-saving requirements, a home must be certified to provide heating and cooling energy savings of 30% to 50% compared to a federal standard. For more information, see IRS Form 8908, *Energy Efficient Home Credit*, and IRS Notices 2006-27 and 2006-11.

Credit for helping your employees

There are a couple of credits you can get if you do some nice things for the people who work for you.

Credit for employer-provided child care. This credit applies to expenses you pay for employee child care and child care resource and referral services. The credit is 25% of qualified expenses you paid for employee child care and 10% of qualified expenses you paid for child care resource and referral services. This credit is limited to $150,000 each year. For more information, see IRS Form 8882, *Credit for Employer-Provided Childcare and Services*.

Credit for small employer pension start-up costs. If you begin a new qualified defined-benefit or defined-contribution plan (including a 401(k) plan), SIMPLE plan, or simplified employee pension, you're due a tax credit of 50% of the first $1,000 of qualified start-up costs. For more information, see IRS Publication 560, *Retirement Plans for Small Business*.

Credit for investing in research

The research and experimentation credit, also called the R & E credit, encourages businesses to invest in scientific research and experimental activities, including energy research. Any technological research qualifies, so long as it relates to a new or improved function, performance, reliability, or quality. The research must involve principles of the physical or biological sciences, engineering, or computer science. It's not available for research in the social sciences, including economics, business management, and behavioral sciences, arts, or humanities.

You can get the credit whether you do the research in-house or contract it out. The credit is generally 20% of the amount by which your research expenses for the year are more than a base amount based on an IRS formula or your business's gross receipts—it's a complex calculation. For more information, see IRS Form 6765, *Credit for Increasing Research Activities*.

USA TODAY Snapshots®

Tactics for growth

Top tactics CEOs would use to grow business in the next 12 months:

New markets, mergers and acquisitions, new products and innovation — 57%

Better penetration of existing markets for existing products — 23%

Better customer service and employee retention — 16%

Source: PricewaterhouseCoopers Annual Global CEO survey of 1,084 CEOs. Margin of error ±3 percentage points.

By Jae Yang and Robert W. Ahrens, USA TODAY 2007

Expats' Delight: Credit for Income Taxes Paid Elsewhere

Here's one for the "Don't change your life around a tax credit" category. But if you're already working in a foreign country and paying income taxes there, you can use a tax credit to make sure you aren't also paying tax on the same income to the U.S. government. You can get a credit for all or part of the amount you paid in foreign tax.

Only foreign income taxes, war profits taxes, and excess profits taxes (or taxes paid in lieu of such taxes) qualify for the credit. Thus, for example, if you've been out shopping for souvenirs or a country estate, you won't get a credit for having paid foreign value-added taxes, sales taxes, or property taxes.

You also can't claim credit for certain foreign income taxes that wouldn't have been double-taxed in the first place—namely exclusions from U.S. income tax under the foreign-earned-income exclusion or the foreign housing exclusion. For more information, see IRS Publication 54, *Tax Guide for U.S. Citizens and Resident Aliens Abroad*.

You get a foreign tax credit only on the portion of your U.S. income tax attributable to your foreign income. This is equal to the lesser of:

- the amount of foreign income taxes you paid, or
- an overall limitation based on the following IRS formula:

Foreign-source taxable income	× U.S. tax before foreign tax credit =
Worldwide taxable income	Overall limit on credit

It's easy to figure out. First, divide your foreign income by your worldwide taxable income (foreign and U.S. taxable income, not including your U.S. personal and dependency exemptions). Multiply this total by the amount of your U.S. income taxes before deducting any foreign tax credits. The total is the overall annual limitation on the credit.

EXAMPLE: Andy, a geologist, earned $10,000 working in a foreign country during part of the year. His U.S. taxable income, not counting his personal and dependency exemptions, is $100,000. Thus, his worldwide taxable income is $110,000. His U.S income tax before taking any foreign tax credit is $20,000. He figures the limitation on his foreign tax credit as follows:

$10,000	× $20,000 = $1,818.
$110,000	

The overall limitation on Andy's foreign tax credit is $1,818. He paid $3,000 in income taxes in the foreign country, but his credit is limited to $1,818, leaving $1,182 in foreign taxes he can't deduct that year ($3,000 – $1,818 = $1,182). He can take a credit for this amount during the next five years, or he can use it to reduce his taxes for the prior two years by amending his tax returns for those years and claiming a refund. The credits he can take for these future or past years are subject to the same limitations as for the current year.

You may also qualify for a foreign tax credit if you own mutual funds that invest in foreign securities. But you may do this only if the fund elects to pass the credit for taxes paid to foreign governments on to its shareholders. If it does, your proportionate share of the foreign taxes paid by your fund will be shown in Box 6 of IRS Form 1099-DIV, *Dividends and Distributions*, which the fund sends you and the IRS at the beginning of each year

Instead of taking a credit for foreign income taxes, you can choose to deduct them as an itemized deduction on your Schedule A. However, it's almost always better to take the credit instead. Only in unusual cases will an itemized deduction for foreign taxes exceed the value of the foreign tax credit.

For more information, see IRS Publication 514, *Foreign Tax Credit for Individuals*.

Bought Your First Home? A Tax Credit That's Really a Loan

The housing bailout legislation passed in July 2008 included some tax help for people buying their first home. As USA TODAY's Sandra Block explains, "First-time home buyers who purchase a primary residence between April 9, 2008, and July 1, 2009, will be eligible for a tax credit of $7,500 or 10% of the purchase price, whichever is less. On the surface, this looks like a pretty good deal. And this tax credit is refundable, which means you'll qualify even if your federal tax bill is less than $7,500, says Bob Scharin, senior tax analyst for Thomson Reuters. For example, a first-time home buyer who owes the IRS $2,000 would receive a refund of $5,500."

But, Block warns, "this provision includes a lot of caveats, including:

- You'll have to pay it back. While this break has been labeled a tax credit, it's really an interest-free loan. Home buyers who claim the credit will be required to pay it back in equal installments over 15 years, starting in the second year after the home is purchased. If you buy a house in 2008 and claim a $7,500 credit on your 2008 tax return, you'll have to pay an additional $500 a year in taxes for 15 years, starting in 2010.
- If you sell your house before the 15 years has elapsed, you'll have to repay the entire balance, unless you sell at a loss.
- If your income exceeds certain thresholds, you're ineligible for the credit. The tax credit phases out for single taxpayers with adjusted gross income of $75,000 to $95,000. For married couples who file jointly, the phaseout is $150,000 to $170,000."

Take Credit for Rehabilitating an Old or Historic Building

Spiffing up an old building—which inevitably involves bringing it up to modern code standards—can cost a bundle. The rehabilitation tax credit helps defray these costs. It's intended to help preserve historic buildings and encourage businesses to stay in older, economically disadvantaged areas, such as inner cities.

To get this credit, your rehabilitation expenditures must exceed the greater of the adjusted basis of the building and its structural components or $5,000. This usually means an extensive rehabilitation project or "gut rehab," as real estate experts call it. To spend this much money on a rehab, you'll usually have to purchase a building that is more or less a shell and restore it—no small task.

Qualifying for the rehabilitation credit

There are actually two different rehabilitation tax credits:

- a credit equal to 10% of part of the cost of rehabilitating a nonhistoric building built before 1936 that will be used for nonresidential, commercial purposes, and

- a 20% credit for part of the cost of rehabilitating any certified historic structure—one listed on the National Register of Historic Places or located in a Registered Historic District and determined to be of significance to the historical district.

If the building is in the area damaged by Hurricane Katrina and part of the Gulf Opportunity Zone, these credits are increased to 13% and 26%, respectively, until the end of 2008.

The two credits are mutually exclusive, and which one fits your project depends on the building—not on your preference.

You can't use the historic building credit to fix up your own home. You can get the 20% credit for commercial, industrial, agricultural, as well as residential rental buildings, but not for property that is used exclusively as the owner's private residence. In addition, the Secretary of the Interior must certify that the project meets their standards and is a "Certified Rehabilitation." You get this by filing a three-part application with the National Park Service. If your building is not already registered as historic, but you think it should be, you can nominate it for historic status by contacting your state historical officer.

No historic certification is needed to obtain the 10% credit. However, the building must be depreciable. That is, it must be used in a trade or business or held for the production of income. It may be used for offices, for commercial, industrial, or agricultural enterprises, or for rental housing. It may not serve exclusively as the owner's private residence. Hotels qualify because they are considered to be in commercial use, not residential.

Collecting the rehabilitation credit

This credit won't help house flippers, who want to get in and out of property ownership fast. First of all, you can't use the credit until the year the building is placed into service—that is, returned to use. What's more, to keep the full credit, you must hold the building for five full years after completing the rehabilitation. If you dispose of the building within a year after it's placed in service, you must pay back 100% of the credit. For properties held between one and five years, the amount you must pay back is reduced by 20% per year.

The following websites provide detailed information on the rehabilitation tax credit:

- National Trust for Historic Preservation at www.nationaltrust.org,
- National Park Service Heritage Preservation at www.nps.gov/history/hps (click "Federal Historic Preservation Tax Incentives").

Benefit From Investing in Low-Income Housing

To spur investment in low-income housing, Congress authorized the states to allocate tax credits to qualifying housing projects. The credit can be used either to construct new or to renovate existing rental buildings.

How much the low-income housing credit is worth

Investors in projects that are not subsidized by the federal government get an annual tax credit of approximately 9% of project construction costs each year for ten years. Investors in federally subsidized projects receive up to a 4% credit for ten years.

The credit for individuals cannot exceed an annual ceiling—generally the amount of tax you would owe on $25,000. For example, if your top tax bracket is 28%, the annual ceiling is $7,000. In addition, to keep the full credit, you must invest in the property for at least 15 years.

How you get the low-income housing credit

No need to rush out and buy an apartment building. Individual investors can get the credit by buying into limited partnerships or limited liability companies (LLCs) put together by syndicators to invest in qualifying low-income housing projects. These partnership or LLC interests can be purchased through brokers and financial planners for as little as $5,000. The investment is made at the beginning of the construction period, which may take a year or more, while the tax credits are paid only when the project is completed and the housing units rented.

The low-income housing credit program is funded by the federal government, but operated by state tax credit allocation agencies. These state agencies choose which projects in their states receive the credit. Each state has only so many credits to hand out, based on its population. For more information, contact your state tax credit allocation agency. You can find a list at www.novoco.com/stcaa.shtml. Also check out the National Housing & Rehabilitation Association's website at www.housingonline.com.

> CAUTION
> **Low-income housing projects are complex, long-term, and often risky investments.** For example, a project could end up losing money if it fails to meet all the requirements for the credit or has trouble attracting tenants. Seek competent advice before making any investment in a low-income housing project.

Delaying the Pain: Deferring Income and the Tax It Brings

A basic, but underutilized tax-saving strategy is to put off paying taxes on your income for as long as you can. Deferring tax on this year's income is like getting a free loan from the government. Just consider: If you pay $1,000 of tax today, it costs you $1,000. But if you postpone paying the $1,000 for five years, you can take that $1,000 and put it in the bank and earn interest.

This no doubt sounds good to you—but how does it work? Everyone knows you can't just announce to Uncle Sam, "Sorry, I think I'll wait until next year to pay my tax bill." In fact, there are a number of ways you can defer paying taxes by a year or two; or in some cases for decades. We'll look at the more common methods and alert you to ones where you'll need professional assistance.

> CAUTION
> **Don't defer paying taxes until you're in a higher tax bracket.** That could leave you worse off than if you'd paid your taxes when you first could have. Deferring payment works best if your top tax rate when you pay is almost the same as or is lower than it was at the time you deferred—something that can be difficult (at best) to predict. But if you can predict a dramatic income increase, try not to defer your taxes into that time period.

Everybody's Deferral Tool: Retirement Accounts

The most common method of deferring income tax is to contribute to a retirement account. You don't have to be working or approaching retirement to have a retirement account—anyone with earned income can open their own individual retirement account (IRA). If you're employed, you may participate in a retirement plan through your employer, such as a 401(k) (or, if you're with a nonprofit, a 403(b)).

Too often, people don't establish or take advantage of retirement plans available to them, and they lose out on tremendous tax-saving opportunities. Maybe retirement seems too far away—or too close. But the fact is, it's never too early or late to think about opening a retirement plan.

Watching your retirement account money grow—tax-free

While plans and options differ, most traditional retirement plans offer you two types of tax deferral opportunities:

- You defer paying tax on the amount you (and/or your employer) contribute to the account.

- You defer paying tax on the money your account earns until you withdraw it (but withdrawals before age 59½ may be subject to tax penalties).

When you contribute to the account, the money either (in the case of a 401(k)) literally flies under the tax radar because your employer deposits it before taxing it, or (in the case of an IRA) it entitles you a tax deduction. You'll have to pay income tax on the money eventually, when you withdraw it upon retirement— but this may be many years, even decades away.

USA TODAY Snapshots®

Americans who expect a defined-contribution plan, such as a 401(k), to be their primary source of retirement income

71% Generation X
63% Baby boomers
45% Seniors

Source: MainStay Investments of New York Life Investment Management survey of 515 respondents ages 26 to 82. Margin of error ±5 percentage points.

By Jae Yang and Dave Merrill, USA TODAY 2005

Just remember, not all retirement accounts allow tax-free contributions: Roth IRAs, Roth 401(k)s, and nondeductible traditional IRAs don't.

> **EXAMPLE:** Art and Agnes, a married couple who file jointly, contribute $8,000 this year to their traditional IRA. That lets them subtract $8,000 from their gross income. Because they're in the 28% tax bracket, they save $2,240 in income taxes (28% × $8,000.) (And they've also socked away $8,000 for retirement.) They won't have to pay any tax on their $8,000 contribution until they start withdrawing the money from their IRA.

With any luck, your retirement accounts will also earn money, in the form of interest or dividends. This is when you get your second gift from the government. With normal investments, you usually must pay taxes on your earnings in the same year that you receive them, plus additional tax if and when you sell (for example, if you sell a stock at a profit).

No need to bother, however, paying taxes on your earnings from a retirement account. You don't owe a bit of tax on the investment earnings until you withdraw the funds. That means that, over time, money in a tax-deferred retirement account will grow much more quickly than the same amount of money in a taxable account, because you'll never have to take money out to pay taxes.

> **EXAMPLE:** Two friends, Baldev and Brian, happen to invest in the same mutual fund. Baldev has a taxable individual account, while Brian invests through a tax-deferred retirement account. They each invest $5,000 per year. They earn 8% on their investments each year and pay income tax at the 28% rate. At the end of 30 years, Brian has $566,416 and Baldev has $272,869. Reason: Baldev had to pay income taxes on the interest his investments earned each year, while Brian's interest accrued tax-free.

Use the online calculator at www.ingfunds.com/investor/content/ resources/calculators/default.aspx to do your own comparisons between deferred and non-tax-deferred accounts for different time periods, amounts, and tax rates.

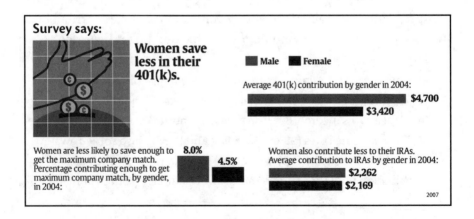

Survey says:

Women save less in their 401(k)s.

■ Male ■ Female

Average 401(k) contribution by gender in 2004: **$4,700** **$3,420**

Women are less likely to save enough to get the maximum company match. Percentage contributing enough to get maximum company match, by gender, in 2004: **8.0%** **4.5%**

Women also contribute less to their IRAs. Average contribution to IRAs by gender in 2004: **$2,262** **$2,169**

2007

Where's the Tax Benefit in Roth Accounts?

Unlike with traditional retirement accounts, the contributions you make to a Roth IRA and Roth 401(k) are not tax deductible—you essentially pay tax on the money before you put it in the account. But once the money is in your Roth account, you're home free: You don't pay any tax on any earnings that grow within the account. And, you don't pay any tax on the earnings or the principal when you take the money out. That's why the earnings you receive from a Roth account are referred to as "tax free," not "tax deferred"—you simply never pay tax on them.

Is a Roth account a good deal? That depends more on the tax rate that applies to your contributions. You've got to pay tax on retirement account contributions sometime, either before you put them into your account (with a Roth) or when you take them out (with a traditional IRA or 401(k), at which time you also pay tax on earnings). So if you can predict that your tax rate will be higher when you retire than it is now, the answer is probably yes, why not take the tax hit on your contribution now and use a Roth? The opposite is true if your taxes go down when you retire, in which case paying taxes on your withdrawals from a traditional retirement account will still be a relatively good deal. The catch is that nobody can know for sure what their tax rate will be when they retire.

Of course, you'll eventually want to withdraw money from your retirement account and, at that point, you'll have to pay taxes on it (except with Roth IRAs and Roth 401(k)s). At what tax rate will you pay? It won't matter what kind of investment you had your money in, whether in stocks or other capital assets—you'll still have to pay ordinary income tax rates. This means you won't be able to take advantage of the lower capital gains rates that would have applied to the sale of these capital assets if only they'd been held outside a retirement account. (See

"Which Investments Belong in Retirement Accounts?" below.) But that's the law, and one of the things you have to weigh when deciding how much money you want to keep in a tax-deferred retirement account.

One last caution before you start trying to squeeze your savings into tax-deferred accounts: Their benefits could be undone if the tax rates skyrocket by the time you retire. Historically, many people's income tax rate at retirement has been lower than it was when they were making the contributions during their working years. If you're one of those people, you'll come out well ahead. However, many people believe taxes will have to be raised in the future to pay for the federal deficit, as well as Social Security and Medicare costs for the hordes of retiring baby boomers. If your crystal ball is telling you that the top income tax rate you end up paying on your account withdrawals when you retire will be higher than your current rate, you might be better off keeping your money in a taxable account and paying tax on it today.

> **EXAMPLE:** Marisol puts $1,000 into a tax-deferred retirement account that earns 8% per year. At the end of 20 years, she has $4,661 in the account. When she withdraws the money, she'll have to pay tax on it at her current tax rate. If, 20 years from now, her tax rate is 35%, she'll have to pay $1,631 in taxes if she withdraws all the money. That would leave her with $3,030. In contrast, if her top tax rate today is 25% and she puts $1,000 into a taxable account that also earns 8%, she'd have to pay a 25% tax on her contribution and then pay income tax every year on her earnings at her applicable tax rate. Let's say Marisol's top rate stays at 25% for ten years, then goes up to 35% because Congress raises income taxes. At the end of 20 years, she'd have $3,451—14% more than in the tax-deferred account. She can withdraw any or all of that money tax-free, because she already paid taxes on it. The result could be even worse for a tax-deferred account if the time frame was shorter. If Marisol left the money in the account for ten years instead of 20, and her tax rate went up to 35% after five years, she'd have $2,159 in the tax-deferred account and $2,626 in the taxable account. After ten years, the taxable account would be worth 22% more than the tax-deferred account.

Which Investments Belong in Retirement Accounts?

If you have a retirement account other than a traditional lifetime employee pension, you'll have to decide how to invest your money. (Your investment options with an employer 401(k) plan may be quite limited.)

Here's a basic rule to follow: Keep investments subject to high taxes in a tax-deferred retirement account so you can defer the tax as long as possible. Keep investments subject to low taxes or no tax at all in taxable accounts. The following chart gives some examples:

Investments to Be Held in Tax-Deferred Retirement Accounts	Investments to Be Held in Taxable Accounts
Corporate bonds	Municipal bonds
Certificates of deposit	Growth stocks
Treasury bills and notes	Dividend-paying stocks
Real estate investment trust (REIT) shares	U.S. savings bonds
	Tax-managed mutual funds
	Index funds
	Tax-deferred annuities

There are thousands of websites, hundreds of books, and several magazines about retirement investing. Two easy-to-understand guides on retirement investing are:

- *Get a Life: You Don't Need a Million to Retire Well*, by Ralph Warner (Nolo), and
- *Investing for Dummies*, by Eric Tyson (Wiley).

No one can predict future tax rates. For most people, the best advice is to hedge your bets. By all means, contribute to tax-deferred retirement plans like a 401(k), especially if your employer will make a matching contribution—this is like found money. But don't put all your savings into tax-deferred plans (which many people are now doing). Instead, keep some money in taxable accounts whose earnings will be taxed at your current tax rates. It's a particularly good idea right now to keep capital assets like stocks and mutual funds in taxable accounts, because of the low capital gains tax rates. Also, take advantage of Roth IRAs and, if available, Roth 401(k)s. You can't deduct your contributions to these accounts, but you don't pay any taxes on your withdrawals.

How much money should you keep in taxable versus tax-deferred accounts? Some investment advisors recommend a 50-50 split. However, this is an individual decision no book can make for you.

Withdrawing your retirement funds: A preview

Someday, you'll get to wave goodbye to the working world and start drawing from those retirement accounts you worked so hard to build

USA TODAY Snapshots®

Many rely on IRAs
Americans who expect IRAs to be their primary source of income:

Seniors **66%**
Baby boomers **61%**
Generation X **58%**

Source: MainStay Investments of New York Life Investment Management survey of 515 respondents ages 26 to 82. Margin of error: ±5 percentage points.

By Jae Yang and Karl Gelles, USA TODAY
2005

up. But you'll have to follow some withdrawal rules—the price, perhaps, of having received those tax-deferral benefits—and it's important to be aware of these rules in advance.

The most important rule is that you're not supposed to withdraw money from your retirement accounts until you're 59½ years old. If you make an early withdrawal (before you're 59½), you must pay regular income tax on the amount you take out, plus a 10% federal tax penalty (unless an exception applies). But don't forget that the money is there, because starting at age 70½, you're expected to withdraw a minimum amount each year and pay tax on it (except with Roth IRAs and Roth 401(k)s).

So, if you aren't prepared to give up your right to use this money freely, you might be better off sticking with taxable accounts, which don't come with restrictions on your use of your money. Or, consider a Roth IRA or Roth 401(k)—you can withdraw your contributions to these accounts at any time without penalty. However, you can't withdraw your earnings from these accounts for five years or your withdrawals will be subject to income tax and early distribution penalties.

Most likely, you'll choose a mix of both taxable investment accounts and tax-deferred accounts such as IRAs and 401(k)s. That raises the question of which you should start withdrawing from first. As a general rule, you'll want to start by taking money from your taxable accounts. Reason: The longer you leave your money in tax-deferred accounts, the more you'll benefit from tax-deferred compounding (see the chart at the beginning of this chapter). Roth IRAs and Roth 401(k)s should be the last accounts you withdraw money from, because they benefit the most from tax-deferred compounding. Keep in mind, however, that the performance of your investments might call for you to break the general rule.

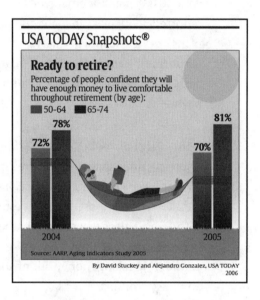

USA TODAY Snapshots®

Ready to retire?
Percentage of people confident they will have enough money to live comfortable throughout retirement (by age):
■ 50-64 ■ 65-74

78%
72%
81%
70%

2004   2005

Source: AARP, Aging Indicators Study 2005

By David Stuckey and Alejandro Gonzalez, USA TODAY 2006

Worried About Foreclosure?
Think Twice Before Tapping Your 401(k)

If your retirement date is still decades away, it's tempting to tap your 401(k) plan for emergency cash. Nearly 20% of companies reported an increase in loans and hardship withdrawals from 401(k) plans during the fourth quarter of 2007, according to a survey of corporate executives and chief financial officers by Duke University and *CFO* magazine. The most common reason: to make mortgage payments.

The IRS allows companies to grant financial hardship withdrawals from 401(k) plans, but only in a limited number of circumstances. Those circumstances include preventing eviction or foreclosure on an employee's primary residence. Individual employers, though, are allowed to impose tougher restrictions or to bar hardship withdrawals altogether, says Jonathan Anderson, an employee benefits expert at Transamerica Retirement Services. So if you're considering taking money out of your 401(k), check with your plan administrator first.

Even if your company allows hardship withdrawals, raiding your 401(k) is almost always a bad idea.

If you're living in a house you can't afford, withdrawing money from your 401(k) might pay the mortgage for a few months. But after that, "You've lost your 401(k) money, and you're still in the same boat," says Catherine Williams, vice president of financial literacy for Money Management International.

A 401(k) loan is less costly than a hardship withdrawal, because as long as you repay the loan, you don't have to pay taxes on it. Even though employers aren't required to allow workers to borrow from their 401(k) accounts, most large companies do permit it.

 "In a terrible bind? Dipping into your 401(k) probably isn't the answer," by Sandra Block, December 11, 2007.

Your retirement plan options

The following chart will give you a closer look at some of the different types of retirement plans available. You'll have to do some research to figure out which plan or plans will work best for you.

Traditional IRA

Description	An investment account where deposits are tax deductible and earnings are not taxable until withdrawn.
Who can start one	Anybody with earned income (from a job, business, or alimony).
Annual contribution rules	Maximum contribution to all your IRA accounts: Single persons $5,000, married persons $10,000, even if one spouse isn't working. (2008). (After 2008, the limit will be adjusted annually for inflation, in $500 increments.) People 50 years or older at the end of the year can make an additional catch-up contribution of $1,000. Note: You should also limit your contributions based on the amount you can deduct, which depends on your income.
Income limits or phaseouts	If neither you nor your spouse (if any) has another retirement plan, all your IRA contributions are deductible regardless of income. If you (or your spouse) are covered by another retirement plan (such as a 401(k)), then: If you're single and have another retirement plan, the possible deductions start phasing out when your modified adjusted gross income (MAGI) reaches $53,000, and disappear completely when your MAGI exceeds $63,000 (in 2008). If you're a married couple filing jointly, the phase out range is from $85,000 to $105,000 or $159,000 to $169,000, depending on circumstances (in 2008).
Other resources	If your income is in the phase out range, the calculator at www.choosetosave.org/calculators will tell you how much you may deduct.
Notes and strategies	If you don't qualify for a deduction, you can contribute to a "nondeductible IRA," in which your money grows tax-free. When making withdrawals from this nondeductible account, you'd pay tax only on the account earnings, not on contributions (which were already taxed). However, figuring out how much is taxable or not can be a headache. (In fact, you could mix deductible and nondeductible contributions in the same account, a potentially greater headache.) In any case, if you'll be paying taxes up front (by making nondeductible contributions), you might as well contribute to a Roth, where you won't have to pay taxes on withdrawals of earnings after age 59½.

Roth IRA

Description	Similar to a traditional IRA, except contributions aren't tax deductible. But you can withdraw the money tax free upon retirement, and never pay any tax on earnings.
Who can start one	Anyone with earned income.
Maximum annual contribution	Assuming it's your only IRA of any sort, the lesser of your taxable compensation or $4,000 ($5,000 if you're 50 or older). But see income phaseouts on contributions, below.
Income limits or phaseouts	If you're single, phaseout begins when your MAGI reaches $101,000; at $116,000, you can no longer make contributions. If you're married and file a joint return, phase out begins when MAGI reaches $159,000, and at $169,000, you can no longer make contributions. (These limits don't apply to conversions of money from traditional IRAs to Roth IRAs.)
Other resources	For help figuring out how much you may contribute, see calculator at www.moneychimp.com/articles/rothira/contribution_limits.htm. For calculators to help you compare a Roth IRA to a traditional IRA, see www.choosetosave.org/calculators. For more information on Roth IRAs, see www.rothira.com and IRS Publication 590, *Individual Retirement Arrangements*.
Notes and strategies	If you leave your money in your Roth IRA when you die, your heirs will inherit it tax free. Establishing a Roth IRA and even transferring money into it from a traditional IRA can be a good way to hedge your bets about future tax rates and avoid deferring too much. Roth IRAs make the most sense for younger people who have many years until retirement. The long time frame leaves more time for the money to grow enough to make up for the taxes paid up front on contributions.

401(k) plan

Description	Most commonly offered retirement plan for employees. You contribute a portion of your salary to your own investment account. The money is deducted directly from your pay by your employer, using pretax dollars. You pay no tax on the money that you contribute (possibly with some matching contributions from your employer) each year. The money in your account grows tax free until you withdraw it, at which point you must pay taxes on it.

Who can start one	Employees whose employer offers a plan (nonprofit employees may be offered a 403(b)). Self-employed persons may establish solo 401(k) plans.
Maximum annual contribution	In 2008, up to $15,500 of your salary, up to a maximum of the lesser of 100% of your salary or $46,000. Employees 50 years of age or over could elect to make an additional catch-up contribution of $5,000 (which doesn't count toward the limit). However, employers are permitted to place percentage caps on their employees' contributions, and many limit contributions to 10% to 15% of employee salary.
Income limits or phaseouts	See above.
Other resources	See www.401khelpcenter.com for detailed information.
Notes and strategies	Many employers match all or part of the employee's contribution, although this is not required. These matching contributions are not taxable income for the employee—they are a tax-free employee fringe benefit.

Roth 401(k)

Description	Similar to the Roth IRA, but offered through an employer. The money contributed to the plan is not paid with pretax dollars, nor is it tax deductible; but in return, withdrawals made after age 59½ are tax free.
Who can start one	Employees whose company offers one (more and more are doing so).
Maximum annual contribution	In 2008, up to $15,500 of your salary, up to a maximum of the lesser of 100% of your salary or $46,000. Employees 50 years of age or over could elect to make an additional catch-up contribution of $5,000 (which doesn't count toward the limit). However, employers are permitted to place percentage caps on their employees' contributions, and many limit contributions to 10% to 15% of employee salary.
Income limits or phaseouts	See above.
Other resources	Detailed guidance on Roth 401(k) issues can be found at www.401khelpcenter.com/cw/cw_roth401k.html.
Notes and strategies	See Roth IRA above.

Roth IRA Conversions

If you like the sound of the Roth IRA and you have other retirement accounts, you may be able to convert them to a Roth IRA. In the past, you could only convert from a traditional IRA to a Roth IRA, so people resorted to convoluted strategies like placing funds in a traditional IRA just so they could convert. Starting in 2008, however, you may directly roll over funds from qualified retirement plans, such as 401(k)s, to a Roth IRA.

Until the year 2010, you may do such a conversion only if your modified AGI is under $100,000. Starting in 2010, anyone will be allowed convert to a Roth IRA, no matter their income.

However, when you convert to a Roth from a traditional IRA or tax-qualified retirement plan, you'll have to pay income tax on the amount of the conversion. For example, if you convert $20,000 from your traditional IRA to a Roth IRA, you'll have to add $20,000 to your taxable income for the year. If you were in the 25% bracket, this would add $5,000 to your income taxes. (If you convert in 2010, you can pay the tax over two years instead of one.) One way to keep these taxes down is to convert only a portion of your traditional IRA or tax-qualified retirement plan into a Roth each year for several years instead of doing it all at once.

Whether a Roth conversion is a good idea or not depends on many factors including your age, your current tax rate, and your tax rate upon retirement. You can find an online calculator http://dinkytown.com/java/RothTransfer.html that allows you to compare the results.

> **TIP**
>
> **Other employer plans also exist.** Beyond the traditional accounts described above, employers may offer their employees SEP-IRAs, SIMPLE IRAs, and Keogh Plans. If you work for an educational or religious institution, or a nonprofit organization, you may have a choice between a 401(k) and a 403(b) or 457 plan (see IRS Publication 571, *Tax-Sheltered Annuity Plans*).

RESOURCE

For additional information on retirement plans, see:

- *IRAs, 401(k)s & Other Retirement Plans: Taking Your Money Out,* by Twila Slesnick and John C. Suttle (Nolo)
- IRS Publication 560, *Retirement Plans for the Small Business,* and
- IRS Publication 590, *Individual Retirement Arrangements.*

You can also find excellent discussions of both the tax and investment aspects of retirement at the websites maintained by major mutual fund companies such as the Vanguard Group (www.vanguard.com) and Fidelity Investments (www.fidelity.com).

No Profits, No Tax: Holding on to Your Investments

Perhaps the simplest way to defer taxes is to purchase investments that produce little or no annual income and then hold on to them for as long as possible while they go up in value. You won't owe any tax on the increased value until you sell the investment. Examples of such investments include stocks that issue few or no annual dividends, tax-managed mutual funds, index funds, and vacant land.

> EXAMPLE: Bugsy bought a small vacant lot near the Las Vegas strip in 1980 for $1,000. Today, it's worth $100,000. As long as Bugsy doesn't sell the land, he owes no tax on his $99,000 paper profit. If he needs money, he can take out a loan using the land as collateral and still not owe any tax.

If you hold on to the investment until you die, no tax will ever be due on the appreciation you earned. This is because the basis of inherited property is ordinarily its fair market value on the date of the owner's death—often called stepped-up basis. This can result in enormous tax savings if the asset has appreciated in value since it was purchased.

USA TODAY Snapshots®

How should the U.S. taxation system be changed?

Top responses:

Flat tax[1]

Significant reform

National retail sales tax[2]

Stay the same

35%

28%

12%

12%

1 – Single-rate tax on wages and pension distributions
2 – Tax on the sale of goods and services from businesses to households
Source: Schwab Institutional Independent Advisor Outlook survey of 1,387 independent financial advisory firm employees. Margin of error: ±3 percentage points.

By Jae Yang and Karl Gelles, USA TODAY 2007

EXAMPLE: Bugsy is murdered by business rivals in 2008, and his vacant land is inherited by his daughter Annette. Annette's basis in the property automatically becomes equal to its fair market value when Bugsy died—$100,000. She quickly sells the property for $100,000. The sales price and her basis are the same, so Annette doesn't owe any tax on the sale. The $99,000 increase in the property's value since Bugsy bought it goes untaxed.

This doesn't mean you should hang on to a losing investment just to defer taxes. Taxes are just one of the factors to consider before deciding whether to keep an investment or get rid of it.

Changes in Tax Basis Rules Looming for 2010

Currently, there's no limit on the amount of inherited property that can receive a stepped-up basis. However, this will change in 2010, when the heirs of anyone who dies will receive a stepped-up basis only on inherited property worth a total of $1.3 million. (Surviving spouses receive a stepped-up basis of an additional $3 million worth.) All property above the limit will carry the same basis as it had for the deceased person. It's unclear whether this new rule will last beyond 2010, or whether the old, unrestricted stepped-up basis rule will return in 2011. Of course, you need to worry about this only if your assets have appreciated by more than $1.3 million since you bought them—not the worst problem. For a detailed discussion, see *Plan Your Estate*, by Denis Clifford (Nolo).

Happy New Year: Deferring Business Income to Next Year

If you're self-employed and are a cash method taxpayer (as most self-employed people are), you have to pay tax only on money you receive during the tax year—usually the calendar year. Thus, you can defer income by billing clients next year for work you've done this year. If this isn't practical, you could break down the payments due into installments and defer some of them until the following year. If clients or customers owe you money, don't press for payment until after the new year.

> **EXAMPLE:** Bettina, a graphic designer, completes a project for Acme, Inc., in November 2008, for which she is owed $10,000. However, she doesn't bill Acme until the beginning of January 2009. This way, she won't have to report the $10,000 as income on her 2008 taxes. She's in the 25% federal income tax bracket, so this saves her $2,500 in federal income tax for 2008. She also saves another $1,340 in self-employment taxes, and $600 in state income tax. She'll have to pay tax on the $10,000 in 2009, but in the meantime, she gets the use of the money, and she doesn't expect to end up in a higher tax bracket by then.

There are rules limiting how you can defer business income. If you're a cash method taxpayer, the IRS won't let you close your eyes to payments that you've "constructively received," meaning the money was credited to your account or otherwise made available to you without restriction. If you authorize someone to be your agent and receive income for you, you're considered to have received it when your agent receives it.

> **EXAMPLE:** Interest is credited to your business bank account in December 2008, but you do not withdraw it or enter it into your passbook until 2009. You must include the amount in gross business income for 2008, not 2009.

Similarly, you cannot hold checks or other payments from one tax year to another to avoid paying tax on the income.

EXAMPLE: On December 1, 2008, Helen receives a $5,000 check from a client. She leaves it on her desk and doesn't cash it until January 10, 2009. She must still report the $5,000 as income for 2008, because she constructively received it that year.

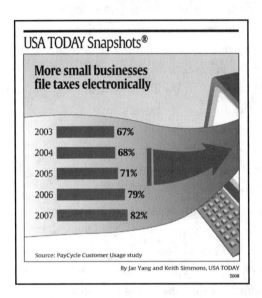

USA TODAY Snapshots®

More small businesses file taxes electronically

Year	Percent
2003	67%
2004	68%
2005	71%
2006	79%
2007	82%

Source: PayCycle Customer Usage study

By Jae Yang and Keith Simmons, USA TODAY 2008

Whether you want to defer business income in any particular year depends upon your circumstances. If you expect your top bracket to be the same next year as this year, or lower, deferral is a good idea. But, if you expect your business income to go up substantially next year, you could be better off not deferring income to that year when you'll be in a higher tax bracket.

Can You Wait for That Bonus? Deferring Employee Compensation

If you're an employee, deferring part of your salary or other compensation to a future year is another way to lower this year's taxes. For example, if you know you'll be paid an annual bonus, you can ask your employer to hold off paying it until January of the following year. True, you'll have to pay tax on it for that year, but again, you'll be able to invest the money in the meantime.

Many employers are willing to go along with compensation deferral requests. If your company uses the accrual method of accounting, as most bigger companies do, it can probably deduct your bonus this year even if it doesn't actually pay it to you until the following year. You could also have your employer pay you your bonus over several years instead of one, and even pay interest on what it owes you.

For such income deferral to work, however, you must elect to have the income deferred before the start of the calendar year in which it will be earned—that is, by December 31 of the current year.

> EXAMPLE: Sid, a crack salesperson for Acme, Inc., gets a substantial bonus every year. He would like to have payment of his 2008 bonus deferred until 2009. He has until December 31, 2007, to ask Acme to defer the bonus. If he waits until 2008, he'll have to include the bonus in his 2008 income.

There's an important exception to the rule described above. An employee can wait as many as six months after the start of the year to elect to defer "performance-based compensation"—in other words, to June 30. Performance-based compensation can be a bonus or other compensation paid to an employee, but it must be tied to written preestablished criteria, such as meeting a certain sales goal over the next year. The services must be performed over at least 12 months.

There are many more sophisticated ways to defer employee compensation—for example:

- salary reduction arrangements in which your employer defers part of your salary to future years
- top-hat plans (also called supplemental executive retirement plans or SERPs) in which extra retirement benefits are provided to a select group of management or highly compensated employees, and
- excess benefit plans that provide benefits to selected employees beyond those allowed for tax-qualified plans.

Deferred compensation plans became subject to complex new tax rules in 2005. If you fail to follow these rules, you could owe tax on the deferred compensation plus a 20% penalty and interest. Your employer should be on top of these requirements and be able to explain them to you. If not, seek guidance from a tax professional.

> ! CAUTION
> **Short-term deferrals are the safest.** Delaying your bonus by a month or two, for example, should be no problem. However, if you end up in a higher tax bracket in the future when you receive the compensation—or if your company goes bankrupt—you could lose out. In a bankruptcy, your money could be claimed by the company's creditors, leaving nothing with which to pay you. Deferring substantial amounts of compensation many years into the future is best done only by highly paid people with the assistance of a professional adviser.

No Need to Ask: Automatic Interest Deferral on U.S. Savings Bonds

A simple way to defer income is to purchase U.S. savings bonds. You don't need to pay federal income taxes on the interest earned on I Bonds or Series EE Savings Bonds until you redeem (cash) the bond or it stops earning interest 30 years from the issue year. This tax deferral feature is automatic—you don't have to do anything to get it. In addition, U.S. savings bond interest is not subject to state or local taxes. But you need to make sure you take this deduction on your state taxes. It's not automatic.

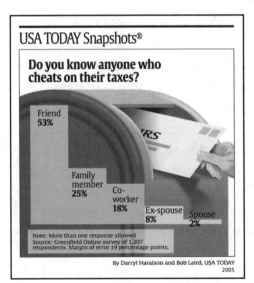

USA TODAY Snapshots®

Do you know anyone who cheats on their taxes?

Friend 53%
Family member 25%
Co-worker 18%
Ex-spouse 8%
Spouse 2%

Note: More than one response allowed
Source: Greenfield Online survey of 1,207 respondents. Margin of error ±9 percentage points.

By Darryl Haralson and Bob Laird, USA TODAY 2005

Moreover, you may not have to pay any federal income tax on your interest if you use the money from these bonds to pay for higher education expenses for yourself or someone else. (See Chapter 3.)

The main difference between I Bonds and Series EE bonds is how the interest is calculated. The interest I bonds pay is indexed for inflation, based on the Consumer Price Index. Thus, the interest rate will go up if inflation goes up. In contrast, Series EE bonds pay a fixed rate of interest based on ten-year Treasury note yields. Series EE bonds usually pay a lower interest rate than I bonds.

You can buy up to $5,000 worth of each type of bond each year. This new annual limit, in effect since 2008, applies separately to Series EE and Series I savings bonds, and separately to bonds issued in paper or electronic form. Under the new rules, an individual can buy a maximum of $5,000 worth of electronic and paper bonds of each series in a single calendar year, or a total of $20,000, in single ownership form.

For more information, see www.savingsbonds.gov and www.publicdebt.treas.gov.

Annuities: Sometimes Worth the Trouble

An annuity is a type of retirement plan, but it differs in many ways from the tax-qualified retirement plans discussed above. Annuities are the only retirement investment that can give you a guaranteed income for the rest of your life. Although your contributions to an annuity are not tax deductible, you aren't limited as to how much you can contribute each year, and the money in your account grows tax-free until you withdraw it.

To start an annuity, you give a life insurance company a single lump sum payment or a series of payments over time. In return, the company promises to pay you (or your beneficiary or heirs) a benefit (money) on an agreed-upon retirement date in the future. The amount of the benefit is based on the plan's earnings. You receive your benefit either as a single lump sum payment or a series of payments over time—usually for the rest of your life.

There are two basic types of annuities—fixed and variable. Fixed annuities pay a fixed interest rate on your investment and, like bank CDs, are conservative investments, except that they're not federally insured. With a variable annuity, you get to choose how your money is invested, typically in mutual funds. Variable annuities are similar to 401(k) plans in that your returns depend on the market performance of your annuity investments. There's no way of knowing how the stock market will perform in the future, so variable annuities are inherently riskier than fixed annuities.

The insurance industry offers something called "tax-deferred annuities." These are not tax-qualified plans, and thus don't offer most of the tax benefits of the retirement accounts discussed above. Moreover, the money you eventually receive from an annuity is taxed at ordinary income rates even if it's invested in capital assets like stocks. So where are the tax advantages? During the years before you start receiving payments, your earnings will grow without being taxed. When you start receiving payments, you don't have to pay tax on the amount of your original investment, because you already paid tax on this money. However, your payments are all considered to be taxable income until you use up all of your earnings; only then will your payments be tax free.

Tax-deferred annuities are not on many experts' list of favorite invest-ments, because the fees and costs currently tend to be higher than you'd pay for IRAs, 401(k)s, and other retirement plans. However, annuities may be a good option if you've already contributed the maximum to your employer-sponsored retirement plans, but still want to set aside more on a tax-deferred basis. Unlike with most retirement accounts, you don't have to make withdrawals by the time you are 70½. But, as with retirement accounts, you'll pay a penalty if you make withdrawals before age 59½. Consult your investment adviser for more information.

Swapping Real Estate: Deferring Taxes on Investment or Rental Property

When you sell property, you usually pay tax on the profit at the time of the sale. But an arrangement called a like-kind exchange (or Section

1031 exchange) lets you defer paying taxes by swapping your property for similar property owned by someone else. Perhaps, for example, you want to trade up to a more valuable property, or you're tired of managing an office building and want to invest in a hotel. The property you receive in the exchange is treated as if it were a continuation of the property you gave up. The result is that you postpone the recognition (taxation) of your gain by shifting the basis of old property to the new property. So you defer paying taxes on any profit you would have received, and own new property instead.

In this type of like-kind exchange, you can only exchange property held for investment or for business use. You can't exchange personal property, including the home you live in or a vacation house, unless you rent it out. And you can't exchange business inventory or stocks and bonds.

> CAUTION
> **Like-kind exchanges are one of the most complex areas of taxation.** They are subject to many rules that are strictly enforced by the IRS and should be done only with professional assistance.

EXAMPLE: Eve exchanges a rental house with an adjusted basis of $250,000 for other real estate held for investment. The fair market value of both properties is $500,000. The basis of Eve's new property is the same as the basis of the old one ($250,000). No gain is recognized on the transaction.

If you keep exchanging your property for property worth at least as much as yours, you'll never recognize any gain on which you must pay tax. However, sooner or later you'll probably want to sell the replacement property for cash, not exchange it for another property. When this occurs, the original deferred gain, plus any additional gain realized since the purchase of the replacement property, is subject to tax. For this reason, a like-kind exchange is tax deferred, not tax free.

EXAMPLE: Assume that five years after the exchange described in the above example, Eve sells her rental house for $800,000 cash. Now she has to pay tax—and quite a lot at that—because she has a $550,000 long-term capital gain. Her gain is $550,000, because her basis in the property is only $250,000 (the basis of the property she exchanged for the building five years earlier). The $800,000 sales price minus $250,000 basis = $550,000 gain.

If you convert the last property you exchange into your personal residence, you can permanently exclude up to $500,000 of your gain from its sale. You must own the property for at least five years and live in it for at least two years to qualify for this exclusion. (See Chapter 2.)

EXAMPLE: Assume that Eve rents out her house for all of 2006 and 2007. On April 15, 2008, she moves into the house and uses it as her personal residence. She can sell the property any time after April 14, 2011, and pay no tax at all on up to $500,000 of her gain, because she is a married taxpayer filing jointly (the exclusion is only $250,000 for single taxpayers).

In addition, you may only exchange property for other similar property, called "like-kind" property by the IRS. Like-kind properties have the same nature or character, even if they differ in grade or quality. Thus, a new car is like kind to a used car. All U.S. real estate is considered to be like kind with all other U.S. real estate, no matter the type or exact location—for example, an apartment building in New York is like kind to an office building in California.

In practice, it's rare that two people want to swap their properties with each other. Instead, one of the property owners usually wants cash for his or her property, not a swap. This transaction can still be structured as a like-kind exchange. This is often done with the help of a third party called a qualified intermediary, or QI, in the business of facilitating like-kind exchanges.

EXAMPLE: Abe owns vacant land he bought for $100,000, which is now worth $200,000. He wants to exchange it for other property instead of selling it and having to pay tax on his $100,000 profit. He puts his property up for sale and in the meantime contacts Carl, a qualified intermediary. Carl locates a small commercial building for sale that Abe likes, but Bob, the owner, has no interest in exchanging it for other property. Carl and Abe enter into an exchange agreement. Carl purchases Bob's building for $200,000 cash that he borrows and then exchanges it for Abe's land. Carl receives a fee for facilitating the exchange and sells Abe's land to repay the funds he borrowed to buy Bob's property. With Carl's help, Abe has exchanged his vacant land for Bob's building, even though Bob didn't want to do a direct exchange.

USA TODAY Snapshots®

Most taxpayers expect refund

More than half of taxpayers expect to get a refund after filing their 2007 taxes.

Getting a refund **53%**

Owing taxes **24%**

Breaking even **12%**

Not sure **11%**

Source: TransUnion's TrueCredit.com survey of 9,497 adults 18 and older conducted by Zogby International. Margin of error ±1 percentage point.

By Jae Yang and Veronica Salazar, USA TODAY 2008

There are strict time limits on such delayed exchanges, which can be more complicated than the above example, involving as many as four parties. You must identify the replacement property for your property within 45 days of its sale. And your replacement property purchase must be completed within 180 days of the initial sale. Because of these time limits, it's a good idea to have a replacement property lined up before you sell your property. Professional exchange companies (also called accommodators or facilitators) can help you find replacement property and handle the transaction for you. You'll find listings for such companies through the website of the Federation of Exchange Accommodators at www.1031.org.

For more information on real property exchanges, see IRS Publication 544, *Sales and Other Dispositions of Assets,* and IRS Form 8824, *Instructions, Like-Kind Exchanges.* Also, refer to *The Real Estate Investor's Tax Guide,* by Vernon Hoven (Dearborn).

Exchanging Your Personal Residence

You can't do a like-kind exchange for your personal residence, because exchanges are allowed only for business or investment property. But you can exchange your residence if you convert it into a rental property before you sell it. To do this, you must move out of the home and rent it out for an appreciable amount of time. There is no time limit set by law, but most tax experts advise that you rent the house for at least one year before exchanging it.

Spreading Out Profits (and Taxes) With Installment Sales

If you sell real estate or other property and are paid the entire purchase price at the close of sale, you'll have to pay tax that year on your entire profits. But, if you want to defer some of the taxes you'll owe to another year, you can structure the sale as an installment sale, with payments spread out over more than one year. You'll pay tax each year only on the part of the profit that came in via these installment payments.

Installment sales can be used for real estate and business or investment property only. You can't use the installment method for sales of business inventory or stocks and securities traded on an established securities market. Also, the installment sale method may be used only where the property is sold at a gain (for a profit), not a loss.

Each payment on an installment sale usually consists of the following three parts:

- interest income
- return of your adjusted basis (investment) in the property, and
- gain on the sale.

In each year that you receive a payment, you must include the interest part in your taxable income, as well as the part that is your gain on the sale. The interest is taxed at ordinary income rates, but the gain may be taxed at lower capital gains rates. You do not include in income the part that is the return of your basis in the property. Basis is the amount of your investment in the property for tax purposes.

> EXAMPLE: In 2008, a buyer agrees to give you $100,000 for land that you bought for $40,000. Your gross profit on the sale is $60,000. You get a $20,000 down payment and the buyer's note for $80,000, which will be paid in four $20,000 annual installments, plus 6% interest, beginning in 2009. Thus, instead of getting $100,000 in 2008, you'll receive $20,000 a year for five years, plus 6% interest for four years. Only $12,000 of each $20,000 payment is counted as income; the other $8,000 is return of your $40,000 basis in the property.

Installment sales are most often used for sales of real estate and purchases of small business. For a detailed discussion of using the installment sale method to sell a business, refer to *The Complete Guide to Selling a Business*, by Fred Steingold (Nolo).

For more general information on this topic, see IRS Publication 537, *Installment Sales*.

Count Every Penny: Reducing Taxable Income With Deductions

Everybody knows that taking tax deductions lowers your taxes. Unfortunately, not everybody takes all the deductions available to them. When the IRS processes your tax return, it won't be looking for deductions you might have missed. It's up to you, with or without the help of a tax professional, to figure out which deductions to claim each year. Your efforts could pay off nicely: For example, if you're in the 25% top tax bracket, you'll pay $25 less in income tax for every $100 in deductions you find.

Something for Everyone: Types of Tax Deductions

A tax deduction (also called a tax write-off) lets you subtract an amount of money from what's called your taxable income (the amount on which you must pay tax). The more deductions you have, the lower your taxable income will be and the less tax you'll have to pay.

There are four basic types of tax deductions. Each has its own special rules and limitations.

- **Standard deduction.** A specified amount taxpayers may deduct each year instead of adding their deductions up one by one, or "itemizing."
- **Itemized deductions.** Expenses that may be deducted individually instead of taking the standard deduction. These include items such as home mortgage interest, state and local taxes, charitable contributions, and medical expenses above a threshold amount.
- **Adjustments to income.** These are a group of expenses that you can deduct whether you itemize or take the standard deduction.
- **Business deductions.** These are for business owners only, who can deduct such expenses as office space rent, supplies, and equipment.

CAUTION

Never, ever, buy anything just to get a tax deduction.
A deduction will never save you as much in tax as you paid to get
the deduction in the first place, so you'll end up out of pocket for
something you didn't want or need.

Nonitemizers: Don't Miss Those Above-the-Line Deductions

Adjustment to income (on our list above) are also called "above-
the-line deductions," because they literally go before the line on
your tax return that lists your adjusted gross income (AGI). They get
subtracted from your gross income, creating a deduction whether
or not you itemize. They're discussed in detail under "Adjust Your
Income With Above-the-Line Deductions," below.

Below-the-line deductions are subtracted from a taxpayer's
AGI. The standard deduction and itemized deductions are below-
the-line deductions. Only those taxpayers who itemize get to
take advantage of these deductions, and many of the itemized
deductions are subject to percentage-of-AGI limitations that don't
apply to above-the-line deductions.

What's in It for You:
The Dollar Value of a Deduction

Most taxpayers don't fully appreciate just how much money they can—
and can't—save with tax deductions. Only part of any deduction will
end up back in your pocket. Because a deduction represents income
on which you don't have to pay tax, the value of any deduction is the

amount of tax you would have had to pay on that income had you not deducted it. So a deduction of $1,000 won't save you $1,000—it will save you whatever you otherwise would have had to pay as tax on that $1,000 of income.

To find out the value of a deduction, you must first figure out your marginal income tax bracket. The U.S. income tax system has six different tax rates for individuals (often called tax brackets), which range from 10% of taxable income to 35% (see the chart "2008 Federal Personal Income Tax Brackets," below). The higher your income, the higher your tax rate.

You don't pay the same rate on all your income, but move from one bracket to the next as your taxable income goes up and reaches the next bracket amount. If, for example, you're a single taxpayer, you pay 10% on all your taxable income up to $8,025. If your taxable income is higher than $8,025, the next tax rate (15%) applies to all your income over $8,025—but the 10% rate still applies to the first $8,025. If your income exceeds the 15% bracket amount, the next tax rate (25%) applies to the excess amount, and so on until you reach the top bracket of 35%.

The tax bracket in which the last dollar you earn for the year falls is called your "marginal tax bracket." For example, if you have $70,000 in taxable income, your marginal tax bracket is 25%. The following table lists the 2008 federal income tax brackets for single and married individual taxpayers.

2008 Federal Personal Income Tax Brackets		
Tax Bracket	Income If Single	Income If Married Filing Jointly
10%	Up to $8,025	Up to $16,050
15%	From $8,026 to $32,550	$16,051 to 65,100
25%	$32,551 to $78,850	$65,101 to $131,450
28%	$78,851 to $164,550	$131,451 to $200,300
33%	$164,551 to $357,700	$200,301 to $357,700
38%	All over $357,700	All over $357,700

The next thing you must do in determining how much tax a deduction will save you is to multiply the amount of the deduction by your marginal tax bracket. For example, if your marginal tax bracket is 25%, you will save approximately 25¢ in federal income taxes for every dollar you're able to claim as a deduction (25% × $1 = 25¢). (This calculation is only approximate, because an additional deduction may move you from one tax bracket to another and thus lower your marginal tax rate, and because some deductions are phased out as your AGI goes up.)

USA TODAY Snapshots®

Top five states with highest median property tax
(In percentage of income)

New Jersey	6.2%
Vermont	5.5%
North Dakota	5.2%
Rhode Island	5.2%
Illinois	5.0%

Source: Zillow.com   By Jae Yang and Sam Ward, USA TODAY 2008

Most federal income tax deductions can also be deducted from any state income tax you owe. The average state income tax rate is about 6%, although seven states (Alaska, Florida, Nevada, South Dakota, Texas, Washington, and Wyoming) don't have an income tax. Two states (Tennessee and New Hampshire) tax only dividend and interest income. (For a list of all state income tax rates, see www.taxadmin.org/FTA/rate/ind_inc.html.)

If you own a business, your business deductions can also reduce your taxable income for purposes of the 15.4% Social Security and Medicare tax, which makes them especially valuable.

Going the Easy Route: The Standard Deduction

Believe it or not, Congress doesn't want to tax you into the poorhouse. To help avoid this, all individual taxpayers are allowed to deduct certain personal expenses, such as medical expenses, home mortgage interest and property taxes, and charitable contributions.

There are two ways to deduct these expenses—by taking the standard deduction or by itemizing your deductions. The easiest way—both for you and the IRS—is to claim the standard deduction. The standard deduction is a specified dollar amount that depends on your filing status. It's adjusted for inflation each year; see the following chart for the standard deduction amounts for 2008.

2008 Standard Deductions	
Filing Status	Standard Deduction
Single or Married filing separately	$5,450
Married filing jointly	$10,900
Head of household	$8,000

The standard deduction is even higher for people who are 65 or older or who are blind. These people get an additional $1,350 if they're single or $1,050 if they're married. Dependents who don't work get $900; those who do work can get as much as adults, depending on how much they earn. (See Chapter 2.)

In addition, for 2008 only, a special rule allows homeowners who take the standard deduction to deduct all or part of their property tax. Ordinarily, only homeowners who itemize their deductions and file Schedule A would get a deduction for real property taxes. You get this deduction by increasing the amount of your standard deduction by the lesser of:

- the amount of real property taxes you paid during the year, or
- $1,000 ($500 for single filers).

EXAMPLE: Mary and Max are a low-income couple who own a small house for which they paid $900 in property tax during 2008. They don't itemize because their total itemized deductions, including property tax, are only $9,000, far below the $10,900 standard deduction for married couples in 2008. However, because of the new rule, Mary and Max can increase their standard deduction to $11,800.

Approximately two-thirds of all taxpayers take the standard deduction instead of itemizing.

Whether to take the standard deduction or itemize your deductions is a choice you must make each year. If you choose the standard deduction, you can't take any itemized deductions. But you can still deduct adjustments to income and business expenses—your above-the-line deductions.

If you add up all your itemized deductions and they don't reach the standard deduction amount, go for the standard deduction. The people who benefit the most from the standard deduction are usually those with modest incomes, particularly those who are not homeowners, and thus have no deductible expenses for mortgage interest or property taxes.

Another benefit of the standard deduction: You'll have a much simpler tax return to fill out and won't have to keep track of so many receipts and other records.

Some People Can't Use the Standard Deduction

You can't take the standard deduction, and must itemize your deductions, if:

- you're married, filing a separate return, and your spouse itemizes deductions, or
- you're a nonresident or dual-status alien during the year. You are considered a dual-status alien if you were both a nonresident and resident alien during the same year. If you're a nonresident alien who is married to a U.S. citizen or resident at the end of the year, you can choose to be treated as a U.S. resident—in which case you can take the standard deduction.

Going for Every Dollar: Choosing to Itemize

If you think you can outdo the standard deduction, you'll need to itemize your deductions, or add up the various qualifying expenses one by one. You must list all the deductions on IRS Schedule A and include the schedule with your tax return. For 2008, if you're a single taxpayer, you should itemize if your total itemized deductions are worth more than $5,450. If you're married and file jointly, you should itemize if your itemized deductions add up to more than $10,900.

Of course, itemizing is a lot more work than taking the standard deduction. You have to know what expenses are deductible (they're covered in the subsections below), and keep track of them. You also need to keep records of your expenses. Bank records or credit card statements are not enough—you need to keep receipts and other bills showing what you spent the money on. You don't need to send these in, but keep them in case the IRS decides to audit you.

Itemized deductions are usually personal in nature, and don't include business expenses (although they do include some job expenses). The largest itemized deductions are those for home mortgage interest, property taxes, and state income tax. It's no wonder homeowners usually itemize while renters often do not.

Most of the deductible expenses cannot be deducted in full. Instead, they are subject to special limitations—for example, medical expenses can be deducted only to the extent that they exceed 7.5% of your adjusted gross income (AGI), and job expenses to the extent they exceed 2% of AGI. In addition, for high-income taxpayers, many itemized deductions are partly phased out because of overall income-level restrictions. You may find that few or none of your personal expenses are deductible.

If you itemized last year, you should probably do so this year, too, unless you've had a major reduction in your deductible expenses. If you took the standard deduction last year, you may be better off itemizing this year if you:

- had large uninsured medical and dental expenses during the year
- paid interest and taxes on your home
- had large unreimbursed job expenses or other miscellaneous deductions
- had significant uninsured casualty or theft losses, or
- made large charitable contributions.

The single biggest mistake people make on their taxes?

Failing to itemize personal deductions. According to a Government Accountability Office report, as many as 2.2 million taxpayers overpay their taxes by an average of $610 per year because they fail to itemize.

The only way to know for sure if you'd be better off itemizing is to keep track of your deductible expenses each year. Through careful planning, you can often increase your deductible expenses so that it pays to itemize.

Have You Reviewed Your Withholdings Lately?

If you're overpaying your taxes, you're shortchanging yourself. Prime candidates for overwithholding include homeowners who had to pay sharply higher interest on their adjustable-rate mortgages says Bob Scharin, senior tax analyst from RIA's Thomson Tax & Accounting. Because mortgage interest is deductible, an increase in your interest rate will fatten your deduction.

Adjusting your withholding now would give you an automatic raise. The IRS offers a withholding calculator, at www.irs.gov, that you can use to estimate how much money you should have withheld. To change your withholding amount, give your employer an updated W-4 form.

"A taxing chore now can save more later," by Sandra Block, November 23, 2007.

Medical and dental expenses

Taxpayers who itemize may be able to deduct medical and dental expenses for themselves, their spouses, and their dependents. Eligible expenses include both health insurance premiums and out-of-pocket expenses not covered or reimbursed by insurance.

Unfortunately, there's a significant limitation on the deduction, which can make it useless for many taxpayers: You can deduct only the amount of your medical and dental expenses that's above 7.5% of your adjusted gross income (AGI). (Your AGI is your total taxable income, minus deductions for retirement contributions and one-half of your self-employment taxes (if any), plus a few other items

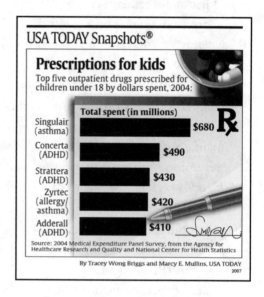

USA TODAY Snapshots®

Prescriptions for kids
Top five outpatient drugs prescribed for children under 18 by dollars spent, 2004:

Total spent (in millions)

Singulair (asthma)	$680
Concerta (ADHD)	$490
Strattera (ADHD)	$430
Zyrtec (allergy/asthma)	$420
Adderall (ADHD)	$410

Source: 2004 Medical Expenditure Panel Survey, from the Agency for Healthcare Research and Quality and National Center for Health Statistics

By Tracey Wong Briggs and Marcy E. Mullins, USA TODAY 2007

(as shown at the bottom of your Form 1040).) So, unless your medical expenses are substantial or your income is low, the 7.5% limitation will eat up most or all of the deduction. The more money you make, the less you can deduct.

> **EXAMPLE:** Al is an employee whose AGI for 2008 is $100,000. He pays $7,600 out of his own pocket for health insurance and uninsured medical expenses for the year for himself and his wife. For Al to deduct any medical expenses, they'd need to exceed 7.5% of his AGI, which is $7,500 (7.5% × $100,000 = $7,500). Because he paid a total of $7,600 in medical expenses for the year, he can deduct only $100. The other $7,500 in medical expenses cannot be deducted.

Many people assume they'll never be able to deduct their medical expenses, so they don't bother to keep track of them. But what if you end up being wrong, perhaps because of a family emergency late in the year? You could end up giving up a valuable deduction without even knowing it, or without having the receipts and records to make sure.

First of all, remember that you may deduct medical expenses for yourself, your spouse, your dependent children, and any other dependents you claim on your tax return. For example, if an elderly parent qualifies as your dependent, you may deduct your out-of-pocket expenses for his or her medical care. These costs can add up fast.

Moreover, lots of things you might not think of as medical expenses are deductible. The IRS broadly defines deductible medical expenses to include any payment for "the diagnosis, cure, mitigation, treatment, or prevention of disease, or treatment affecting any structure or function of the body." That covers a lot of territory.

It includes, of course, money you spend on doctors and dentists, as well as nursing care, hospitalization, lab fees, and long-term care. But IRS-recognized medical expenses include much more—for example, fees you pay to chiropractors, psychiatrists, optometrists, psychologists, osteopaths, acupuncturists, podiatrists, and even Christian Science practitioners. You can also deduct things like transportation costs for health treatment and the cost of remodeling your home to accommodate a handicap (adding wheelchair ramps, for example).

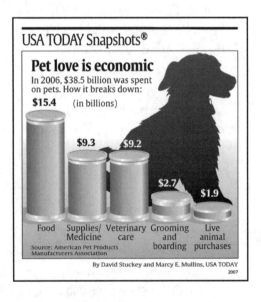

USA TODAY Snapshots®

Pet love is economic
In 2006, $38.5 billion was spent on pets. How it breaks down:
$15.4 (in billions)
$9.3
$9.2
$2.7
$1.9

Food | Supplies/Medicine | Veterinary care | Grooming and boarding | Live animal purchases

Source: American Pet Products Manufacturers Association

By David Stuckey and Marcy E. Mullins, USA TODAY 2007

Some health-related expenses are not deductible, including non-prescription drugs or the cost of cosmetic surgery (but reconstructive surgery is deductible). Nor can you deduct veterinary fees (sorry, Fido).

Interest payments

Certain types of interest you pay on loans are deductible, including interest on a mortgage, investment loan, or home equity loan.

Home mortgage interest. Home mortgage interest is any interest you pay on a loan secured by your home (either your main home or a second home). The loan may be a mortgage to buy your home, a second mortgage, a line of credit, or a home equity loan.

If the purpose of the loan is to buy, build, or substantially improve (for example, remodel) your main or second home, it's called a home acquisition loan. You can deduct the annual interest you pay on acquisition loans of up to $1 million.

If you use the loan secured by your main or second home for purposes other than to buy, build, or improve your home, it's a home equity loan. For example, you might get a home equity loan to help pay for school or buy a car—but not to remodel your kitchen. You can deduct the interest on home equity loans of less than $100,000 as an itemized personal deduction.

To get your home mortgage loan, you may have paid all sorts of charges not labeled interest (such as points, loan origination fees, maximum loan charges, and premium charges). Good news: If any of these charges were solely for the use of the money and not for a specific service (such as an appraisal), they're considered prepaid interest and can be deducted.

But if you paid points on your loan, you need to know a little more before deducting them: As a general rule, taxpayers can deduct points only a little at a time, over the life of the loan. However, if you took out a mortgage to buy or build your main home, you can deduct the points in the year you paid them, as you can with points on a mortgage used to improve your main home—for example, if you add a new bathroom. With refinancings, by contrast, you usually must deduct the points over the life of the new mortgage.

Paying PMI? Deduct Your Premiums

If you paid private mortgage insurance last year, a new tax deduction could take some of the sting out of your monthly premiums.

Most home buyers who can't afford a 20% down payment must pay private mortgage insurance, which is intended to protect lenders against default.

A 2006 law lets eligible borrowers deduct private mortgage premiums for mortgages issued after December 31, 2006. The full deduction is limited to those with adjusted gross income of $100,000 or less. (Home buyers with AGI of up to $109,000 can claim a partial deduction.) The income cutoff applies to both married and single borrowers, says Barbara Weltman, a tax lawyer and contributing editor to *J.K. Lasser's Your Income Tax 2008.*

Mortgage Insurance Companies of America, a trade group, estimates that the deduction will save the average borrower $350 a year. The deduction was originally scheduled to expire at the end of 2007, but Congress voted to extend it through 2010.

 "Bone up before you tackle those taxes," by Sandra Block, February 15, 2008.

Most other expenses you pay to get a mortgage can't be deducted as interest. But they still have tax benefits, since they're added to your basis in the property and can thus reduce your capital gains when you sell. These include legal fees, appraisal fees, mortgage commissions, transfer taxes, title insurance, and any amounts the seller owes that you agree to pay, such as back taxes or recording fees.

It's easy to keep track of how much interest you pay each year on a home mortgage loan. If you paid $600 or more of mortgage interest (including certain points) on any one mortgage, you'll receive an IRS Form 1098 from the lender, listing the interest you paid.

Mortgage Trouble? Your Options Have Gotten Tax-Friendlier

If you lost your home to foreclosure last year, filing your taxes won't help you get your house back. But at least you won't have to deal with an unexpected tax bill on phantom income.

After a foreclosure, lenders often sell the home for less than the amount left on the mortgage and write off the debt. Many borrowers are shocked to learn, though, that this "forgiven debt" is considered taxable income. Say, for example, you owe $400,000 on a home that goes into foreclosure. Your lender sells the home for $300,000 and writes off the remaining $100,000. The IRS will treat the $100,000 as taxable income.

In the past, the only way that taxpayers could avoid tax on forgiven debt was to seek bankruptcy protection or prove to the IRS that they were insolvent.

In response to rising foreclosures, President Bush signed a law that excludes most mortgage debt that was canceled in 2007 from income taxes. The legislation is scheduled to expire at the end of 2009.

In addition to foreclosure, the change will benefit taxpayers who had debt forgiven from a loan restructuring or a short sale. A short sale occurs when a home is sold for less than the amount of the loan.

Debt written off on a home-equity line of credit or a home-equity loan is also eligible for the tax break, as long as it was used to build, buy, or improve your home, says Robert Houskeeper, a certified public accountant who teaches accounting at San Diego State University. If you used home equity for other purposes, he says, such as to pay off credit cards, forgiven debt remains taxable.

The law is limited to up to $2 million in forgiven debt on the sale of a principal residence. Forgiven debt on the sale of an investment property or vacation home is still taxable.

To claim this relief, you'll need to fill out the revised version of IRS Form 982. You can download it at www.irs.gov.

 "Bone up before you tackle those taxes," by Sandra Block, February 15, 2008.

Investment interest. You can take an itemized deduction for interest on money you borrow to invest, but you can't deduct more than your net annual income from your investments. Any amount that you can't deduct in the current year can be carried over to the next year and deducted then.

Personal interest. Interest you pay to buy something for your personal use is not deductible (except for interest on a mortgage for a personal residence or second home, and some interest on student loans). You can't deduct interest on credit cards, car loans, or other loans where you used the money for personal purposes.

Because personal interest is not deductible, but home equity loan interest is, some people borrow against their home to make consumer purchases instead of charging them on their credit card or taking out a consumer loan. For example, if you need a $20,000 loan to buy a car for personal use, you can deduct all the interest on that loan if you get the money through a home equity loan. Of course, you must have a home, and have equity to obtain such a loan, and you risk losing your home if you don't pay the loan back.

State and local taxes

Several types of state and local taxes can be deducted from your federal taxes.

State income taxes. All but seven states (Alaska, Florida, Nevada, South Dakota, Texas, Washington, and Wyoming) impose their own income taxes. If you itemize, these taxes are deductible in full. This is one of the largest itemized deductions.

Property taxes. You can deduct state and local property taxes on your home and other nonbusiness property as an itemized deduction. There is no dollar limit on the deduction, and you can claim as many vacation homes as you own. However, you may not deduct charges for improvements that increase the value of your property—for example, a special assessment for new sidewalks or sewers.

State sales taxes. Alaska, Florida, Nevada, South Dakota, Texas, Washington, and Wyoming don't have any state income taxes. If you live in one of these states, you were formerly able to deduct your state and local sales taxes as an itemized deduction. This deduction expired at the end of 2007, but Congress may eventually decide to reenact it.

If you live in one of the 43 states that has income taxes, you may be able to choose to deduct your sales taxes instead of your state income taxes—you can't deduct both. You could get a larger deduction from sales taxes if, for example, you purchased expensive items during the year and paid substantial sales tax—for example, you bought a car. Or, maybe your state income taxes are small because you took state income tax credits— for example, a state credit for installing solar power in your home.

There are two ways to figure out how much sales tax you can deduct: the easy way and the hard way.

The easy way involves using IRS tables to figure your deduction. If you use this method, you don't need to keep receipts or keep track of what you actually spent on sales tax. Instead, you use your income level and number of exemptions to find the sales tax amount listed in the tables for your state. This number is an IRS estimate of the average sales tax a person with your income and exemptions would pay. You may add to this any sales taxes you paid during the year for a car, aircraft, boat, home (including mobile or prefabricated), or home building materials.

The hard way means you figure out how much you actually spent on sales taxes and you deduct that amount. You must save all your sales receipts and then add them up—probably a lot of work. You might get a bigger deduction this way, but first consider whether it's worth it.

Personal property taxes. State and local taxes on personal property are deductible if they're based on the property's value (an "ad valorem" tax) and charged on a yearly basis. How often the taxes are collected doesn't matter.

Personal property taxes vary from state to state. Some states don't have any. However, more and more states are charging personal property taxes on things like cars, motorcycles, boats, mobile homes, trailers, and aircraft. Your state's annual automobile registration fee is wholly or partly deductible if it's based on your car's value. Check your state taxing agency's website for more information on state property taxes. Links to these websites can be found at www.bankrate.com/brm/itax/ state/state_tax_home.asp.

Foreign income taxes. You can take either a deduction or a credit for income taxes imposed on you by a foreign country or a U.S. possession. Generally, you're better off using the credit. (See Chapter 3.) However, you cannot take a deduction or credit for foreign income taxes paid on income that's exempt from U.S. tax under the foreign earned income exclusion or the foreign housing exclusion.

Charitable contributions

Charitable contributions can be a big itemized deduction. In 2005, Vice President Dick Cheney took over $6.8 million in charitable deductions.

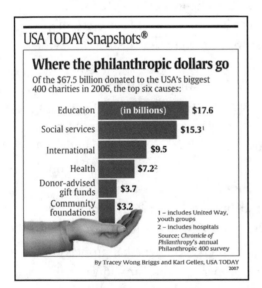

USA TODAY Snapshots®

Where the philanthropic dollars go

Of the $67.5 billion donated to the USA's biggest 400 charities in 2006, the top six causes:

(in billions)

Education — $17.6
Social services — $15.3[1]
International — $9.5
Health — $7.2[2]
Donor-advised gift funds — $3.7
Community foundations — $3.2

1 – includes United Way, youth groups
2 – includes hospitals
Source: *Chronicle of Philanthropy's* annual Philanthropic 400 survey

By Tracey Wong Briggs and Karl Gelles, USA TODAY 2007

You're probably not in Dick Cheney's league, but you can still reap valuable tax benefits by doing good.

Don't get the idea that making charitable contributions will end up saving you money, however. Dick Cheney is a good case in point: He saved over $2.4 million in 2005 income taxes because of his contributions, but he contributed $6.8 million to get those tax savings.

But, if you want to make a charitable contribution, you will lower your taxes (assuming you itemize), which will leave you more money with which to make even larger contributions—keep it up, and they'll be naming a building after you. The best time to make cash donations is at the end of the year. You get the same deduction, but more time in which to earn interest on your money.

What contributions are deductible? Subject to overall limits, you may take an itemized deduction for contributions of either money or property to charity. However, not every organization or cause qualifies as a charity. Only contributions to "qualified organizations" are deductible. These include:

- churches, temples, synagogues, mosques, and other religious organizations
- most nonprofit charitable organizations, such as the Red Cross and United Way
- most nonprofit educational organizations, including the Boy and Girl Scouts of America, colleges, museums, and day care centers for working parents, and
- nonprofit hospitals and medical research organizations.

You can ask any organization you're considering giving to whether it's a qualified organization. They should have an IRS letter saying so, and be able to give you a copy. You can also call the IRS at 877-829-5500 to ask, or check IRS Publication 78, which lists most qualified organizations (except churches, synagogues, temples, and mosques, which don't need to apply for IRS recognition and are frequently not listed). You can also check the website www.guidestar.org, which lists 1.5 million qualified charities and contains in-depth financial information about them as well.

You can't deduct gifts to foreign charities or governments (except certain Canadian, Israeli, and Mexican charities). If you want to help people in a foreign country, you can donate to a qualified U.S. charity providing aid in that country and then deduct your donation.

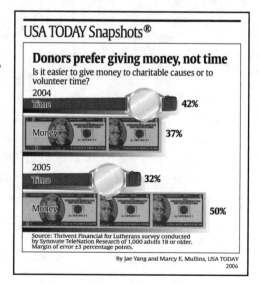

USA TODAY Snapshots®

Donors prefer giving money, not time

Is it easier to give money to charitable causes or to volunteer time?

2004
Time 42%
Money 37%

2005
Time 32%
Money 50%

Source: Thrivent Financial for Lutherans survey conducted by Synovate TeleNation Research of 1,000 adults 18 or older. Margin of error ±3 percentage points.

By Jae Yang and Marcy E. Mullins, USA TODAY 2006

How much can you deduct? Unless your charitable contributions are quite substantial, you won't have to worry about the overall limits. These limits vary depending on whether you give cash or property, but overall you can't take a deduction for contributions of over 50% of your AGI for the year. Any contributions you make over this amount may be carried forward for up to five years.

Contributions of money. It's easiest to give cash, which is usually most welcome by charities. Cash includes currency, checks, and credit card contributions.

Ordinarily, cash contributions can be deducted until they reach the 50% of AGI limit. However, a few types of cash contributions are subject to the 30% limitation; namely, contributions to veteran's organizations, fraternal societies, nonprofit cemeteries, and certain private foundations that fail to timely distribute all the donations they receive.

Buying Tickets and Goods From a Charity

When you give money to a charity and get a benefit in return—such as a banquet ticket, thank-you gift, or an auctioned item—you can deduct only the amount that is more than the value of the benefit you receive.

EXAMPLE: You pay $250 to a qualified charity for a ticket to attend a football game. The ticket is worth $50, so that portion of the ticket price is not deductible because it benefited you—you get to go to the game. The remaining $200 is deductible.

The charity will often be able to tell you the exact value of the benefit you received. Indeed, charities are required to give donors written confirmation of the value of any benefit they receive that's worth more than $75.

Contributions of property. Donating property to charity is very popular—you get rid of stuff you no longer need and get a tax deduction too. However, it's more complicated than contributing hard cash, because you have to figure out what the property you donate is worth.

Let's say you clean out your closets and give your old clothes to charity. How much do you get to deduct? You may be tempted to overvalue those old sweaters, but beware, the IRS is cracking down on abuses by setting tougher standards for valuations.

If you're donating property worth more than $5,000, you'll need to get an appraisal from a qualified appraiser. Otherwise, you can deduct no more than the property's "fair market value," which means the amount that a "willing buyer would pay and a willing seller would accept for the property, when neither party is compelled to buy or sell, and both parties have reasonable knowledge of the relevant facts." In other words, it's a fair price—not too high or too low.

However, you may take a deduction for an item in poor condition if it's worth more than $500 and you obtain an appraisal of its value that you include with your tax return.

To help you determine how much your property is worth, several well-known charities have created price guides for frequently donated items such as clothing, household goods, and furniture. These can be found at the following websites (the Salvation Army guide is the most detailed):

- Salvation Army Donation Value Guide: www.salvationarmysouth .org/valueguide.htm
- Goodwill Industries: www.goodwillpromo.org
- Children's Home Thrift Shop Guide to Valuing Donated Goods: www.childrens-home.org/valuationguide.htm

Online auction sites, such as eBay, can also provide a good idea of what prices people are putting on used goods.

EXAMPLE: Barry wants to buy a new computer and get rid of his old one. He decides to donate the old computer to a local charity and try to figure out its value by viewing sales data for similar computers on eBay. Three computers identical to his recently sold for $950, $1,150, and $900—an average price of $1,000. Thus, Barry determines that his used computer's fair market value is $1,000. Barry should keep a copy of the eBay sales data with his tax records.

Specialized software programs can also help determine the fair market value of used property—*It'sDeductible* from Intuit (www.itsdeductible .com) and *DonationPro* from H & R Block (www.hrblock.com).

No Deductions for Used Socks and Underwear

The IRS is taking a harder line on deductions for used clothing and household items. Under a law that took effect in August 2006, these items must be in good or better condition to qualify for a tax deduction. The IRS hasn't defined "good or better," but the law indicates that used socks and underwear won't make the cut.

 "Bone up before you tackle those taxes," by Sandra Block, February 15, 2008.

Donating used cars and other vehicles. If you have an old car you want to get rid of, donating it to charity can seem like a great idea—it's easy to do and you'll get a tax deduction. Unfortunately, hundreds of thousands of taxpayers already had this idea, and many of them abused the charitable deduction rules by grossly inflating the value of their clunky old cars. In one case, a taxpayer claimed a $2,915 deduction for a 1980 Mercury station wagon that was ultimately sold by the charity for $30.

With the IRS losing hundreds of millions of dollars every year, the rules for deducting donated used cars were significantly tightened in 2005. Today, if you donate a car or other vehicle to charity and claim a deduction greater than $500, your charitable deduction is limited to the amount the charity receives when it actually sells the car. Thus, the owner of the Mercury station wagon described above would get only a $30 deduction.

The charity must provide you with IRS form, 1098-C, *Contributions of Motor Vehicles, Boats, and Airplanes*, documenting the sale price. You must file a copy with your tax return and also file IRS Form 8283, *Noncash Charitable Contributions*.

There are a few situations where you can claim your car's fair market value as your deduction amount, such as when:

- your claimed deduction is $500 or less
- the charity keeps the vehicle for its own use, or
- the charity gives or sells the vehicle to a needy person at a price significantly below fair market value.

For more information, see IRS Publication 4303, *A Donor's Guide to Vehicle Donations*.

Donating stock and other capital gain assets. If you want to donate to charity and you own property—such as stocks, bonds, or mutual funds—that has gone up in value since you bought it, a great tax strategy is to donate the property directly to the charity. You may deduct the fair market value of the property on the date of the donation and you don't have to pay any capital gains taxes on the property's increase in value since you purchased it. The charity can then sell the property and pay no tax at all on the proceeds.

EXAMPLE: Ivan bought 1,000 shares of Acme Gun Co. stock for $1,000 back in 1995, and they're now worth $10,000. He gives the stock to his favorite charity, the Red Cross, and deducts its $10,000 fair market value as a charitable contribution. Ivan doesn't have to pay the 15% capital gains tax on the $9,000 gain in the value of his stock. The Red Cross sells the stocks and pays no taxes on the $10,000 it receives. Had Ivan sold the stock, he would have had to pay a $1,350 long-term capital gains tax on his $9,000 profit (15% × $9,000 = $1,350). This would have left him only $8,650 from the stock sale to donate to charity.

Don't contribute stocks you've held in a tax-free retirement account such as an IRA or 401(k). If you do, you'll have to pay tax on the earnings. Only contribute property held in taxable accounts. Also, don't distribute stocks or other capital assets that have gone down in value, because you won't be able to deduct your loss. Instead, you should sell the asset, deduct the loss, and give the sales proceeds to charity.

For a detailed discussion of capital gains taxes, see Chapter 6.

Contributions of services. Many people volunteer their services to a charity, whether as board members or by performing other services. Unfortunately, you get no deduction for the value of your time or services. However, you can take an itemized deduction for your out-of-pocket expenses such as travel expenses, uniforms that you're required to buy and wear (such as an apron showing that you're a museum volunteer), and phone calls.

USA TODAY Snapshots®

Doing their part
Top volunteering rates in the USA from 2003 to 2005:

Utah	48%
Nebraska	43%
Minnesota	41%
Iowa	39%
Alaska	39%

Source: Corporation for National and Community Service

By David Stuckey and Robert W. Ahrens, USA TODAY 2006

> EXAMPLE: Dr. Smith, a radiologist, volunteers ten hours of his time every week to a nonprofit hospital in his community. He may deduct the cost of his gas and parking, but not the value of his time or medical services.

Out-of-pocket expenses incurred while performing services for a charity are deducted in the same way as cash contributions. You must have adequate records to prove the amount of your expenses, and get an acknowledgement from the charity describing the services you provided and a good faith estimate of the value of any goods or services you received as reimbursement.

Record-keeping requirements. What sort of records you must keep depends on what you donate. Starting in 2007, you must keep a cancelled check, bank record, or receipt for all your cash contributions, however small. This is a significant change from the law in effect prior to 2007, which required a receipt only for donations over $250. You may want to make all your monetary contributions by check or credit card, rather than by cash. If you do give cash, be absolutely sure to get a receipt.

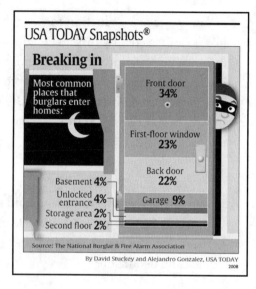

For most property donations, you'll need a receipt or written acknowledgment (such as a thank-you letter mentioning the amount you gave) from the charity. You don't have to file any records with your tax return, unless you make a contribution of property worth more than $500. In that case, you'll need to file IRS Form 8283, *Noncash Charitable Contributions.*

Here's an easy way to keep track of all your donations during the year: Get a file folder, label it "Donations," and use it for all your cancelled checks to charities, receipts for cash contributions, credit card bills and electronic transfer notices for contributions, and acknowledgements of donations for property contributions.

For more on how to value donated property, see IRS Publication 561, *Determining the Value of Donated Property.* For more on donations in general, see IRS Publication 526, *Charitable Contributions.*

Casualty and theft losses

If a fire, theft, vandalism, earthquake, storm, floods, terrorism, or some other sudden, unexpected, or unusual event damages your property, you may have undergone a casualty loss, which is potentially deductible.

Some external force needs to have been at work—you get no deduction if you simply lose or misplace property, or it breaks or wears out over time.

You can take a deduction for casualty losses only to the extent that the loss is not covered by insurance. However, the deduction for casualty losses to personal property (as opposed to real property) is severely limited: You can deduct only the amount of the loss that exceeds 10% of your adjusted gross income for the year. To add insult to injury, you must also subtract $100 from each casualty or theft you suffered during the year.

> **EXAMPLE:** Javier suffers $5,000 in losses when a fire strikes his home and destroys some furnishings and a home treadmill. His adjusted gross income for the year is $75,000. He can deduct only that portion of his loss that exceeds $7,500 (10% × $75,000 = $7,500). He lost $5,000, so he gets no deduction.

How much you may deduct depends on whether the property involved was stolen, completely destroyed, or only partially destroyed. If more than one item was stolen or destroyed, figure your deduction separately for each item and then add them all together.

If the property is stolen or completely destroyed, your deduction is figured as follows: Adjusted Basis – Salvage Value – Insurance Proceeds = Casualty Loss. (Your adjusted basis is the property's original cost, plus the value of any improvements.) Obviously, if an item is stolen, it will have no salvage value.

> **EXAMPLE:** Sean's computer is stolen from his apartment by a burglar. The computer cost $2,000. Sean has taken no tax deductions for it because he purchased it only two months ago, so his adjusted basis is $2,000. Sean's casualty loss is $2,000. ($2,000 adjusted basis – $0 salvage value – $0 insurance proceeds = $2,000 loss.)

If the property is only partly destroyed, your casualty loss deduction is the lesser of the decrease in the property's fair market value or its adjusted basis (your basis is reduced by any insurance you receive).

EXAMPLE: Assume that Sean's computer (from the example above) is partly destroyed due to a small fire in his home. Its fair market value in its partly damaged state is $500. Because he spent $2,000 for it, the decrease in its fair market value is $1,500. Sean didn't receive any insurance proceeds, so the computer's adjusted basis is $2,000. Thus, his casualty loss is $1,500.

Unreimbursed job expenses

If you work as an employee, you may end up paying some work-related expenses out of your own pocket, such as

- work-related travel, transportation, meal, and entertainment expenses
- business liability insurance premiums
- depreciation on a computer or cellular telephone your employer requires you to use in your work
- dues to a chamber of commerce if membership helps you do your job
- dues to professional societies
- education (work-related)
- home office expenses for part of your home used regularly and exclusively in your work
- expenses of looking for a new job in your present occupation
- legal fees related to your job
- malpractice insurance premiums
- a passport for a business trip
- research expenses of a college professor
- subscriptions to professional journals and trade magazines related to your work
- tools and supplies used in your work
- union dues and expenses, and
- work clothes and uniforms (if required and not suitable for everyday use).

If your employer doesn't reimburse you for these costs, you can deduct them as a personal itemized deduction, so long as they are ordinary, necessary, and reasonable in amount. (Special restrictions are placed on unreimbursed education and home office expenses, however, as described below.)

The unreimbursed employee expense deduction is, for the most part, subject to the same rules and limitations as the business expense deductions. There are some differences, however—the most important one being that employee expenses are deductible only if, and to the extent that, they (along with your other miscellaneous deductions) exceed 2% of your adjusted gross income.

> **CAUTION**
>
> **If you have a choice about how to pay for work-related job expenses**—don't pay them yourself! Use a company credit card or have your employer billed directly for the expense. If you must pay for something out of your own pocket, have your employer reimburse you. Provided they are for work-related expenses and are properly documented, these reimbursements are not taxable income to you and should not be included in the W-2 form your employer files with the IRS. Your employer, meanwhile, gets to deduct these expenses as a business expense.

You're much better off being reimbursed than paying for something yourself and deducting it, because any deduction you get will only recoup part of the expense. For example, if you spend $1,000 for a business trip and deduct it as an unreimbursed job expense, you'll get at most a $1,000 deduction. If you're in the 28% tax bracket, you'll save $280 on your taxes. Thus, your trip will end up costing you $720. If, on the other hand, your employer reimburses you for the $1,000, the trip will cost you nothing because the $1,000 is not taxable income.

Make sure you know what your employer's reimbursement policy is. If you have a right to reimbursement from your employer but fail to claim it, you can't take a personal deduction for work-related expenses, because they aren't considered "necessary." In some states (like California), employers are required by law to reimburse employees for work-related expenses.

Any reimbursement from your employer must be made under an "accountable plan." If you fail to follow these rules, any reimbursements you receive must be treated as employee income and included on your W-2. Instead of the nonreportable event that you'd get with a properly documented reimbursement, you'll have to report and pay tax on the reimbursement and deduct the expense on your personal tax return.

Accountable plan rules require that you:

- make an "adequate accounting" of the expense—that is, follow all the applicable record-keeping and other substantiation rules for the expense; for example, you must keep receipts (except for travel, meal, and entertainment expenses below $75; or travel and meal expenses paid on a per diem basis)
- timely submit your expense report and receipts to your employer, and
- timely return any payments that exceed what you actually spent.

Home-office deductions for employees. If you sometimes take your job home, you may wonder whether you qualify for the home office deduction. Doing so is hard to do for an employee, however. First of all, you must satisfy the ordinary requirements for the home office deduction, which means that (1) you must use a part of your home regularly and exclusively for work, and (2) your home office must be your principal workplace or you must regularly perform administrative or management tasks there. In addition, employees must meet the convenience of the employer test, which means they maintain a home office because it is:

- a condition of employment
- necessary for the employer's business to properly function, or
- needed to allow the employee to properly perform his or her duties.

If you simply decide to work at home some days because, for instance, you can get more done there, you won't meet the convenience of

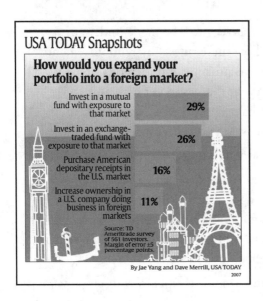

USA TODAY Snapshots

How would you expand your portfolio into a foreign market?

Invest in a mutual fund with exposure to that market — 29%

Invest in an exchange-traded fund with exposure to that market — 26%

Purchase American depositary receipts in the U.S. market — 16%

Increase ownership in a U.S. company doing business in foreign markets — 11%

Source: TD Ameritrade survey of 561 investors. Margin of error ±5 percentage points.

By Jae Yang and Dave Merrill, USA TODAY 2007

employer test. You have to show that your employer doesn't provide you with an office, or that there is some valid business reason why you must work at home. In one case, an employee succeeded in claiming the home office deduction because her employer required her to perform work during off-hours when her regular office was closed.

If you don't qualify for the home office deduction, but regularly use your home office for work, try to get your employer to reimburse you for your home office expenses. The reimbursement would not be taxable income so long as you properly account for your expenses.

Education expense deductions for employees. If you pay to attend a business-related course, seminar, convention, or professional meeting, and your employer doesn't reimburse you, the costs are deductible only if the education:

- maintains or improves skills required in your profession, or
- is required by law or regulation to maintain your professional status.

This includes the cost of attending continuing professional education classes. Deductible education expenses include tuition, fees, books, and other learning materials. They also include transportation and travel.

However, you cannot deduct education expenses you incur to qualify for a new line of work or profession or to meet the minimum level educational requirements for a job or profession. Thus, for example, you can't deduct the expense of going to law school, medical school, or dental school.

Investment expenses

You can earn money by engaging in personal investing—for example, by having personal bank accounts that pay interest, or investing in stocks that pay dividends and appreciate in value over time (hopefully). The IRS calls activities like these—that are pursued primarily for profit but aren't businesses—income-producing activities.

You can deduct the ordinary and necessary expenses you incur to produce income, or to manage property (including real estate) held for the production of income. These expenses include such items as clerical help and office rent for investment-related work, investment fees and expenses, legal and tax advice, and more.

As miscellaneous itemized deductions, these are deductible only if and to the extent they, along with your other miscellaneous deductions, exceed 2% of your adjusted gross income.

For detailed guidance on tax deductions for investments, refer to IRS Publication 550, *Investment Income and Expenses*.

Miscellaneous itemized deductions

A large group of deductions is lumped together in a category called "miscellaneous itemized deductions." They're deductible only to the extent they exceed 2% of a taxpayer's adjusted gross income (with exceptions, noted below). Income thresholds also affect how much you can deduct (discussed below).

> **EXAMPLE:** Ladonna, a single taxpayer, has an adjusted gross income of $50,000. She may deduct her miscellaneous itemized deductions only to the extent that they exceed 2% of $50,000, or $1,000. This year she had $100 in tax preparation fees and $1,100 in unreimbursed employee expenses. Her total miscellaneous itemized deductions are $1,200, but because of the 2% of AGI limit, she may only deduct $200 of this amount—the amount that exceeds $1,000.

Unreimbursed job expenses (discussed above) are by far the most important miscellaneous itemized deduction. Others include:

Tax preparation fees. This includes costs for hiring a tax pro or buying tax preparation software or tax publications. It also includes any fee you pay for electronic filing of your return. If you have a tax pro prepare both your personal and business taxes, ask for a separate bill for your business return. Reason: This amount will be fully deductible as a business expense whether or not you itemize your deductions, but the costs of preparing your personal return are deductible only as a miscellaneous itemized deduction and subject to the 2% of AGI threshold.

Fees to fight the IRS. You may deduct attorney fees, accounting fees, and other fees you incur to determine, contest, pay, or claim a refund of any tax.

Gambling losses. These are deductible up to the amount of your gambling winnings for the year. You cannot simply reduce your gambling winnings by your gambling losses and report the difference. You must report the full amount of your winnings as income and claim your losses (up to the amount of winnings) as an itemized deduction. These losses are not subject to the 2% limit on miscellaneous itemized deductions.

Hobby expenses. A hobby is an activity you engage in primarily for a reason other than to earn a profit—for example, to have fun. Expenses from a hobby are deductible only if you have income from the hobby and only up to the amount of hobby income earned during the year. (See "Hobby Expenses," below.)

For more information, see IRS Publication 529, *Miscellaneous Deductions.*

Limit on itemized deductions for high-income taxpayers. High-income taxpayers lose the benefit of some of their itemized deductions because of income thresholds. If you exceed the thresholds, you must reduce your deductions by a certain percentage. This percentage is scheduled to go down over the next several years, and by 2010, there will be no limit at all (unless Congress changes the law again). The limit will be reinstated in its original form starting in 2011, unless Congress acts to eliminate it permanently.

Here's how it works: If your AGI exceeds the threshold amount ($159,950 in 2008), you total whichever of your itemized deductions are subject to the limit. (Don't include your deductions for medical expenses, investment interest, casualty and theft losses, and some gambling losses, because they aren't subject to the limit.) Apply the 2% of AGI limit on miscellaneous itemized deduction and the limits on charitable deductions. Take this total and reduce it by the smaller of either 3% of the amount of your AGI that exceeds the threshold, or 80%. The upshot is that in no event can your affected itemized deductions be reduced by more than 80%.

Now, about the phaseout: Here's a schedule of the changes.

Year	Reduction in Itemized Deduction Limit
2008–2009	66.67%
2010	100%
2011 and later	0%

The effect of this phaseout is that, up until 2010, after you've done the other calculations, you reduce your itemized deduction limitation by two-thirds or 66.67%.

If your AGI is in the reduction range, but not too far above it, you can try to reduce it by increasing your adjustments to income or business deductions. For example, increase your contributions to your retirement accounts such as a 401(k) or IRA—these reduce your AGI. If you own losing stocks, you can sell them and deduct up to $3,000 of your losses from your AGI.

Adjust Your Income With Above-the-Line Deductions

Some expenses, you can deduct whether you itemize or take the standard deduction. Technically speaking, these are not deductions at all, but adjustments to income, also called above-the-line deductions. But, just like a deduction, they reduce your taxable income.

You deduct these expenses directly from your gross income (on the first page of your IRS Form 1040), not from your adjusted gross income as you do with itemized deductions (which you list on Schedule A). (See Chapter 1 for a detailed explanation of gross income and adjusted gross income.) Above-the-line deductions are not subject to any of the limits that apply to itemized deductions.

The only problem with these adjustments to income is that there aren't very many of them. The most significant ones are health insurance expenses and retirement contributions by self-employed people. If you're not self-employed, you can still deduct IRA contributions and contributions to health savings accounts. However, many taxpayers have no adjustments to income at all.

Adjustments to income include:

Self-employed health insurance. People who are self-employed can deduct:

- contributions to health savings accounts (but payments for health insurance paired with HSAs must be itemized), and
- health insurance premiums (deductible up to the amount of profit from the business).

Health savings account contributions. You can deduct HSA contributions you make with personal funds. See Chapter 2.

Retirement plan contributions by self-employed taxpayers. These include annual contributions made by self-employed people to their retirement plans, such as SEP-IRAs, SIMPLE IRAs, Keogh Plans, and solo 401(k) plans.

IRA contributions. Contributions to IRA accounts of up to $5,000 ($6,000 for taxpayers over 50) may be deductible, depending on your income (2008 figures).

Educator expenses. Because of inadequate school funding, teachers sometimes pay for needed supplies out of their own pockets. A special tax deduction allows kindergarten-through-grade-12 teachers to deduct up to $250 of what they pay for books, supplies, equipment, and other materials used in the classroom. This deduction began in 2005 and is extended by Congress on a year-to-year basis, so be sure it's in effect during the current year.

Employee moving expenses. If you moved because of a change in your job location or because you started a new job, you may be able to deduct your moving expenses as a nonitemized deduction. To qualify for the deduction, you must meet tests concerning both distance and the amount of time that you continue to work after moving. For more information, see IRS Publication 521, *Moving Expenses.*

50% of self-employment taxes. If you're self-employed, you can deduct half of the 12.4% Social Security tax on net self-employment income, up to an annual ceiling, and a 2.9% Medicare tax on all net self-employment income.

Penalty on early savings withdrawals. You can deduct from your income for penalties you had to pay to banks and other financial institutions because you withdrew your savings early from certificates of deposit or similar accounts.

Alimony. You can also subtract amounts you paid in alimony, that is, a court-ordered payment to a separated spouse or divorced ex-spouse. You can't include child support payments. For more details, see IRS Publication 504, *Divorced or Separated Individuals.*

Student loan interest. Up to $2,500 of student loan interest is deductible from your gross income provided that your AGI—before subtracting any deduction for student loan interest—is below a ceiling amount. For 2008, the student loan interest deduction starts to be phased out

USA TODAY Snapshots®

Why workers change jobs

Although 97% of workers think financial compensation is one of the most important aspects in the workplace, it's not the main reason they change jobs. Most important reasons to change jobs:

Growth and earnings potential	30%
Time and flexibility	23%
Financial compensation	22%
Culture, work environment	22%
Benefits	12%

Note: Multiple responses allowed.
Source: Spherion survey of 1,996 employed adults 18 and older. Margin of error ± 2 percentage points

By Jae Yang and Frank Pompa, USA TODAY
2007

if your AGI is over $55,000 ($115,000 for joint filers) and is eliminated if your AGI exceeds $70,000 ($145,000 if filing jointly).

College tuition and fees. For tax years 2006 and 2007, you could deduct up to $4,000 of the tuition and fees you paid so that you, your spouse, or child or other dependent could attend any accredited college, university, or other postsecondary school such as a vocational school (provided you didn't claim a Hope or Lifetime Learning credit). This deduction expired at the end of 2007, but Congress could act to extend it to future years.

Own a Business? Deduct Your Expenses

If you own a business, you don't have to pay tax on every dollar your business takes in (your gross income). Instead, you owe tax only on the amount left over after your business's deductible expenses are subtracted from your gross income (your "net profit"). Virtually any business expense is deductible as long as it is:

- ordinary and necessary—that is, common, accepted, helpful, and appropriate for your business or profession
- directly related to your business—that is, not a personal expense, and
- for a reasonable amount.

EXAMPLE: Noemi, a sole proprietor, earned $50,000 (gross income) this year from her consulting business. Fortunately, she doesn't have to pay income tax on the entire $50,000. Instead, she can deduct from it various business expenses, including a $5,000 home office deduction and $5,000 spent on equipment. These leave her with a net profit of $40,000. She pays income tax only on this net profit amount.

If, like a majority of small business owners, you're a sole proprietor, you deduct your business expenses on IRS Schedule C, *Profit or Loss From Business*. Your net profit (or loss) is then transferred to the first page of your Form 1040.

Business deductions are above-the-line deductions from your gross income, just like adjustments to income. However, business expenses are even more valuable than itemized deductions or adjustments to income, because they reduce the amount of self-employment tax (Social Security and Medicare tax) you owe along with your income taxes. Reason: The amount of self-employment tax you have to pay is based on your net self-employment income. Business deductions reduce this income and thus lower your self-employment taxes. The self-employment tax is a combined 15.3% Social Security and Medicare tax up to an annual income ceiling.

If the money you spend on your business exceeds your business income for the year, your business incurs a loss. This isn't as bad as it sounds, because you can use a business loss to offset your other income—like interest income or your spouse's income if you file jointly. You can even accumulate your losses and apply them to reduce your income taxes in future or past years.

CAUTION

You must keep track of your business expenses. You can deduct only those expenses that you actually incur. You need to keep records of these expenses to (1) know for sure how much you actually spent, and (2) prove to the IRS that you really spent the money you deducted, in case you are audited.

RESOURCE

This section provides only an overview of a complex subject, but one well worth careful study by any business owner. For a detailed discussion of business deductions, refer to one or more of the following:

• *Deduct It! Lower Your Small Business Taxes*, by Stephen Fishman (Nolo)
• *Home Business Tax Deductions: Keep What You Earn*, by Stephen Fishman (Nolo), and
• *Tax Deductions for Professionals*, by Stephen Fishman (Nolo).

Start-up expenses

To get your business up and running, you may have to pay license fees, advertising costs, attorney and accounting fees, travel expenses, market research, office supply costs, and more. You may deduct up to $5,000 of these start-up costs the first year your new business is in operation. You may deduct amounts over $5,000 over the next 15 years.

> EXAMPLE: Cary, a star hairdresser at a popular salon, decides to open his own salon. Before it opens to customers, Cary has to rent space, hire and train employees, and pay for an expensive preopening advertising campaign. These cost Cary $20,000. Cary may deduct only $5,000 of this $20,000 the first year he's in business. He may deduct the remaining $15,000 in equal amounts over the next 15 years.

Operating expenses

Operating expenses are the ongoing day-to-day costs of staying in business. They include such things as the following (assuming you buy them for business, not personal use):

- advertising costs—for example, for a yellow pages ad, brochure, or business website
- attorney and accounting fees
- bank fees
- car and truck expenses
- costs of renting or leasing office space, vehicles, machinery, equipment, and other property
- education expenses—for example, the cost of attending professional seminars or classes required to keep up a professional license
- expenses for the business use of your home

- fees you pay to self-employed workers you hire—for example, the cost of paying a marketing consultant to advise you on how to get more clients
- health insurance for yourself and your family
- insurance—for example, liability, workers' compensation, and business property insurance
- interest on business loans and debts—for example, interest you pay for a bank loan you use to expand your business
- license fees
- office expenses, such as supplies
- office utilities
- postage
- professional association dues
- professional or business books you need
- repairs and maintenance for business equipment, such as a photocopier or fax machine
- retirement plan contributions (see Chapter 4)
- software
- subscriptions for professional or business publications
- business travel, meals, and entertainment, and
- wages and benefits you provide your employees.

These expenses (unlike start-up expenses) are currently deductible—that is, you can deduct them all in the year you pay them.

EXAMPLE: After Cary's salon opens, he begins paying $5,000 a month for rent and utilities. This is an operating expense that is currently deductible. When Cary does his taxes, he can deduct from his income the entire $60,000 that he paid for rent and utilities for the year.

Capital expenses

Capital assets are things you buy for your business that have a useful life of more than one year, such as land, buildings, equipment, vehicles, books, furniture, machinery, and patents you buy from others. Their costs, called capital expenses, are considered to be part of your investment in your business, not day-to-day operating expenses.

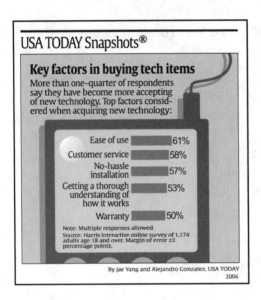

USA TODAY Snapshots®

Key factors in buying tech items

More than one-quarter of respondents say they have become more accepting of new technology. Top factors considered when acquiring new technology:

Ease of use 61%
Customer service 58%
No-hassle installation 57%
Getting a thorough understanding of how it works 53%
Warranty 50%

Note: Multiple responses allowed
Source: Harris Interactive online survey of 1,174 adults age 18 and over. Margin of error ±3 percentage points.

By Jae Yang and Alejandro Gonzalez, USA TODAY 2006

Large businesses—those that buy at least several hundred thousand dollars of capital assets in a year—must deduct these costs using depreciation. To depreciate an item, you deduct a portion of the cost in each year of the item's useful life. Depending on the asset, this could be anywhere from three to 39 years (the IRS decides the asset's useful life).

Small businesses can also use depreciation, but they have another option available for deducting many capital expenses: They can deduct a substantial amount in capital expenses per year under a provision of the tax code called Section 179. For 2008, this amount was raised to $250,000 from $128,000, under an economic stimulus package— see "Congress Accelerates Capital Expense Deductions for One Year—2008," below.

Certain capital assets, such as land and corporate stock, never wear out. Capital expenses related to these costs are not deductible; the owner must wait until the asset is sold to recover the cost.

Congress Accelerates Capital Expense Deductions for One Year—2008

In early 2008, Congress enacted the Economic Stimulus Act, a $168 billion tax package designed to prevent a recession. Among other things, the Act enables businesses to speed up their deductions for capital expenses. One provision increases the annual limit for the Section 179 deduction to $250,000 for 2008, replacing the $128,000 that had been scheduled. The Act also allows bonus depreciation for equipment and other tangible personal property placed in service during 2008. This means that the purchaser can deduct half the cost of the property in the first year, along with any additional normal depreciation on the other half of the property's cost, along with any available Section 179 expensing. Allowable first-year depreciation for passenger vehicles was increased to $11,060, rather than the scheduled $3,060. These provisions apply only to property placed in service during 2008. After 2008, there will no longer be bonus depreciation and the Section 179 deduction will go back to $128,000 (adjusted for inflation), unless Congress acts to extend the Act.

Inventory

Inventory includes almost anything you make or buy to resell to customers. It doesn't matter whether you manufacture the goods yourself or buy finished goods from someone else and resell them to customers. Inventory doesn't include tools, equipment, or anything else that doesn't actually become part of the item you are selling.

You must deduct inventory separately from all other business expenses —you deduct inventory costs as you sell the inventory. Inventory that remains unsold at the end of the year is a business asset, not a deductible expense.

EXAMPLE: In addition to providing hair styling services, Cary sells various hair care products in his salon, which he buys from cosmetics companies. In 2008, Cary spends $15,000 to buy his inventory of hair care product, but sells only $10,000 worth of the product. He can deduct only $10,000 of the inventory costs in 2008.

Home office expenses

Many business owners qualify for the home office deduction. To do so, (1) you must use a part of your home regularly and exclusively for work, and (2) your home office must be your principal workplace or you must regularly perform administrative or management tasks there. For a detailed discussion about the special rules for claiming the home office deduction, see:

- *Deduct It! Lower Your Small Business Taxes*, by Stephen Fishman (Nolo), or
- *Home Business Tax Deductions: Keep What You Earn*, by Stephen Fishman (Nolo).

 CAUTION

You must be in business to claim business deductions. Unfortunately, even though you might believe you're running a business, the IRS may beg to differ. If your business doesn't turn a profit for several years in a row, the IRS might decide that you're engaged in a mere hobby—leading to disastrous tax consequences. People engaged in hobbies are entitled to very limited tax deductions. Make sure you understand the rules and how to avoid having the IRS treat your business as a hobby.

Plan Ahead to Maximize Tax Savings From Deductions

As a general rule, you want to deduct as much as possible, as fast as possible. That way you'll pay the least tax possible. Some smart planning can help.

Bunch deductions into years you can itemize

If you don't have enough itemized deductions to itemize every year, consider bunching your itemized deductions. This means that you pile on your itemized deductions every other year, giving yourself the maximum itemized deduction for that year. You then take the standard deduction in the alternate years, when you have fewer itemized deductions.

During the year you plan to itemize, do everything you can to make your itemized deductions exceed your standard deduction. Pay every bill that will result in an itemized deduction.

You particularly want to bunch expenses for those itemized deductions that are subject to a deduction floor—medical expenses and most miscellaneous itemized deductions. This way, you don't have to struggle to satisfy the 2% of AGI threshold for miscellaneous itemized deductions and 7.5% of AGI for medical expenses in the years that you itemize.

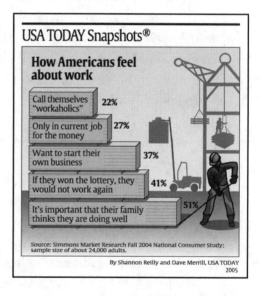

USA TODAY Snapshots®

How Americans feel about work

Call themselves "workaholics" 22%

Only in current job for the money 27%

Want to start their own business 37%

If they won the lottery, they would not work again 41%

It's important that their family thinks they are doing well 51%

Source: Simmons Market Research Fall 2004 National Consumer Study; sample size of about 24,000 adults.

By Shannon Reilly and Dave Merrill, USA TODAY 2005

Here are some ways to bring expenses into the current year.

Charitable contributions. You could contribute double what you ordinarily do and donate nothing the following year.

Property taxes. If you own a home, pay the next year's property taxes before the end of the current year.

State income taxes. If you pay your state income taxes by paying estimated tax four times per year, you ordinarily make your fourth payment for the current year in January of the following year. Make this payment in December instead of January so you can deduct it this year.

State sales taxes. You might choose to deduct your state sales tax instead of your state income tax if your income taxes are small. To maximize this deduction, you could buy any big-ticket items you want this year—for example, if you're thinking about buying a new car, buy it by the end of the year.

Medical expenses. If you or a family member need to have elective surgery or an expensive dental procedure like orthodontia, have it this year. Stock up on prescription medications. Get new eyeglasses. If your doctor has advised you to make home improvements to safeguard your health—for example, installing an air filtration system to protect from allergies—make them this year.

Employee expenses. If you've been thinking about spending money on any employee expenses that won't be reimbursed by your employer—for example, subscriptions to work-related publications, professional or union dues, or education expenses—this would be the year in which to do it.

Investment expenses. If you need to buy things for your investment activities, do it this year. For example, renew your subscriptions to investment publications.

Hobby expenses. If you have a hobby from which you earn money, stock up on things you need for the hobby, and make this your year to go to conferences and the like. Hobby expenses are deductible up to the amount of hobby income. Any expenses that exceed hobby income are not deductible at all. Thus, ideally, in any year you wish to itemize your deductions, your annual hobby expenses should match your hobby income. For example, a hobby artist who sells two paintings during the year for $1,000, and wants to itemize his deductions for the year, should have $1,000 in art expenses he can deduct. If you don't itemize, no hobby expenses are deductible, so try to spend as little as possible in any year you take the standard deduction.

Take a gambling vacation. If you like to gamble and you've won more than you've lost during the year, take a gambling vacation. If you lose no more than your total winnings for the year, your losses will be made up by your tax savings since they're deductible against your gambling winnings. If you don't lose, you won't save on taxes, but you'll have even more winnings. Either way, you're ahead.

In What Year Was an Expense Actually Paid?

In the IRS's eyes, you've actually paid an expense when you draw and mail a check, use a credit card, make an electronic funds transfer, or hand over your cash. So, for example, a check dated December 31, 2009 is considered paid during 2009 only if it has a December 31, 2009 postmark. If you're using a check to pay a substantial expense, you may wish to mail it by certified mail so you'll have proof of when it was mailed.

Bunch income adjustments into years you itemize

You can deduct adjustments to income whether or not you take the standard deduction—so why should you worry about putting them into the same year as you itemize? Here's the reason: If you bunch your itemized deductions, maximizing your adjustments to income for that year helps keep your AGI as low as possible. And that helps you deduct more of your itemized deductions, since most of them can be deducted only to the extent they exceed a certain percentage of your AGI—7.5% for medical expenses, and 2% for most miscellaneous itemized deductions.

For example, if your AGI is $100,000, you'll be able to deduct only those medical expenses that exceed $7,500 (7.5% × your AGI). But if your AGI is $75,000, you'll be able to deduct medical expenses that exceed $5,625 (7.5% × $80,000 = $5,625)—likewise for miscellaneous itemized deductions subject to the 2% of AGI floor.

To keep your AGI as low as possible, you can:

- make an IRA contribution
- if you're self-employed, contribute to your retirement accounts
- if you have a health savings account, make the maximum annual contribution
- move by year end so you can take the moving expense deduction (but only if the move is job-related)

- if you're a teacher, take the educator's deduction (if available, see above)
- prepay college tuition and fees (if this deduction becomes available again; note that you're allowed to deduct these expenses even if they aren't due until the following year)
- prepay student loans if you qualify for the student loan interest deduction (you can prepay this expense just like tuition and fees), or
- if you pay alimony to an ex-spouse, pay part of next year's payments this year.

Of course, you can also reduce your AGI by deferring income until a later year. (See Chapter 4.)

Buy what your business needs by year-end

To get your business tax deductions as soon as possible, go ahead and buy or prepay for items you know you'll need. For example:

- make any needed equipment purchases before the end of the year (be sure to place the equipment into service by the end of the year or you'll get no deduction)
- deduct the cost of business assets in one year under Section 179 rather than depreciating them over several years
- pay any business-related fees this year—for example, attorney fees or accounting fees, and
- if you plan to borrow money for your business, do so before the end of the year so you can deduct your interest payments this year.

Defer deductions to avoid the AMT

If you could be subject to the Alternative Minimum Tax (AMT), you may want to defer to later years certain deductions that the AMT doesn't allow. These expenses include taxes, employee business expenses, and investment expenses. (See Chapter 1 for more on the AMT.)

Don't Prepay Expenses More Than One Year in Advance

If you're a cash basis taxpayer, you generally can't prepay business expenses and deduct them from the current year's taxes. An expense you pay in advance can be deducted only in the year to which it applies.

However, there's an important exception called the 12-month rule. It lets you deduct a prepaid expense in the current year if the expense is for a right or benefit that extends no longer than the earlier of:

- 12 months, or
- until the end of the tax year after the tax year in which you made the payment.

EXAMPLE 1: You're a calendar-year taxpayer and you pay $10,000 on July 1, 2008 for a malpractice insurance policy that's effective for one year beginning July 1, 2008. The 12-month rule applies, because the benefit you've paid for—a business insurance policy—extends only 12 months into the future. Therefore, the full $10,000 is deductible in 2008.

EXAMPLE 2: You're a calendar-year taxpayer and you pay $3,000 in 2008 for a business insurance policy that's effective for three years, beginning July 1, 2008. This payment doesn't qualify for the 12-month rule, because the benefit extends more than 12 months. Therefore, you must use the general rule: $500 is deductible in 2008, $1,000 is deductible in 2009, $1,000 is deductible in 2010, and $500 is deductible in 2011.

To use the 12-month rule, you must apply it when you first start your business. You must get IRS approval if you haven't been using the rule and want to start doing so. Such IRS approval is granted automatically. You must file IRS Form 3115, *Application for Change in Accounting Method,* with your tax return for the year you want to make the change.

Join the Low-Rate Club:
Reduce Taxes Through Investing

Tax rates make a big difference. If you have to pay a 35% tax on $1,000, you're out $350. But if you pay a 15% tax instead, you lose only $150. That's already a $200 incentive to learn ways to pay taxes at the lowest rate possible.

But aren't you trapped within your tax bracket? Not entirely. Tax rates vary depending on how much income you have and the type of income being taxed. Income you earn from investments is taxed at the lowest rates. This includes things like stocks, bonds, mutual funds, and real estate. The profits you earn from these investments are taxed at capital gains rates. Right now, these rates are lower than they've been at any time since 1933—as low as 5%. In fact, between 2008 and 2010, some investors will owe 0% tax on their capital gains. In contrast, the average working stiff must pay income tax on salary or business income at ordinary income rates, which can be as high as 35%. So, now's the perfect time to start saving and investing your hard-earned money—and join the club of people who make money from money.

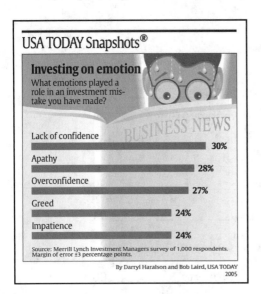

USA TODAY Snapshots®

Investing on emotion
What emotions played a role in an investment mistake you have made?

Lack of confidence	30%
Apathy	28%
Overconfidence	27%
Greed	24%
Impatience	24%

Source: Merrill Lynch Investment Managers survey of 1,000 respondents. Margin of error ±3 percentage points.

By Darryl Haralson and Bob Laird, USA TODAY 2005

CAUTION

Investments held in retirement accounts are taxed differently. The information in this chapter about the lower tax rates for capital gains and dividends is not applicable to mutual funds, stocks, and other investments held in retirement accounts such as a traditional IRA, 401(k), or SEP-IRA. These types of accounts are tax deferred—that is, you don't pay any tax on your contributions or the income they earn until the money is withdrawn (normally at retirement), at which time it's taxed at ordinary income rates. It makes no difference if the money in the account comes from capital assets like stocks and bonds or dividends. The only exception is a Roth IRA or Roth 401(k); withdrawals from these accounts are all tax free, but contributions are not tax deferred. See Chapter 4 for a detailed discussion of retirement accounts.

Keeping Your Capital Gains Tax Low

Two separate sets of tax rates apply to income. One is for ordinary income; the other is for capital gains. Ordinary income is what most people think of as income—your salary from a job, interest on savings accounts or bonds, rental income, profits from owning a business, and income from retirement accounts and pensions. Ordinary income is taxed at ordinary income rates with tax brackets ranging from 10% to 35%—something we're all familiar with.

Another way you can receive income is to sell something you own—a house, mutual fund shares, stocks, bonds, or collectibles like coins and stamps. These are all capital assets, and any profit you receive from selling them is taxable income. However, this profit is classified as a capital gain, which you pay tax on at capital gains tax rates. These rates can be significantly lower than those for ordinary income—in some cases, as low as 5% or (in limited circumstances) even 0%. There are things you can do to make sure you pay the lowest capital gains tax rate. But first you must understand how capital gains are taxed.

RESOURCE

This chapter only scratches the surface of a complex subject. For more information on capital gains and losses, refer to the following IRS publications:

• Publication 550, *Investment Income and Expenses*
• Publication 551, *Basis of Assets*, and
• Publication 564, *Mutual Fund Distributions*.

The book *Capital Gains, Minimal Taxes*, by Kaye A. Thomas (Fairmark Press), also provides excellent in-depth coverage of tax issues for investors in mutual funds and stocks.

What property gets capital gains tax treatment?

Almost everything you own for any purpose, other than business, is a capital asset. This includes both tangible property like your home, and intangible property like stocks and mutual funds. There are two main types of capital assets: personal use property and investment property. Personal use property consists of things you use in your daily life such as:

- your main home
- a vacation home or boat
- household furnishings
- a coin or stamp collection
- clothing and jewelry, and
- any vehicle used for pleasure or commuting.

Investment property consists of things like:

- corporate stocks and bonds (including stock in a small company that is not publicly traded)
- mutual funds
- government bonds
- vacant land, and
- partnership and limited liability company ownership interests.

The one significant type of property that's not a capital asset is business property. This includes:

- inventory or merchandise held mainly for sale to customers (or property that will become part of merchandise)
- equipment and other personal property used by a business—for example, office furniture and computers
- real property used for business or as rental property, and
- the copyright in a literary, musical, or artistic work you create yourself, pay someone to create, or purchase from someone else.

Because business property is not considered a capital asset, different tax rules apply (see "Different Rules When You Sell Business Property," below.)

Adding up your profits or losses (your "basis")

Whenever you sell a capital asset, you must figure out whether you've earned a profit, incurred a loss, or broken even. This will tell you whether you've had a capital gain or loss for tax purposes. To start with, you'll need to know your basis in the property.

The basis of a capital asset is its initial cost (the amount you paid for it), plus any other costs at the time of the purchase or sale, such as sales fees and commissions, shipping expenses, sales tax, and installation costs.

To determine whether you have a capital gain or loss, subtract your basis from what you are selling it for (its selling price): Selling Price – Basis = Capital Gain or Loss. If the selling price is higher than your basis, you have a capital gain.

> **EXAMPLE:** Sue buys ten shares of BigTech stock for $1,000 ($100 per share). She pays a $20 sales commission to an online broker. She later sells all of her shares for $1,520. She paid another $20 brokerage fee to close the sale. Her basis in the ten shares is $1,000 + $20 + $20 = $1,040. Her capital gain on the sale is $460 ($1,500 – $1,040).

Unfortunately, capital assets aren't always sold for a profit. If you lose money on the sale, you have a capital loss. These losses are treated very differently for tax purposes than other types of losses (see "What if you lose money on the sale?" below).

> **EXAMPLE:** Assume that Sue from the above example sold her ten shares of stock for $900. She has a capital loss of $140 ($900 – $1,040).

What if you didn't buy the asset you are selling? For example, you received the item as a gift, or inherited it. With gifted property, your basis in the property is the same as the giftor's if the value of the property has gone up since the time you received it (which is likely). This is called a "carryover basis."

EXAMPLE: Assume that Sue received her BigTech shares as a gift from her father. Her father paid $500 for the shares plus $50 in broker fees. Sue's basis is $550. Sue sells the shares for $1,500. Her capital gain is $950.

If someone has the nerve to give you property that has gone down in value since its purchase, your basis is the lower of its fair market value at the time of the gift or the giftor's basis.

In contrast, the basis of inherited property is its fair market value on the date of the owner's death—often referred to as stepped-up basis. This can result in enormous tax savings if the asset has appreciated in value, because no tax is ever owed on the property's gain in value between the time of the asset's purchase and the owner's death.

EXAMPLE: Let's say that Sue inherited her BigTech stock from her late Uncle Ralph. He had bought his ten shares for $1,000. On the date he died, the stock was worth $1,500. Sue sells the shares for $1,500 and has no capital gain—the sale is tax free.

If property is transferred to you from your spouse (or former spouse, if the transfer is part of your divorce), your basis is the same as your spouse's or former spouse's basis at the time of the transfer.

It's in your interest to keep track of your basis—only you may have the information that will show the IRS that your profit on a sale wasn't as high as it appeared, or that when all the costs were added up, you actually sold at a loss. This isn't always simply a matter of keeping your original purchase records, because a property's basis can change over time. For example, your original basis in stock can go down if you receive more stock from stock splits or nontaxable stock dividends.

The basis of real property (houses and real estate) can also change—for example, it will go up by the cost of any capital improvements you make like adding a room to your home or replacing the roof. The basis of real property used in business is decreased by any depreciation you take.

You can use computer software to help you keep track of your basis, such as *Quicken* and *Microsoft Money*. Specialized programs are also available for this purpose—*Gainskeeper*, for example. Brokerages and fund companies like Fidelity Investments and Vanguard also have online tools to help you keep track of the basis in your investments.

If you haven't kept good records, you may still be able to reconstruct your basis in an asset. In the case of stocks, bonds, and mutual fund shares, ask your brokerage or fund company for the relevant information. Also, if you know when you bought a stock, you can find out the price on the website www.bigcharts.com. It has a free database of historical stock prices, adjusted for stock splits, back to 1985.

Don't Toss These Records

Keep copies of all the statements and reports you receive from your mutual fund or broker. The 1099 forms you receive each year are particularly important. When you buy or sell shares (including those purchased by reinvesting your dividends or fund distributions), keep the confirmation statements you receive. The statements show the price you paid for the shares when you bought them and the price you received for the shares when you disposed of them. The information from the confirmation statement when you purchased the shares will help you figure your basis in the shares. Keep track of any adjustments to the basis of the shares as they occur.

How long did you hold the property before selling?

How long you own a capital asset (the holding period) is a huge factor in determining what tax rate will apply when you sell. There are two holding periods for capital assets: long-term and short-term. Different tax rates apply depending on whether you have a long-term or short-term gain or loss.

If you own property for more than one year, any profit or loss you receive from its sale is a long-term capital gain or loss. If you hold it for one year or less, any gain or loss is a short-term capital gain or loss. The holding period begins the day after you acquire the asset and ends on the day you sell it. The day you sell the asset is part of your holding period.

> **EXAMPLE:** Harry buys a vacation home on February 5, 2008 for $200,000, and sells it on February 5, 2009, for $250,000. His holding period is not more than one year, so he has a short-term capital gain of $50,000. If he'd sold it one day later, his holding period would have been more than one year and he would have had a long-term capital gain, instead.

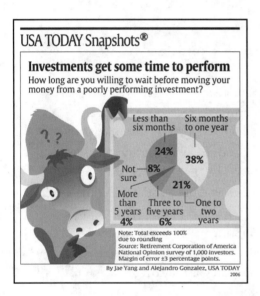

USA TODAY Snapshots®

Investments get some time to perform
How long are you willing to wait before moving your money from a poorly performing investment?

Less than six months: 24%
Six months to one year: 38%
One to two years: 21%
Three to five years: 6%
More than 5 years: 4%
Not sure: 8%

Note: Total exceeds 100% due to rounding
Source: Retirement Corporation of America National Opinion survey of 1,000 investors. Margin of error ±3 percentage points.
By Jae Yang and Alejandro Gonzalez, USA TODAY 2006

When you buy stocks, bonds, mutual fund shares, and other securities traded on an established securities market, your holding period begins the day after the trade date when you buy the securities, and ends on the trade date when you sell them. Be careful not to confuse the trade date with the settlement date. The trade date is the day you enter into the transaction. The settlement date, which usually comes a few days later, is the date ownership of the shares is delivered to you and you pay for them.

The holding period for gifted assets is the giftor's holding period, plus the time the person receiving the gift holds the property. In contrast, all inherited property is deemed to be a long-term capital asset, no matter how long it is actually held by the deceased person and the heir.

What tax rate will apply to your profits?

You don't have to pay any tax on the appreciation of a capital asset while you own it—you can earn millions of dollars on paper and never have to pay the IRS a cent. But once you sell a capital asset, you have to pay taxes on any profits you receive—your capital gains.

Capital gains tax rates vary depending on the type of asset involved, how long you owned it (your holding period), and your top income tax bracket. The IRS knows about most of your capital gains because the proceeds of any stock, bond, or other securities sold during the year are reported on IRS Form 1099-B by the brokerage or financial institution that carried out the sale.

Long-term capital gains. To encourage people to make long-term investments, long-term capital gains receive the most favorable tax treatment, with the lowest tax rates. The following chart shows the long-term capital gains rates in effect from May 7, 2003, through December 31, 2010. As you can see, your long-term capital gain tax rate depends on your top income tax bracket.

Long-Term Capital Gain Rates—5/7/2003 through 12/31/2010		
If your taxable income is (2008 tax rates):	Then your top income tax bracket is:	And your capital gains tax rate is:
Up to $65,100 if married filing jointly, or up to $32,550 if single	10% or 15%	0% from 1/1/08 through 12/31/10
$65,101 and over if married filing jointly, or $32,551 and over if single	25% to 35%	15%

EXAMPLE: Harry, a dentist whose taxable income is $100,000, buys 100 shares of stock for $1,000 on May 1, 2008. He sells the stock for $1,200 on June 1, 2009. He owned the stock for over one year, so he'll have to pay long-term capital gains tax rates. He's in the 25% to 35% tax bracket, so his long-term capital gains tax rate for the stock sale is 15%. He pays 15% tax on his $200 profit, resulting in a $30 tax.

Taxpayers in the 10% and 15% tax brackets will owe *no tax at all* on long-term capital gains from January 1, 2008 through December 31, 2010. But that doesn't mean they should go wild selling off property. Here's why: Any capital gains that push someone into the 15% income tax ceiling are taxed at the higher 15% capital gains rate. The zero percent rate applies only to those capital gains that fall between the taxpayer's ordinary income and the income limit for the 15% federal tax bracket in 2008 to 2010.

> **EXAMPLE:** Carl and Charlotte, a married couple filing jointly, have $50,000 in ordinary income in 2008 and $20,000 in long-term capital gains. They pay zero taxes on $15,100 of their $20,000 in long-term capital gains. Reason: Their $50,000 ordinary income plus $15,100 in capital gains equals the $65,100 income limit for the 15% bracket. They must pay a 15% long-term capital gains tax on the remaining $4,900 in capital gains, because this amount puts them over the 15% tax bracket.

CAUTION

The capital gains rate is scheduled to increase in 2011. The 0%, 5%, and 15% long-term capital gains tax rates are set to expire at the end of 2010. Starting in 2011, the rates will go back to what they were before May 7, 2003, unless Congress acts to change them. These rates were 10% for taxpayers in the 10% and 15% income tax brackets, and 20% for all other taxpayers. In addition, 8% and 18% rates applied to capital gains for assets held at least five years. No one (not even Congress at this point) knows whether these rates will go into effect in 2011, whether Congress will extend the 5% and 15% rates, or whether they will enact other rates.

Short-term capital gains. If you hold a capital asset for less than a year before selling it, you'll have a short-term capital gain. Short-term capital gains are all taxed at ordinary income tax rates. The tax you'll pay will be at your highest income tax rate (also called your marginal tax rate), which can be determined from the chart below.

2008 Federal Personal Income Tax Brackets		
Tax Bracket	Income If Single	Income If Married Filing Jointly
10%	Up to $8,025	Up to $16,050
15%	From $8,026 to $32,550	$16,051 to 65,100
25%	$32,551 to $78,850	$65,101 to $131,450
28%	$78,851 to $164,550	$131,451 to $200,300
33%	$164,551 to $357,700	$200,301 to $357,700
38%	All over $357,700	All over $357,700

EXAMPLE: Bill bought stock on March 15, 2008 and sold it for a $1,000 profit on December 30, 2008. He owned the stock for less than 12 months, so the short-term capital gains rates apply. This means his $1,000 profit will be taxed at his top personal income tax rate. Bill's taxable income for the year is $125,000, so his top rate is 28%. He must pay a 28% capital gains tax on his $1,000 gain, for a $280 tax. Had he waited a little longer—at least one year and one day—to sell the stock, his profit would have been taxed at the lower, 15% long-term capital gains rate instead.

Real estate. Your personal residence is a capital asset, and any profit you make when you sell it is taxed at the long- or short-term capital gains rates described above. However, there is a special exclusion from tax for profits from home sales—up to $250,000 if you're single and $500,000 if you're married filing jointly. The home sale tax exclusion is discussed in detail in Chapter 2. Real estate that is not your principal home, but is used for personal purposes—a vacation home, for example—is taxed like any other capital asset.

Rental real estate gets different tax treatment. When you sell rental property at a profit, you must pay a 25% tax on the total amount of depreciation you deducted for the property in prior years. Any profit left over is taxed at the normal capital gains rates.

TIP

Borrow against your equity in capital assets. Do you need to free up some cash, but without adding to your tax liability for the year? Instead of selling capital assets like real estate, stocks, bonds, and mutual fund shares, you can borrow against them. A loan is not taxable income, because you must pay it back. Moreover, if you use the money for a business purpose, the interest is deductible as a business expense. If you have equity in a house or other real estate, you might be able to get a loan or a line of credit (but be sure you have a plan for paying the money back—you're risking your house being foreclosed on). You can also get a stock loan using stocks or other securities as collateral. Another option is to establish a margin account at a brokerage that permits you to borrow against stock and other securities; this is similar to a line of credit.

Collectibles. Collectibles include such things as stamps, coins (there are exceptions for certain coins minted by the U.S. Treasury), artwork, baseball cards, antiques, rugs, gems, alcoholic beverages like rare wines, and metals like gold and silver (there are exceptions for certain kinds of bullion). Although these are capital assets, they're taxed differently from other capital assets. All gains from selling collectibles are taxed at a single 28% rate, no matter how long you own the asset. Before buying coins or artwork as an investment, keep in mind that you'll have to pay a much higher tax on any profits you earn when you sell than on investments like stocks.

Small business stock. The stock in certain types of small corporations receives special capital gains treatment. If you hold stock at least five years, 50% of any capital gain you realize from its sale is exempt from tax. The remaining 50% is taxed at a single 28% rate. In effect, this means a 14% capital gains tax is paid on the total gain.

There are many restrictions on who can qualify for this tax break. Among other things:

- The corporation must be a regular C corporation, not an S corporation.

- You must own the stock for at least five years.
- The corporation can't be one that provides personal services—for example, a professional corporation formed by a doctor, dentist, or lawyer.
- The corporation can't have more than $50 million in assets.
- You must purchase the stock directly during its initial issuance.

For a complete discussion of all the restrictions on this tax, see IRS Publication 550, *Investment Income and Expenses*.

Getting the lowest capital gains rate

You usually have little or no control over how well an investment in stock or property does. But you can control how much tax you pay on the profits from your investments. Here are some tips and strategies for getting the most out of your investments and paying the least in taxes.

Always try to sell property at lowest capital gains rates. Long-term capital gains rates are the lowest you'll get. To take advantage of these rates, you'll have to hold onto your property or investment for at least one year. Don't hang onto a losing investment just to pay a lower capital gains rate, but do consider the effect of long-term versus short-term capital gains rates, and try to sell at the long-term rate whenever possible. The capital gains calculator at www.moneychimp.com lets you compare the taxes for short-term versus long-term and show the advantage of waiting at least one year before selling.

Take advantage of low capital gains rates before 2011. Currently, long-term capital gains tax rates are the lowest they've been since 1933. And, never in U.S. history has there been a zero tax on capital gains, as there will be for lower-income taxpayers during 2008 through 2010. These low rates are scheduled to end after 2010 and return to their pre-2003 levels. No one really knows what long-term capital rates will be after 2010. If you have long-term capital assets that have appreciated in value, consider selling them by the end of 2010 to take advantage of the low capital gains rates.

Give capital assets that have gone up in value to your favorite charity.
You can save on taxes by giving stocks, bonds, other securities, and real
estate that has gone up in value to a charity. You save because you don't
have to pay any tax on your gain, and will be allowed to deduct the fair
market value of the asset, which should be more than you paid for it.

> EXAMPLE: Jake owns 100 shares of the Acme Mutual Fund he bought for
> $1,000 ten years ago. The shares are now worth $11,000. If he sold the
> shares, he'd have to pay a 15% capital gains tax on his $10,000 profit, for
> $1,500 tax. Instead of selling, he donates the shares to his favorite charity.
> He pays no taxes on the shares' gain in value. He also gets to deduct as a
> charitable deduction their full $11,000 value which, because he's in the
> 28% income tax bracket, saves him $3,080 in income taxes.

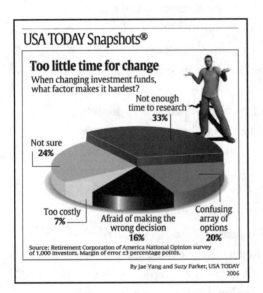

Of course, giving to charity
makes sense only if you really
want to help a charity, since your
tax savings will always be less
than the value of the gift.

See Chapter 5 for a detailed
discussion of charitable gifts.

**Give capital assets to family
members in lower tax brackets.**
If you don't want to give
appreciated assets to charity,
consider giving them to your
children or grandchildren, or
other family members who are
in the 10% or 15% income tax bracket. You don't get the benefit of an
increased basis as with charitable contributions, but if the recipient is
in the 10% or 15% tax bracket, and sells the gift, he or she will owe
only a 5% capital gains tax on all or part of the profit. Moreover, during
2008–2010, all or part of the profit will be taxed at 0% (assuming the
asset is held for over one year). Fortunately, the giver's holding period is
added to the holding period of the recipient for this purpose.

> **EXAMPLE:** Assume that Jake (from the example above) gave his Acme shares to his 16-year-old daughter, Maria, who is in the 10% income tax bracket. Jake's ten-year holding period for the shares is added to Maria's holding period. Maria sells the stock for a $10,000 profit and pays only a 5% long-term capital gains tax on the profit, for a $500 tax.

If a child is under 19 years of age, he or she will be subject to the kiddie tax. This requires the child to pay income tax at the parents' top tax rate on all unearned income over $1,800 from capital gains, interest, and dividends. So, there will be a tax benefit only if the all the child's unearned income, including income from selling gifted capital assets, is less than $1,800.

What if you lose money on the sale?

Any losses you incur when you sell personal use property, like your principal home or collectibles, are not deductible at all.

> **EXAMPLE:** Virginia bought a drawing she thought was by Picasso for $10,000. It turned out the drawing was a fake. She sold it to an art dealer for $100. Her $9,900 loss is not deductible.

You can deduct a loss on personal use property only if it results from a casualty loss or theft—for example, your house is destroyed in a hurricane.

Losses on investment property, like stocks and real estate, are deductible, but they cannot be deducted directly from your ordinary income like a business loss or casualty loss. Instead, all your capital losses from investment property must be subtracted from your investment property capital gains. You have to do the following:

- Tally up all your long-term and short-term gains and losses for the year.
- Subtract the short-term losses from the short-term gains.
- Subtract the long-term losses from the long-term gains.

- If you have a loss in one category and a gain in another, subtract the loss from the gain—the result is considered to be in the same category as the larger of the two numbers.

You'll end up with either a short-term gain, short-term loss, long-term gain, or long-term loss. Or, if gains and losses are equal, you'll have zero gains and losses.

EXAMPLE: Ken bought and sold stock during the year as follows:

Asset	Cost	Holding Period	Gain on Sale	Loss on Sale
100 shares XYZ stock	$25,000	6 months		$5,500
50 shares ABC stock	$5,000	3 months	$500	
Vacation home	$100,000	2 years	$10,000	
Mutual fund	$50,000	1 year, 1 day		$9,000

Ken subtracts his short-term capital losses ($5,500 on XYZ stock) from his short-term capital gains ($500 on ABC stock), resulting in a net $5,000 short-term loss for the year. Ken then subtracts his long-term capital loss ($9,000 from mutual fund) from his long-term capital gain ($10,000 from vacation home), resulting in a $1,000 net long-term capital gain for the year. He subtracts the loss from the gain. Thus, he subtracts his $5,000 short-term loss from his $1,000 long-term gain. The result is a net $4,000 short-term capital loss for the year.

If you have a lot of capital gains in a year, you can try to reduce those gains through a strategy known as tax-loss harvesting. To do this, you sell securities or other investment properties that have dropped in value, to create a capital loss for the year. Then you use the losses to offset your capital gains. If you have enough losses, you can offset all your gains for the year.

EXAMPLE: Dave purchased 100 shares of XYZ Corp. a few years ago. Unfortunately, the stock has steadily gone down in value. However, Dave has also picked some winners: his shares in the ABC Mutual Fund and Acme Mutual Fund have shot up in value. Dave sells his XYZ shares for a $10,000 loss and realizes a long-term capital loss, since he owned the shares for more than one year. He also sells the Acme and XYZ shares for $7,000 and $3,000 gains, respectively. These are short-term capital gains. Come tax time, Dave has a $10,000 long-term capital gain for the year and a $10,000 short-term capital loss. The $10,000 capital loss offsets the $10,000 capital gain, so Dave pays no taxes on his $10,000 profit. Had Dave not realized the losses, he would have had to pay income tax on his short-term capital gains at ordinary income tax rates. His top tax bracket is 28%, so he would have had to pay $2,800 in taxes on his short-term gains (28% × $10,000 = $2,800).

But wait, it gets even better. If your total capital losses exceed all your capital gains for the year, you may deduct each year up to $3,000 of these extra losses from your ordinary income, such as salary income, interest, and dividends.

EXAMPLE: Lara sells some mutual fund shares for a $3,000 loss. She may deduct the $3,000 from her salary income for the year. Lara is in the 33% income tax bracket, so this saves her $990 in taxes.

Keeping the Tax on Your Dividends Low

If you own stock in a corporation, you may occasionally receive dividends. These might come in the form of money (cash) or additional stock shares, based on the corporation's earnings and profits. Dividends are taxable income. They're reported to the IRS by the company that distributes them, on IRS Form 1099-DIV. Income from bonds and government obligations (such as Treasury bills and notes) is interest, not dividends, so it falls under different tax rules.

Until 2003, dividend income was taxed at ordinary income rates—anywhere from 10% to 35%, depending on your tax bracket. However, Congress changed the tax rate for many dividends to the same rate as for long-term capital gains—a 15% tax for most taxpayers and 10% for taxpayers in the lowest two income brackets. But don't get too comfy: These reduced dividend rates are scheduled to expire at the end of 2010. Starting in 2011, dividends will again be taxed at ordinary income rates, unless Congress steps in again.

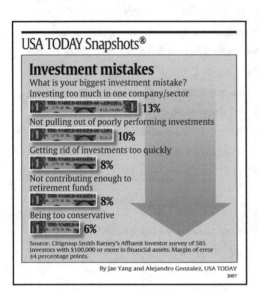

USA TODAY Snapshots®

Investment mistakes

What is your biggest investment mistake?
Investing too much in one company/sector
13%

Not pulling out of poorly performing investments
10%

Getting rid of investments too quickly
8%

Not contributing enough to retirement funds
8%

Being too conservative
6%

Source: Citigroup Smith Barney's Affluent Investor survey of 585 investors with $100,000 or more in financial assets. Margin of error ±4 percentage points.

By Jae Yang and Alejandro Gonzalez, USA TODAY 2007

To benefit from the current, lower rates, your dividends must be "qualified dividends." This means your stock is in a U.S. corporation, or a foreign corporation traded on a U.S. stock exchange, or from a country with which the United States has signed a tax treaty (this includes most major countries—see IRS Publication 550 for a list). In addition, you must hold the stock for at least 60 days—but not just any 60 days. The 60 days must be during a 121-day window that begins 60 days before what's called the corporation's "ex-dividend date" and ends 61 days after that date. The ex-dividend date is the day after the company's record date—the date the corporation's books are closed.

The idea is that you can't purchase a stock just before the company issues a dividend, collect the dividend, and then immediately sell the stock at the lower rate. You must hold on to the stock for at least 61 days to qualify for the lower tax rates. When counting the number of days you held the stock, include the day you disposed of the stock, but not the day you acquired it.

EXAMPLE: Yumi buys 5,000 shares of XYZ Corp. stock on June 30, 2008. XYZ Corp. pays a cash dividend of ten cents per share. The ex-dividend date is July 8, 2008. Yumi sells the shares on August 3, 2008. She held her shares of XYZ Corp. for only 34 days during the 121 day window—from July 1, 2008, through August 3, 2008. The 121-day period began on May 9, 2008 (60 days before the ex-dividend date), and ended on September 6, 2008 (61 days after the ex-dividend date). Yumi has no qualified dividends from XYZ Corp. because she held the XYZ stock for less than the required holding period. This means she must pay income tax on her XYZ dividends at ordinary income tax rates.

Lost Track of Money That's Already Yours?

Sandra Block found that about $32.8 billion in unclaimed property is sitting in state treasuries. This property includes stocks, uncashed dividend checks, forgotten bank accounts, lawsuit settlements, and undelivered refunds.

Some companies offer to help consumers find unclaimed property, for a fee. But you don't need to pay someone to find out if any of the money belongs to you, says Noreen Perrotta, deputy editor of *Consumer Reports Money Adviser*. You can search for free at www.missingmoney.com, a website operated by the National Association of Unclaimed Property Administrators. The site also provides an online form you can use to file a claim with the state that's holding your property.

Occasionally, people discover they've inherited money from long-lost relatives, Perrotta says, but the average value of lost property claims is about $100.

 "A little extra cash can come in handy—especially if it's already yours," by Sandra Block, December 18, 2007.

> (♡) TIP
> **Reinvesting dividends won't avoid tax.** Investors often use their dividends to buy more stock in the company, instead of taking them in cash. Many companies have dividend reinvestment plans that allow shareholders to do this automatically. It may not seem fair, but you must still report the dividends as income, even though you use the money to buy more stock. If you're allowed to buy more stock at a discount, you must report as dividend income the fair market value of the additional stock on the dividend payment date.

Minimizing the Taxes on Your Mutual Fund Earnings

Mutual funds are some of the most popular investments around, yet many people have little idea of how their profits and earnings will be taxed—and thus how to avoid certain tax traps.

First, what is a mutual fund? It's a company that pools money from investors (people like you who buy shares in the mutual fund). They take that money and build an investment portfolio of stocks, bonds, money market funds, or a hybrid of bonds and stocks. There are all sorts of mutual funds you can invest in—different funds specialize in everything from Asian stocks to tax-exempt municipal bonds to blue chip companies.

You can make money from a mutual fund in two ways, each of which leads to different tax results:

- **By selling your mutual fund shares at a profit.** This occurs when you sell your fund shares back to the fund and are no longer an investor in the mutual fund company. Any profit you earn from the sale will be either a short-term or long-term capital gain, depending on whether you owned the shares of the mutual fund for over one year.

- **From annual distributions the mutual fund sends you, represent-ing your share of any profits, dividends, and interest the fund earned.** Your tax rate on these distributions will depend on what kind of income the fund earned—ordinary income or short-term or long-term capital gains. This, in turn, will depend on what the fund invested in—stocks, bonds, tax-exempt bonds, and so on. You'll be given this information each year, when the fund sends you IRS Form 1099-DIV. Many funds also issue their own tax reports and provide extensive information about taxes on their websites and in their literature—these can be a great resource.

> ## CAUTION
> **Reinvesting your distributions won't avoid tax.** Mutual fund shareholders choose whether to receive their distributions in cash or have them reinvested in the fund through the purchase of new shares. Don't base your choice on the tax consequences—the distributions will be subject to income tax either way. The only exception is if your mutual fund shares are held in a tax-deferred account like an IRA or 401(k).

You can't control how well your mutual fund performs—you've handed that job over to the fund that picks the investments for you. But there are certain things you can do to minimize your taxes and thus maximize your earnings from a mutual fund.

Don't buy mutual funds just before year-end distributions. Mutual funds need to distribute 98% of their profits to their shareholders by the end of each year. For this reason, they often make large distributions of capital gains in December. If you invest in a mutual fund near the end of the year, you'll have to pay tax on the distributions, even though you really don't benefit from them, given that the fund's share price will drop by the amount of the distribution. Most mutual funds have websites that can tell you when capital gain distributions are scheduled.

EXAMPLE: You want to invest $1,000 in the Acme Mutual Fund. Its shares currently cost $5. Acme has announced that it will distribute a $1 dividend to its shareholders on December 15. If you buy 200 Acme shares on December 14, you'll have to pay tax on the $200 dividend you receive. Moreover, on December 16, the price of the shares will drop to $4 per share to reflect the $1 dividend distribution. So you end up with 200 shares worth only $800 and a $200 dividend you must pay tax on. Had you waited until December 16 or later to buy Acme shares, you could have purchased 250 shares for $1,000 and not had to pay tax on a distribution.

Sell highest-cost shares first. Investors often purchase shares in the same mutual fund in separate lots over time. Each lot will typically have a different selling price, and therefore your shares will have a different basis, depending on when you bought them.

If you want to sell only part of your holdings of a mutual fund, how do you decide which ones to sell? Always sell the shares with the highest basis (the ones you paid the most for) first. This will result in the smallest taxable profit for you (your profit is the selling price minus your basis). The same is true if you're selling shares in a company.

To accomplish this, you must use the "specific identification method" to advise your broker or the mutual fund company which of your shares to sell. You identify the shares by specifying their cost and purchase dates. You're also supposed to receive a written confirmation of your instructions from the broker. Many discount and online brokers won't do this. In this event, keep a record of your oral instructions and put this in your tax file for safekeeping.

EXAMPLE: Caroline owns 200 shares of the Acme Mutual Fund. She purchased 100 of the shares five years ago for $1,000 and the other 100 shares two years ago for $5,000. Acme shares are currently worth $75 per share. Caroline decides to sell half of her shares. She instructs her broker to sell the shares she purchased two years ago for $5,000 ($50 per share). She earns $2,500 on the sale, leaving her with a $2,500 long-term capital gain on which she must pay tax at the long-term capital gains rate.

Using the specific identification method requires careful record keeping. You can use easier methods, but these will often result in higher taxes. In the case of mutual funds, you can use the first-in, first-out method, or one of two averaging methods. The averaging methods may not be used when you sell individual stocks—that is, shares in companies other than mutual funds. Think carefully about that method you want to use, because you'll have to stick with your choice for as long as you own the mutual fund or stock.

With the first-in, first-out (FIFO) method, the shares you buy first are considered sold first. The shares you buy first probably have the lowest basis, thus you'll have the largest taxable gain if the FIFO method is used. The IRS assumes that you use the FIFO method unless you choose another method.

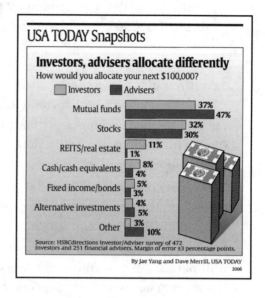

USA TODAY Snapshots

Investors, advisers allocate differently

How would you allocate your next $100,000?

☐ Investors ☐ Advisers

Mutual funds — Investors 37%, Advisers 47%
Stocks — Investors 32%, Advisers 30%
REITS/real estate — Investors 11%, Advisers 1%
Cash/cash equivalents — Investors 8%, Advisers 4%
Fixed income/bonds — Investors 5%, Advisers 3%
Alternative investments — Investors 4%, Advisers 5%
Other — Investors 3%, Advisers 10%

Source: HSBCdirections Investor/Adviser survey of 472 investors and 251 financial advisers. Margin of error ±3 percentage points.

By Jae Yang and Dave Merrill, USA TODAY
2006

> **EXAMPLE:** Assume that Caroline from the example uses the FIFO method to value her shares. This means that the shares she purchased first are the shares that are deemed sold by the IRS. These shares cost $1,000 ($10 per share), so Caroline would have a $6,500 taxable capital gain ($7,500 − $1,000 = $6,500). That's $5,500 more taxable gain than Caroline has using the specific identification method.

With the single-category method, you figure the average cost of all of your shares and use this average as your basis. You simply add up the purchase price of all your shares and then divide that number by the total number of shares. This is the most commonly used method, and most funds will calculate and provide this figure to you.

> **EXAMPLE:** Caroline from the above examples bought 100 shares of the Acme Mutual Fund for $1,000 and 100 shares for $5,000. The average cost of her shares is $30 ($6,000 ÷ 200 = $30), so she uses $30 as her basis. In fact, 100 of the shares cost $10 per share and the other 100 shares cost $50 per share.

As if you didn't have enough methods to choose from, someone refined the single-category method into a variation called the multiple-category method. With this method, you average your long-term and short-term holdings separately, potentially resulting in a lower basis than you'd get by simply using the single-category method.

Invest in tax-efficient mutual funds. When you purchase a mutual fund (or exchange traded fund "ETF"—see "What's an Exchange-Traded Fund (ETF)?" below), you have no control over how much money the fund distributes to you, as a shareholder, each year. The fund's managers control this. But you can control which mutual funds you buy. Some funds are more tax efficient than others—that is, they keep taxable distributions to a minimum. By investing in a tax-efficient mutual fund, you defer paying most of your taxes until you sell your shares.

This doesn't mean you shouldn't invest in mutual funds that are not tax efficient. Such funds—for example, those that invest in growth stocks—can be highly profitable. However, it's best to place these funds in tax-deferred accounts such as IRAs, 401(k)s, and traditional IRAs. That way, you won't have to pay any tax on the distributions the fund makes each year (so long as you leave them in your account). Of course, you must pay income tax at ordinary rates when you withdraw your earnings upon retirement.

So how do you know if a mutual fund is tax efficient? Some mutual funds, such as index funds, are inherently tax efficient, because they are not actively managed; rather, their holdings simply mirror a stock index or some other criterion such as investing in specific industries or countries. The securities in these funds ordinarily don't have to be traded very often.

Other funds are managed so as to keep distributions to a minimum. These funds sell shares as infrequently as possible and use other techniques to avoid having to distribute capital gains to their shareholders. Such funds often bill themselves as "tax managed."

Since 2002, the Securities and Exchange Commission has required mutual funds to show their after-tax investment returns in their prospectuses.

A mutual fund that claims to be tax efficient or tax managed must also show after-tax returns in its marketing literature and prospectuses. These should be easy to find on the mutual fund and broker websites. And for help comparing the before- and after-tax returns from mutual funds, you'll find a useful calculator at www.ingfunds.com/investor/content/resources/calculators.

What's an Exchange Traded Fund (ETF)?

Exchange traded funds (ETFs for short) are a new type of investment that combine many of the attributes of individual stocks and mutual funds. They are traded on stock exchanges, just like regular stocks, which makes them easier to buy than mutual funds. You can also buy just one share (a boon for small investors). Like mutual funds, most ETFs are registered investment companies that offer investors a share of a portfolio of stocks or other investments. Almost all ETFs are index funds, and, as such, are highly tax efficient. Moreover, they often have the lowest operating expenses around— lower than comparable mutual funds—which saves you money. You can find good information on ETFs at the Vanguard Group website at http://flagship2.vanguard.com/VGApp/hnw/FundsVIPER.

Different Rules When You Sell Business Property

If you've been following along through this whole chapter, you may remember that business property is not a capital asset. Just to confuse matters, however, income from certain business property sales—namely, depreciable business property—are taxed at long-term capital gains rates. If you have depreciable business property (you probably do), you'll want to at least be familiar with the unique set of tax rules that will apply when you sell it.

Depreciable business property (also known as Section 1231 property), includes most business property:

- business real estate
- business equipment, automobiles, trucks, and furniture, and
- intangible property like patents and copyrights.

Whenever a business sells Section 1231 property, any profit it receives is taxed at everyone's favorite tax rate—the long-term capital gains rate. However, there's one catch: Any depreciation you deducted for the property while you owned it is recaptured—meaning it is taxed at ordinary income rates, or a flat 25% rate for business real estate.

> EXAMPLE: Phil, an optometrist, owns a small office building. He bought it for $200,000 several years ago, and has taken a total of $100,000 in depreciation deductions for the property. He sells the property this year for $300,000. His profit—$100,000—is taxed at long-term capital gains rates (15% because Phil is in the 28% tax bracket). However, he must pay a flat 25% income tax on the $100,000 of depreciation he previously deducted.

If business property is sold at a loss, the losses are ordinary losses, not capital losses. This means you can deduct them directly from your gross income. In contrast, if you sell a capital asset at a loss, you deduct this loss from your capital gains. Because you can deduct only $3,000 of capital losses from your gross income each year, depreciable business property losses have an important tax advantage over capital asset losses.

Remember, however, that the depreciation deductions you take on business property each year reduce your basis in the property, and therefore increase your taxable profit or decrease your deductible loss when you sell the property.

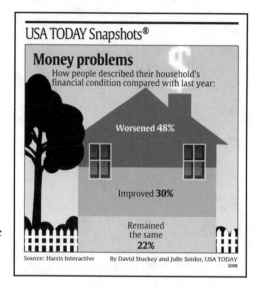

USA TODAY Snapshots®

Money problems

How people described their household's financial condition compared with last year:

Worsened 48%

Improved **30%**

Remained the same **22%**

Source: Harris Interactive   By David Stuckey and Julie Snider, USA TODAY
2008

EXAMPLE: Assume that Phil purchased his computer for $1,000 and has depreciated 52% of its cost. His basis in the computer has gone down from $1,000 to $480 (52% × $1,000 = $520). He sells the computer for $400. He has only an $80 loss he can deduct.

RESOURCE

For detailed guidance on the tax and other legal issues involved in selling business property, refer to *The Complete Guide to Selling a Business,* by Fred S. Steingold (Nolo).

All in the Family:
Shifting Income Within
Your Household

U.S. taxpayers pay rates ranging from a low of 10% to a high of 35%. That's a 25% difference. If you're in one of the higher brackets you could save a lot by shifting your income to someone in a lower tax bracket—say, your children. There is a way to do this—it's called income shifting or income splitting. Recent changes in the tax laws have made income shifting more difficult than in the past, but not impossible.

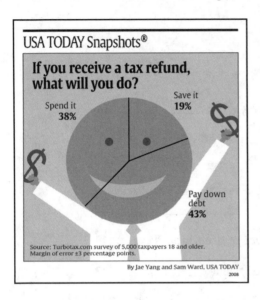

USA TODAY Snapshots®

If you receive a tax refund, what will you do?

Spend it
38%

Save it
19%

Pay down debt
43%

Source: Turbotax.com survey of 5,000 taxpayers 18 and older. Margin of error ±3 percentage points.

By Jae Yang and Sam Ward, USA TODAY 2008

Income shifting works best for well-off people in high tax brackets. It's especially useful for those with assets like stocks that have greatly appreciated in value. It can also work well for people who own their own business. But, if you're an average 9 to 5 stiff, this game is probably not for you. Instead, think about socking away as much money as possible in retirement accounts like IRAs and 401(k)s (see Chapter 4). If you want to save for your children's education, Coverdell ESAs and 529 savings plans are good options (see Chapter 2).

All Aboveboard: How Income Shifting Works

Income shifting works because, as far as earned income is concerned, the IRS views a family as a collection of separate individual taxpayers. Except for husbands and wives who can (and usually do) file a joint return, each family member pays taxes on income at his or her own tax rate. Family members with lower incomes pay taxes at a lower rate than those with higher incomes.

2008 Federal Personal Income Tax Brackets		
Tax Bracket	Income If Single	Income If Married Filing Jointly
10%	Up to $8,025	Up to $16,050
15%	From $8,026 to $32,550	$16,051 to 65,100
25%	$32,551 to $78,850	$65,101 to $131,450
28%	$78,851 to $164,550	$131,451 to $200,300
33%	$164,551 to $357,700	$200,301 to $357,700
38%	All over $357,700	All over $357,700

As the "2008 Federal Personal Income Tax Brackets" chart shows, a married couple with $100,000 in taxable income in 2008 will have a top tax bracket of 25%. However, if they could arrange things so that $25,000 of their income was, for example, taxable to their 20-year-old son, his top tax rate would be only 15%. But how can someone do this?

You can't simply allocate or assign part of your salary or income to your children or others and have them pay tax on it. The IRS says that the person who earns money for doing work is the one who must pay tax on it. The same goes for earnings from investments, such as savings accounts or stocks. The person who reports earnings from investment property must actually own the property.

The two main ways to achieve income shifting are to:

- transfer ownership of income-producing property to your children, grandchildren, or others in a lower income tax bracket, or
- hire your children or other family members to work in your business and pay them a salary or other compensation.

Other Tax Advantages of Income Shifting

Income shifting can not only lower the tax rates that have to be paid on income, it can have other beneficial effects:

Lowering your AGI below other phaseout levels. Income shifting reduces your adjusted gross income (AGI) for the year. That lets you reverse the process by which many deductions and exemptions are phased out as your AGI goes up. Also, many personal deductions are deductible only to the extent they exceed a specified percentage of your AGI. For example, medical expenses are deductible only to the extent they exceed 7.5% of your AGI. The lower the AGI, the more you can deduct. (See Chapter 5.)

Reducing the size of your estate. Gifting assets to your children or others will also reduce the size of your estate when you die, reducing the chance that estate taxes will take a chunk out of your legacy. For detailed information on estate taxes, see *Plan Your Estate*, by Denis Clifford (Nolo).

CAUTION
The more money a child has in his or her name, the less college financial aid will be available. So if you're counting on financial aid, think twice before giving your children money or property. Colleges and universities figure students should spend at least 35% of all assets in their name on their college expenses. In contrast, they expect parents to kick in only 5.6% of their assets. This is one important reason income shifting to children is used mainly by well-off families—their children won't qualify for financial aid anyway, or will only be able to obtain loans. Coverdell ESAs and 529 savings plans are a good option if you want to save for your children's college and don't want to ruin their chances of getting aid (see "Education accounts," below). For more information, see the Department of Education's website at www.studentaid.ed.gov.

Thanks, Mom: Giving Your Kids Income-Producing Property

The simplest way to shift income is to give income-producing property to your lower-tax-bracket children (or other relatives or friends with whom you don't mind sharing). Your chosen recipients won't need to pay any tax when they get the gift—though when the property starts to generate income, they'll owe tax on that income. But that's where your strategy actually starts paying off, because they'll be paying tax at their own, presumably lower tax rates.

Gifts to People Other Than Your Children

Most income-shifting gifts are made to children or grandchildren, but you can give money or investment property to any lower-income taxpayer—perhaps your parents, other relatives, or friends. Don't bother trying to shift income to your spouse, however. If you file a joint return, your income is already combined. If you file separate returns, the tax brackets have been adjusted to largely eliminate the marriage penalty. (See Chapter 6.)

The Kiddie Tax—The IRS Puts the Brakes on Income Shifting

The IRS has never been thrilled with income-shifting, and adopted the "kiddie" tax in the 1980s to limit the strategy's usefulness. Under the kiddie tax, children pay tax at their own income tax rate on unearned income they receive up to a threshold amount ($1,800 in 2008). That part is fine—here's the hitch: All unearned income kids receive above the threshold amount is taxed at their parent's highest income tax rate. That rate could be as high as 35%, compared to the 10% rate that most children would be paying. Any unearned income below the standard deduction amount—$900 in 2008—is not taxed or reported to the IRS.

USA TODAY Snapshots®

Learning and working
Percentage of 16- to 24-year-old full-time college students with jobs:

1975   35%
1985   44%
1995   47%
2005   49%
Source: Department of Education

By David Stuckey and Robert W. Ahrens, USA TODAY
2007

The net effect is that you get the benefit of the child's lower tax rate only for unearned income over the standard deduction amount ($900 in 2008) and below the threshold amount ($1,800 in 2008). Everything else above the threshold amount is taxed at the parent's highest rate.

The kiddie tax applies only to unearned income a child receives from income-producing property (or investment property), such as cash, stocks, bonds, mutual funds, and real estate. Any salary or wages that a child earns through full- or part-time employment is not subject to the kiddie tax rules—that income is taxed at the child's tax rate.

Until recently, the kiddie tax applied only to children under 14 years old. Its reach has been greatly expanded in recent years and, starting in 2008, applies to:

- children under 19 years of age (by the end of the year), and
- children age 19 through 23 (by year end) who are full-time students and whose earned income does not exceed half of the annual expenses for their support.

To be considered a student, a child must attend school full time during at least five months of the year. It doesn't matter whether the child is claimed as a dependent on the parent's return. However, the tax does not apply to a child under 24 who is married and files a joint tax return. (See Chapter 8, "Are you really 'supporting' those dependents?" for a detailed discussion of support.)

EXAMPLE: Sam and Sarah give their youngest child Anne a $50,000 savings account that generates $3,000 in interest income during 2008. The first $900 of the income is tax free. Sarah must pay a 10% income tax on the next $900. The remaining $1,200 is taxed at Anne's parent's highest income tax rate—35%.

Obviously, you don't want a child subject to the kiddie tax to have investment income over the kiddie tax threshold amount—$1,800 in 2008. However, this is not a negligible amount. For example, a child whose investments earn 5% per year would have to have a total of $36,000 in cash or property to earn $1,800.

There is another way to stay within the limit—give your child investments that appreciate in value over time but don't generate much or any taxable income until they're sold. If you wait until after the child turns 24 to sell, there's no need to worry about the kiddie tax. Here are some ideas for these kinds of investments:

- **U.S. savings bonds.** You could purchase U.S. savings bonds for your child and defer the payment of interest until the child is no longer subject to the kiddie tax. All the interest would then be taxed at the child's tax rate.

- **Municipal bonds.** You could buy a muni bond for your child that matures after your child is no longer subject to the kiddie tax. You won't owe federal tax on the interest the bond earns while your child is younger (and subject to the kiddie tax) because muni

USA TODAY Snapshots®

Women are more risk averse in stock market

If both the stock market and a stock you owned dropped 25% in three months, what would you do?

	Women	Men
Buy more shares while the price is low	35%	52%
Hold shares and wait for a turnaround	54%	40%
Sell some of shares	10%	5%
Sell all shares	2%	3%

Source: ShareBuilder Women and Investing survey of 965 women and 1,066 men 18 and older. Margin of error ±3 percentage points.

By Jae Yang and Bob Laird, USA TODAY
2006

bonds are exempt from federal income tax. If the muni bond is ultimately sold at a profit, it would be taxed as a capital gain at the child's capital gains tax rate, provided you waited until the child was no longer subject to the kiddie tax. (See below for discussion of child's capital gains rate.)

- **Growth stocks or growth mutual funds.** You can buy your child stocks, or funds made up of stocks, from companies that reinvest their profits for future growth rather than paying them to shareholders as taxable dividends. You could then wait until after the child ceases to be subject to the kiddie tax to sell—for example, the year he or she graduates from college (or drops out of college) or turns 24, and the profit will be taxed at the child's capital gains rate.

- **Index funds.** You could also look into buying funds whose investments mirror a stock index or some other criterion and usually generate minimal taxable annual income.

- **Tax-managed mutual funds.** These are specifically designed to generate little taxable income. Again, you could sell them after the child ceases to be subject to the kiddie tax and the profits are taxed at the child's capital gains rate. (See Chapter 4 for more information on these funds.)

- **Treasury bills.** If your child is almost at the age when he or she will not be subject to the kiddie tax, buy a treasury bill that won't mature until the no-kiddie-tax year. That way, the child won't earn any interest while the kiddie tax still applies.

There is no kiddie tax for children 24 years old and over, even if they are their parents' dependents, or for children age 19 to 23 who are not full-time students or who provide more than half of their own support from their earned income. These children are taxed like adults—all their income is taxed at their own income tax rates. If the kiddie tax is inapplicable, you can give your child all the money or property you want and their unearned income will be taxed at their individual rates, which will most likely be lower than yours.

EXAMPLE: Bill and Linda have a 20-year-old son named Victor, who lives at home and does not go to school full time; thus his unearned income is not subject to the kiddie tax. They take $100,000 out of their own savings account and use it to establish an account in Victor's name. The account earns $5,000 in interest per year. Victor pays income tax on the entire amount of his unearned income at his individual income tax rate, which is 10%.

Giving Assets to Children Not Subject to the Kiddie Tax

It's fine to give cash to children who aren't subject to the kiddie tax, but the real tax savings come from giving them assets that have appreciated (gone up) in value since you bought them—for example, investment properties like stocks, mutual funds, and real estate.

If these properties (also called capital assets) are sold at a profit after one year or more, they're taxed at long-term capital gains tax rates. Right now and for the next few years, long-term capital gains tax rates are the lowest they've been in decades, especially in the bottom tax brackets. That means that if your children sell the assets fairly soon, your family could walk away with some tax-free gains.

Long-Term Capital Gains Rates		
Single Person's Income Level	Tax Bracket	Long-Term Capital Gains Rate 2008–2010
Up to $8,025	10%	0%
From $8,026 to $32,550	15%	0%
$32,551 to $78,850	25%	15%
$78,851 to $164,550	28%	15%
$164,551 to $357,700	33%	15%
All over $357,700	35%	15%

There's one potential catch: To qualify for the long-term capital gains rate, your child needs to have owned the asset for over one year. But if you've already owned it for that long, no problem: The giver's holding period is added to the holding period of the recipient for this purpose.

From January 1, 2008 through December 31, 2010, the long-term capital gains tax rate for taxpayers in the lowest two brackets will be an incredible, unheard-of, 0%—that's right, zero. However, this zero tax rate applies only so long as the taxpayer's taxable income, including income from long-term capital gains, is within the 15% tax bracket. This all means a child not subject to the kiddie tax could collect as much as $30,650 in long-term capital gains in 2008–2010 and pay absolutely no taxes. Obviously, if you have long-term assets that have appreciated in value, transferring them to your children not subject to the kiddie tax and then selling them during 2008–2010 presents a tremendous, once-in-a-lifetime tax-savings opportunity.

> **EXAMPLE:** Lance purchased shares in a mutual fund ten years ago for $10,000. By 2008, they're worth $40,000. He gives the shares to his 22-year-old granddaughter, Victoria, who is a self-supported salesperson. She immediately sells the shares and pockets the $30,000 profit, which is a long-term capital gain. Victoria's total taxable income for 2008 is $31,000, which places her in the 15% income tax bracket. Thus, the applicable 2008 long-term capital gains rate for her profit is 0%. She gets the $30,000 profit tax-free. Had Lance kept the shares and sold them himself, he would have had to pay a 15% long-term capital gains rate on his profit, for a $4,500 tax.

It's unlikely we'll ever see a zero capital gains tax rate again. The long-term capital gains rate for taxpayers in the lowest two tax brackets is scheduled to rise to 10% in 2011.

If your child is subject to the kiddie tax, you won't benefit nearly as much from the lower capital gains tax rate. Any long-term capital gains that result in a child earning more than $1,800 for the year will be taxed at the parent's capital gains rate, most likely 15%. So, there will be a tax benefit only if all of the child's unearned income, including income from selling gifted capital assets, is less than $1,800 in 2008.

Don't Give Away Loser Investments

Don't give your children or others investment property that has declined in value since you purchased it. A person who receives such a gift cannot deduct a loss upon sale of the property, and neither can the person who gives the gift. It's much better to sell the property yourself—that way you can deduct the loss from your own taxes. Then, if you wish, you can make a gift of the money you earned from the sale, plus the amount of tax you saved from your deductible loss.

Minor Detail? You Can't Take Your Gifts Back

If you give property to your children or others, the gift must be real and it must be irrevocable—that is, you can never take the property back, no matter how your financial needs or your relationship with your child change. If you don't want the child to get the property so young, you may want to use a trust.

Trusts have some income-shifting benefits, because any trust income that's spent on a child is taxed at the child's tax rate. Of course, the kiddie tax rules apply to this income, so children subject to the kiddie tax will pay their own tax rate only on the first $1,800 of unearned income they receive for the year.

The trust itself pays tax at its own rates on any income the trust earns that's not spent on the child or other beneficiary. Trust income tax rates are somewhat higher than rates for individuals, so you'll have to figure out whether on balance, the tax and other benefits (like asset control and asset protection) that you get with a trust are worth it.

To create a trust, you give a person, called a trustee, title to money or property that must be managed on behalf of your child or other beneficiary. You can set up a trust for a single child (a child's trust) or for several of your children (a family pot trust). Any adult can act as trustee—for example, your spouse, yourself, or another relative. The trust must be irrevocable (permanent, with no amendments allowed), for it to be effective for income-shifting purposes. You must create a trust document instructing the trustee how to manage the money.

Ordinarily, the trustee is allowed to spend trust money for the child's health, education, and living expenses. However, if you are the trustee and spend trust money on your basic child support obligation, you may be required to pay personal income tax on the trust income. This is similar to the rule for custodial accounts explained above.

When the child reaches the age you specify, the trustee ends the trust and gives the trust property to the beneficiary.

Education accounts. If your main goal is to save money for your child's college education, you might want to consider an education account—a Coverdell ESA, 529 savings plan, or both. Transferring your money to these accounts accomplishes income shifting, and has one other huge advantage: No tax need ever be paid on the income the money in the account earns, so long as it's used for educational expenses.

In addition, keeping money in these accounts (rather than a trust) will make it easier for a child to qualify for college financial aid. (See Chapter 2 for a detailed discussion of these accounts.) These education accounts may be a better option than a trust, especially now that the kiddie tax applies to all children under 19.

However, these accounts do have some drawbacks. Higher-income taxpayers are not allowed to contribute to Coverdell ESAs, and the annual contribution limit for those who can contribute is small—only $2,000. The 529 plans don't have these limitations, but you have little control over how the money is invested.

In addition, you can only contribute cash to education accounts. You can't contribute property, such as stock or mutual funds. This means you can't enjoy the tax advantages of giving appreciated assets to your children, as discussed above. If you want to give assets, you'll have to use a trust. This doesn't mean you must give up on having education accounts. You may have an education account and trust for the same child.

How to Give Away Plenty Without Gift Tax Concerns

Giving away money or property to your children or others is another way to lower your taxes. When you give money away while you're alive, it reduces the size of your estate, and thus the amount of estate taxes that may be owed when you die.

Many people wrongly believe that the gift tax requires the people who receive the money or property to pay tax on it, or that the giver will owe tax anytime they make a financial gift. In fact, most people have nothing to worry about when it comes to the gift tax. The people who receive money certainly don't. And the giver must distribute more than $1 million in money or property over a lifetime to be subject to any gift taxes. In fact, there are ways to give away even more than $1 million and still incur no gift taxes.

USA TODAY Snapshots®

People most difficult to buy gifts for

Everyone	28%
Adult men	27%
Adult women	21%
Teen boys	10%
Teen girls	10%
Children	1%
Babies	1%
Other	2%

Source: Harris Interactive online study via QuickQuery for Gifts.com of 2,730 adults, April 20-24. Margin of error: ±3 percentage points.

By Mary Cadden and Sam Ward, USA TODAY 2006

The gift tax exists to prevent people from avoiding all estate taxes by giving away all their money during their life. However, there are generous exclusions from the gift tax. First, there's the annual exclusion of $12,000 per person. This means that you may give up to $12,000 a year in cash or assets to any number of people each year without any gift tax implications. Married couples can combine their $12,000 annual exclusions and give, as a couple, a $24,000 gift per year to as many people as they want.

EXAMPLE: Wendell and Wanda are a married couple with four children. This year they give each of their children a gift of $24,000, for a total of $96,000. None of these gifts is subject to the gift tax, because they each fall within the annual gift tax exclusion.

USA TODAY Snapshots®

All in the family
Do you plan to bring your children into the family business?

No **43%**
Undecided **31%**
Yes **26%**

Source: SunTrust Bank Private Wealth Management survey of 201 business owners of companies with revenue of $10 million or more.

By Jae Yang and and Bob Laird, USA TODAY 2007

Even if you give more than $12,000 or $24,000 to a single person in a single year, you're still not likely to incur any gift tax liability. You will have to file a gift tax return, but that's just to let the IRS know about the gift (it's keeping track). You won't actually have to pay any gift tax unless you've exceeded the lifetime, $1 million exclusion, and then only on the excess amount.

EXAMPLE: Assume that Wendell and Wanda give one of their children $50,000 in a single year. This is $26,000 more than their annual combined gift tax exclusion. Thus, $26,000 is deducted from their $1 million lifetime gift tax exclusion, leaving them with a mere $974,000 lifetime exclusion. The couple must file a gift tax return with the IRS when they do their taxes for the year, but they won't owe any gift taxes.

By the way, spouses can give each other gifts of any size completely gift-tax free. The gift tax also does not apply to gifts to qualified charities.

RESOURCE

For more information about gift taxes, see *Plan Your Estate*, by Denis Clifford (Nolo).

Give Junior a Job and Shift Your Tax Burden

If you own a business, there's another way to shift your income to lower income taxpayers: Hire your children. If they do legitimate work, you may deduct their salaries from your business income as a business expense. Your children pay tax on their salaries at their own tax rates, which should be lower than yours (unless you earn little or no income). Let's look at just how this can work.

Can You Make Junior Work in a Salt Mine?

You're probably aware that certain types of child labor are illegal under federal and state law. However, these laws generally don't apply to children under 16 who are employed by their parents, unless the child is employed in mining, manufacturing, or a hazardous occupation. Hazardous occupations include driving a motor vehicle; being an outside helper on a motor vehicle; and operating various power-driven machines. So it's perfectly legal to hire your under-16 year old for office work, product assembly, cleanup, and so on.

A child who is at least 16 may be employed in any nonhazardous occupation. Children at least 17 years of age may spend up to 20% of their time driving cars and trucks weighing less than 6,000 pounds as part of their job if they have licenses and no tickets, drive only in daylight hours, and go no more than 30 miles from home. They may not perform dangerous driving maneuvers (such as towing) or do regular route deliveries. For detailed information, see the Department of Labor Website (www.dol.gov).

First of all, there is no kiddie tax on a child's earned income—that is, salaries and other amounts for work actually done. Regardless of a child's age, all earned income is subject to taxation at the child's income tax rates, not the parent's. This means that parents can hire their children when they're under 18 years of age and they won't have to pay tax on any part of their salaries at their parent's tax rates.

One of the great tax advantages of hiring your children is that you don't have to pay FICA (Social Security and Medicare) taxes for your children under age 18 who work in your trade or business or your partnership if it's owned solely by you and your spouse. FICA is a 15.4% tax paid half by the employer and half by the employee, so this is a major tax savings. Moreover, you don't have to pay federal unemployment (FUTA) taxes for services performed by your child who is under 21 years old.

Yet another benefit of a child-employee is that you won't have to withhold any income taxes from your child's pay unless:

- your child has more than $250 in unearned income for the year and a total income of over $900 (in 2008), or
- your child's pay exceeds the standard deduction for the year.

A child who works can have a much larger standard deduction than a child who just has investment income. A working child gets a standard deduction that is the larger of:

- $900, or
- the amount of the child's earned income for the year plus $250 (but this amount can't be more than the standard deduction for single adults—$5,450 in 2008).

Thus, a child can have a standard deduction of as much as $5,450 in 2008 (the deduction for adult single taxpayers), provided that the child had at least $5,200 in earned income from a job.

Let's put all these rules together and see how they can benefit a parent who owns a business.

EXAMPLE: Carina hires Mark, her 16-year-old son, to perform computer inputting services for her medical transcription business during 2008. He works ten hours per week and she pays him $20 per hour (the going rate). Over the course of a year, Carina pays Mark a total of $9,000. She doesn't have to pay FICA tax for Mark because he's under 18, but she must withhold income taxes from his salary because he makes more than the standard deduction. When Carina does her taxes, she may deduct his $9,000 salary from her business income as a business expense. Mark pays income tax only on the portion of his income that exceeds the $5,450 standard deduction—so he pays federal income tax only on $3,550 of his $9,000 salary. With such a small amount of income, he is in the lowest federal income tax bracket—10%. He pays $355 in federal income tax for the year. (Mark gets no personal deduction because he is his mother's dependent.) Had Carina done the transcription work herself and kept the $9,000, she would have had to pay income tax and self-employment tax on it. In her bracket, this amounts to a combined 39.4% tax.

Had Carol paid Mark $5,450 in 2008 (the amount of his standard deduction), his entire income would have been tax-free.

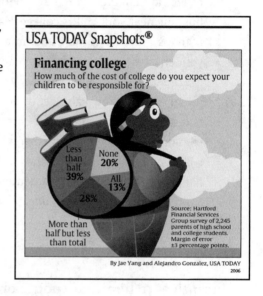

USA TODAY Snapshots®

Financing college

How much of the cost of college do you expect your children to be responsible for?

Less than half **39%**
None **20%**
All **13%**
28%
More than half but less than total

Source: Hartford Financial Services Group survey of 2,245 parents of high school and college students. Margin of error ±3 percentage points.

By Jae Yang and Alejandro Gonzalez, USA TODAY 2006

A child can get even more tax-free income by opening an IRA and deducting the contribution. If the child makes the maximum $5,000 annual contribution, up to $10,450 can be earned tax-free ($5,450 standard deduction + $5,000 IRA contribution = $10,450). If the child is not subject to the kiddie tax, this may be both earned and unearned income. But, as described above, children subject to the kiddie tax must pay income tax on all unearned income over $900 (but not on earned income).

Buy Animal House and Rent It to Your Kids

Here's a tax-savings strategy that can work well for families with college age children: Purchase a house, condo, or apartment building near your child's college. Have your child move in—perhaps with one or more roommates—and pay you rent. Hire your child as your employee to manage the building and perform maintenance. The salary you pay your child will be a tax deductible rental expense. You'll also get to deduct mortgage interest, property taxes, depreciation, and repair costs—all of which will reduce or eliminate any tax you must pay on your rental income. Your child will pay income tax on the salary at his or her own lower tax rates. For more information on tax deductions for landlords, see *Every Landlord's Tax Deduction Guide*, by Stephen Fishman (Nolo).

Incentives to hire your spouse or other relatives

You don't get the benefits of income shifting when you employ your spouse in your business. Your income is combined when you file a joint tax return, and there's usually little or no tax savings if you file separate returns—indeed, you could end up paying more tax.

But there are tax advantages to be gained if you hire your spouse and provide employee benefits. You can deduct the cost of these benefits as a business expense, and your spouse doesn't have to declare the benefit as income, so long as the IRS requirements are satisfied. This is a particularly valuable tool for health coverage—you can give your spouse health insurance coverage and reimbursements for uninsured expenses as a tax-free employee benefit. (See Chapter 5 for a detailed discussion.)

Family employees must do real work for realistic pay

If you were hoping to pay your child $100 an hour to cut snowflakes out of your discarded documents, we've got some bad news. The IRS is on the lookout for taxpayers who claim tax benefits without having their family members do real work in their business. If the IRS decides you've crossed the line, you'll lose your tax deductions for the family member's salary and benefits. Here's how to avoid questions.

Rule 1. The family member must be a real employee. Their work must be ordinary and necessary for your business, and their pay must be for services actually performed. Their services don't have to be indispensable, only common, accepted, helpful, and appropriate—for example, you could employ your child or other family member to clean your office, answer the phone, perform word processing, do photo-copying, stuff envelopes, input data, or do filing. You get no business deductions when you pay your child or other person for personal services, such as babysitting or mowing your lawn at home. On the other hand, money you pay for yard work performed on business property could be deductible as a business expense.

The IRS won't believe that an extremely young child is a legitimate employee. How young is too young? The IRS has accepted that a seven-year-old child may be an employee (*Eller v. Comm'r,* 77 T.C. 934 (1981)), but that's probably the lower limit.

Keep track of the work and hours your children or other family members do by having them fill out time sheets or timecards. You can find these in stationery stores or make them yourself. List the date, the services performed, and the time spent. Although not legally required, it's also a good idea to have the child or other family member sign a written employment agreement specifying job duties and hours. These duties should only be related to your business.

Junior's Timesheet

Date	Time In	Time Out	Total Work Time	Services Performed
1/9/04	3:30 pm	5:30 pm	2 hours	copying, some filing
1/14/04	3:30 pm	5:00 pm	1 1/2 hours	printed out bills and prepared for them for mailing
1/15/04	3:45 pm	5:15 pm	1 1/2 hours	copying and filing
1/24/04	10:00 am	3:00 pm	5 hours	answered phones
1/30/04	3:30 pm	5:30 pm	2 hours	copying, filing
?1/04	10:00 am	2:00 pm	4 hours	cleaned office

Rule 2. Compensation must be reasonable. No fair overpaying your children (to shift the maximum income) or underpaying your spouse (since you get no benefits from income shifting).

Reasonable wages are determined by comparing the amount paid with the value of the services performed. You should have no problem as long as you pay no more than what you'd pay a stranger for the same work. Find out what workers performing similar services in your area are being paid. For example, if you plan to hire your teenager to do word processing, call an employment agency or temp agency in your area to see what these workers are being paid. The absolute minimum you can pay your spouse is the minimum wage in your area.

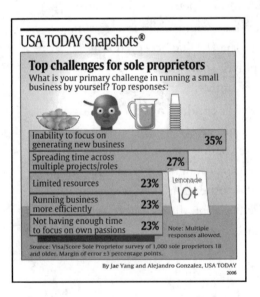

USA TODAY Snapshots®

Top challenges for sole proprietors
What is your primary challenge in running a small business by yourself? Top responses:

Inability to focus on generating new business — 35%
Spreading time across multiple projects/roles — 27%
Limited resources — 23%
Running business more efficiently — 23%
Not having enough time to focus on own passions — 23%

Note: Multiple responses allowed.

Source: Visa/Score Sole Proprietor survey of 1,000 sole proprietors 18 and older. Margin of error ±3 percentage points.

By Jae Yang and Alejandro Gonzalez, USA TODAY 2006

To prove how much you paid (and that you actually paid it), you should pay your child or spouse by check, not cash. Do this once or twice a month as you would for any other employee. The funds should be deposited in a bank account in your child's or spouse's name. Your child's bank account may be a trust account.

Rule 3. Follow legal requirements for employers. You must meet most of the same legal requirements when you hire a child, spouse, or other family member as you do when you hire a stranger. This means you must withhold taxes from their pay if required, and file the appropriate tax forms:

- IRS Form W-2, showing how much you paid the employee and how much tax was withheld, if any
- Form 941, *Employer's Quarterly Federal Tax Return*, or Form 944, *Employer's Annual Federal Tax Return*, and
- Form 940 or Form 940-EZ, *Employer's Annual Federal Unemployment (FUTA) Tax Return*.

RESOURCE

IRS Circular E, *Employer's Tax Guide*, **and Publication 929,** *Tax Rules For Children and Dependents*, **provide detailed information on these requirements.**

Making the Most of Your Filing Status and Tax Exemptions

ow we're on to two subjects that may not sound exciting, but can be big money-savers—your filing status and tax exemptions. Every tax exemption you qualify for gives you an extra $3,500 tax deduction in 2008. And, choosing the best filing status can reduce your top tax rate, so that you owe less in taxes. No one (especially not the IRS) is going to make sure you choose the best filing status and take all the exemptions you're due. You must figure these out yourself—or better yet, with the help of this chapter.

Choosing the Classification for You

The number one, most important thing you must decide when you file your taxes is your filing status. There are five possible choices:

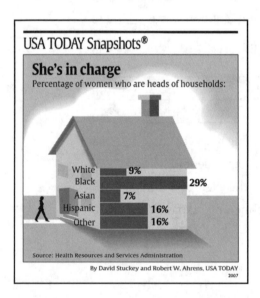

USA TODAY Snapshots®

She's in charge
Percentage of women who are heads of households:

White 9%
Black 29%
Asian 7%
Hispanic 16%
Other 16%

Source: Health Resources and Services Administration

By David Stuckey and Robert W. Ahrens, USA TODAY
2007

- single
- married filing jointly
- married filing separately
- head of household, or
- widow(er) with dependent child.

Do you find yourself always checking the same box, automatically? That may be okay, but some people actually have a choice between categories and don't know it. For example, a single person whose parent moves in might qualify as a head of household—and for lower tax rates as a result. So it's worth reexamining your assumptions.

Why is your filing status so important? Well, for one thing, it determines the income levels for your tax brackets. You can see how this works in the chart below.

Tax Brackets Based on Filing Status					
Tax Bracket	Taxable Income If Single	Taxable Income If Married Filing Jointly	Taxable Income If Married Filing Separately	Taxable Income If Head of Household	Taxable Income If Widow(er) with Dependent Child
10%	Up to $8,025	Up to $16,050	Up to $8,025	Up to $11,450	Up to $16,050
15%	From $8,026 to $32,550	$16,051 to 65,100	From $8,026 to $32,550	From $11,451 to $43,650	$16,051 to 65,100
25%	$32,551 to $78,850	$65,101 to $131,450	$32,551 to $65,725	$43,651 to $112,650	$65,101 to $131,450
28%	$78,851 to $164,550	$131,451 to $200,300	$65,726 to $100,150	$112,651 to $182,400	$131,451 to $200,300
33%	$164,551 to $357,700	$200,301 to $357,700	$100,151 to 178,850	$182,401 to $357,700	$200,301 to $357,700
35%	All over $357,700	All over $357,700	All over $178,850	All over $357,700	All over $357,700

Applying these tax brackets, a single person who has $50,000 in taxable income must pay $8,844 in federal income taxes in 2008. A married couple filing jointly with the same taxable income pays only $6,698. Married couples filing jointly and widows(ers) with dependent children have the lowest (best) tax brackets. The next best rates go to heads of households, then single people, and finally married people filing separately.

Your filing status is also crucial for calculating your standard deduction, personal exemptions, and income levels for phaseouts of your itemized deductions and personal exemptions. This is shown in the following chart (the numbers are for 2008).

Effects of Filing Status				
Single	Married Filing Jointly	Married Filing Separately	Head of Household	Widow(er) with Dependent Child
Personal Exemption				
$3,500	$7,000 (two $3,500 deductions)	$3,500	$3,500	$3,500
Standard Deduction				
$5,450	$10,900 (two $5,450 deductions)	$5,450	$8,000	$10,900
Income Levels for Deduction Phaseout				
$159,950 to $282,450	$239,950 to $362,450	$119,975 to $181,225	$199,950 to $322,450	$239,950 to $362,450

Once again, married couples filing jointly and widow(er)s with dependent children do best, followed by the people who are heads of household, single, and then married filing separately.

Oops—I Chose the Wrong Status Last Year

If you discover that you could have paid less tax in a prior year had you chosen a different filing status, you can file an amended return for that year and change your filing status. However, you must do so within three years of the date you filed your original return (including extensions to file—so if you got a six-month extension and filed in October, you have until October of three years later). Big exception: If you file a joint return, you cannot later amend your return to file separately (except in some cases where your spouse died). For detailed guidance on how to file amended tax returns, see the IRS publication *Instructions for Form 1040X*.

Filing as a single person

If you're not married, have no relatives living with you, and are not supporting your parents, you must file as a single. If relatives live in your home or you support your parents, see if you can qualify for head of household status (or widow or widower status if your spouse died), so as to pay less tax.

You're considered unmarried for the whole year if, on December 31, you are divorced or legally separated from your spouse under a final divorce decree or separate maintenance decree.

Married filing jointly status

You can choose married filing jointly as your filing status if you are legally married and both you and your spouse agree to file a joint return. A joint return is a single return for a husband and wife that combines their incomes, exemptions, credits, and deductions. You can file a joint return even if one of you had no income or deductions.

You are considered married for tax purposes for the entire year if, by December 31:

- you are married and living together as husband and wife
- you are living together in a common law marriage recognized in the state where you live or in the state where the common law marriage began
- you are married and living apart, but not legally separated under a decree of divorce or separate maintenance, or
- you are separated under an interlocutory (not final) decree of divorce. (For purposes of filing a joint return, you are not yet considered divorced.)

For IRS purposes, a marriage is only a legal union between a man and woman as husband and wife. Same-sex marriages and domestic partnerships don't count, although they may be recognized under some state laws (in Massachusetts, for example).

Couples who live together but are not legally married under their state law cannot file as married. However, it may be possible for one member of an unmarried couple to file as a head of household.

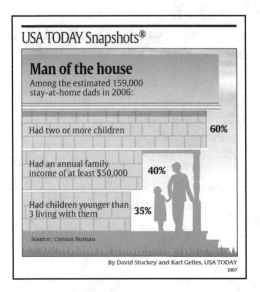

USA TODAY Snapshots®

Man of the house
Among the estimated 159,000 stay-at-home dads in 2006:

Had two or more children — 60%

Had an annual family income of at least $50,000 — 40%

Had children younger than 3 living with them — 35%

Source: Census Bureau

By David Stuckey and Karl Gelles, USA TODAY
2007

If your spouse dies and you do not remarry in the same year, you may file a joint return for that year. This is the last year for which you may file a joint return with that spouse.

Most married couples file jointly. You'll usually pay the lowest taxes by filing this way, particularly if one spouse earns substantially more than the other. This is because the tax brackets are lower for married people filing jointly, and several deductions and tax credits are not allowed for married people filing separately.

> EXAMPLE: Jack and Jill are a married couple. Jack had $100,000 of taxable income in 2008. Jill, a stay-at-home mom, had no income. If they file jointly, they will pay $17,688 in income taxes. If they file separately, Jack will have to pay $21,978 in income tax, and Jill will pay no taxes. Filing separately, Jack's top tax rate is 28%. Filing jointly, the top tax rate for Jack and Jill is only 25%.

The so-called marriage penalty—where a couple filing jointly pays more tax than if they filed separately—was for the most part eliminated in 2003. Prior to this law change, a couple's combined income could push them into a higher tax bracket than they would have been in if they filed separately. This is unlikely to happen anymore.

Nevertheless, if you're married and don't want to be personally responsible for your spouse's taxes, you should choose the married filing separately status (see "Does Married Life Mean Filing Taxes Together?" below). If your incomes and deductions are about the same, filing separately may not have a significant impact on what you owe in taxes. (But see "Married filing separately status," below, for more on this topic.)

Does Married Life Mean Filing Taxes Together?

As a general rule, when a married couple files a joint return, each spouse is jointly and individually liable for the entire tax owed. This means that either spouse can be required to pay the tax due, plus any interest, penalties, and fines. In a marriage with open communication, this usually isn't an issue. But numerous cases have arisen where one spouse handles most of the household finances, cheats on the taxes, and then cuts out, leaving the other spouse to deal with back taxes and potential penalties. A spouse can claim "innocent spouse relief" and avoid personally paying the other spouse's taxes if he or she can show the IRS that (1) the understatement of tax was due to the other spouse, and (2) the spouse did not know, or have reason to know, that there was an understatement of tax when he or she signed the joint return. However, both propositions can be hard to prove. You'll avoid being personally responsible for your spouse's taxes if you file a separate return. This is something you should seriously consider if your marriage is rocky or you've got a strong suspicion that your spouse cheats on your joint taxes.

Married filing separately status

If you're married, you always have the option to file your taxes separately. If one of you won't agree to file a joint return, you'll have to file separately, unless you qualify for head of household status. When you file a separate return, you report only your own income, exemptions, credits, and deductions.

Filing separately can result in a couple paying the same as, more than, or less than they would pay filing jointly. It all depends on their incomes and deductions. If their incomes are similar and they have similar deductions, filing separately will usually make little or no difference. By the same token, if one spouse earns much more than the other, filing separately could mean the high earner ends up paying more.

A particularly good time to file separately is if one spouse has large itemized deductions for miscellaneous itemized deductions (such as unreimbursed employee expenses), medical expenses, or casualty losses. Why? Because you must reduce these deductions by a certain percentage of your adjusted gross income. If filing separately gives the spouse with the deductions a lower AGI, then there would also be a smaller reduction in the spouse's itemized deductions.

> EXAMPLE: Oleg and Oksana are a married couple. Oksana had an adjusted gross income in 2008 of $150,000 and Oleg had an AGI of $50,000. Oleg had surgery and follow-up treatment that year, which together with new glasses and other minor health expenses cost him $20,000. Oksana had $5,000 in medical expenses. Medical expenses are deductible only to the extent they exceed 7.5% of the taxpayer's AGI. If Oleg and Oksana file jointly, their combined AGI is $200,000, so they can deduct their medical expenses to the extent they exceed 7.5% of $200,000 (or $15,000). Their combined medical expenses were $25,000, so they could deduct only $10,000, and would end up paying a total income tax of $44,716. If they file separately, Oleg can deduct any medical expenses that exceed 7.5% of his $50,000 income, or $3,750. Subtracting that from his $20,000 in medical expenses, he'll get a $16,250 deduction on his separate return, leading to a separate income tax bill of $4,781. Oksana gets no deduction for her medical expenses on her separate return because they were less than 7.5% of her AGI. Her income tax bill is $38,865. They end up saving $1,070 in taxes by filing two separate returns instead of one joint return.

If you live in a community property state, the income you and your spouse earn is split evenly between you, as are your expenses (unless one spouse pays expenses with separate, non-community funds—for example, money earned or inherited before marriage). There are nine community property states: Arizona, California, Idaho, Louisiana, Nevada, New Mexico, Texas, Washington, and Wisconsin. In these states, each spouse's taxable income will be similar whether they file separately or jointly, so it usually makes little difference which they choose. However, they may get tax benefits if either or both of their adjusted gross incomes exceed the income threshold for personal exemptions ($119,975 in 2008) and one of them pays for all of their combined medical expenses or miscellaneous itemized deductions from separate funds. That spouse could then deduct the entire amount on a separate return.

There are several disadvantages to filing separately, however, which can easily outweigh the other benefits:

- You cannot take various tax credits, such as the Hope or Lifetime Learning education credits, earned income tax credit, and, in most cases, the credit for child and dependent care expenses.

- The amount you can exclude from income under an employer's dependent care assistance program is limited to $2,500 (instead of $5,000 if you file a joint return).

- You cannot take the deduction for student loan interest or the tuition and fees deduction.

- You cannot exclude from your income any interest income from qualified U.S. savings bonds that you used for higher education expenses.

- If you live with your spouse at any time during the tax year, you'll have to include in income more (up to 85%) of any Social Security benefits you receive.

- If you live with your spouse at any time during the tax year, you cannot roll over amounts from a traditional IRA into a Roth IRA.

- The following credits and deductions are reduced at income levels that are half of those for a joint return: child tax credit, retirement savings contributions credit, itemized deductions, and the deduction for personal exemptions.

- Your capital loss deduction limit is $1,500 (instead of $3,000 if you filed a joint return).

- You may not be able to deduct all or part of your contributions to a traditional IRA if you or your spouse was covered by an employee retirement plan at work during the year.

- If you own and actively manage rental real estate, it will be more difficult for you to deduct any losses.

- If your spouse itemizes deductions, you cannot claim the standard deduction. If you can claim the standard deduction, your basic standard deduction is half the amount allowed on a joint return.

The only way to know for sure if you'll pay less taxes filing separately or jointly is to figure your taxes both ways. This isn't hard to do if you use tax preparation software.

Head of household filing status

If you're not married, but pay for the upkeep of a home where a relative lives or you support your parents, you may qualify for head of household status. Filing as head of household is better than filing as single because you get a larger standard deduction and the tax brackets are more favorable.

Head of household is the most difficult filing status to understand. However, the basic idea is that you qualify as a head of household if you pay more than half the cost of keeping up a home where you and at least one of your dependents lives.

You can file as head of household if:

- you are unmarried on December 31 of the tax year

- you paid more than half the cost of keeping a home for the year, and

- a dependent child or other dependent relative lived with you in the home for more than half the year (however, a dependent parent does not have to live with you).

It's usually not difficult to tell if you're married or not (see the discussion in the "Married filing jointly status" section, above). The second and third requirements are the hard parts.

First of all, you must have a home where a dependent lives over half the year (temporary absences for things like schooling, medical treatment, vacations, business, or military service are not counted). The home doesn't have to be your main residence, but you must still spend a substantial amount of time there.

A dependent is a person for whom you can claim a dependency exemption (as explained more below in this section). So long as the requirements for the dependent exemption are met, dependents can include:

USA TODAY Snapshots®

Who heads adoptive families

Married couple 68%
Single woman 27%
Single man 3%
Unmarried couple 2%

Source: Department of Health and Human Services

By David Stuckey and Alejandro Gonzalez, USA TODAY 2007

- **Qualifying children.** Children under 19 years old (or under 24 if full-time students), including your son, daughter, stepchild, adopted child, foster child, brother, sister, stepbrother, stepsister, or a descendant of any of them (for example, your grandchild, niece, or nephew), who lives with you over half the year, and doesn't pay for over half of his or her own support.

- **Qualifying relatives.** No matter what their age, your children who are not qualifying children, parents and stepparents, grandparents, siblings, aunts, uncles, nephews, nieces, and people married to your children, parents, or siblings, who earn less than $3,500 per year (in 2008), and for whom you provide more than 50% support. People who aren't related to you cannot be qualifying relatives for these purposes, even if you can get a dependency exemption for them.

A dependent parent (or parents) does not have to live in the same home as you; but, then you must pay for more than half the cost of maintaining the home where the parent does live for the entire year. For these purposes, a home includes a rest home or home for the elderly.

You also must be able to show that you paid for more than half the cost of maintaining the home where the qualifying relative lives. These payments can include upkeep expenses such as rent, mortgage interest, real estate taxes, home insurance, repairs, utilities, and food eaten in the home. Do not include expenses for clothing, education, medical treatment, vacations, life insurance, or transportation. IRS Publication 501, *Exemptions, Standard Deduction, and Filing Information*, contains a worksheet you can use.

> EXAMPLE: Kevin and Kate, who are unmarried, live together with their 12-year-old son Mike. Because they aren't married, they can't file a joint return. Kevin works full-time and pays 75% of the cost of keeping up the home. Kate works part-time and pays only 25%. Kevin may file as head of household instead of single because he's unmarried and paid for more than half the cost of maintaining the home where his dependent child lived during the year. Kate must file her tax return as single. Filing as head of household gives Kevin a $8,000 standard deduction instead of the $5,450 deduction for singles—$2,550 more. His top tax bracket is 25%, so he saves an extra $638 in tax (25% × $2,550 = $638).

As the above example shows, head of household status may be used by members of many nontraditional families. However, its use in these situations is limited under new rules (adopted in 2005) that a person must be related to you by blood or marriage to be a qualifying relative. Thus, you can't use head of household status if you help maintain a home where someone not related to you lives.

> EXAMPLE: Assume that Mike, Kate's son from the previous example, was not fathered by Kevin. Mike is not a qualifying relative of Kevin because he is not related to him by blood or marriage. This means that

Kevin cannot qualify for head of household status even though he pays for more than half the cost of maintaining the home where Mike lives. To avoid filing as single, Kevin would have to marry Kate, which would entitle him to file a joint return.

Under the new rules, some people who qualified for head of household status in the past no longer qualify. For example, a single parent formerly qualified as a head of household as long as he or she paid more than half the cost of maintaining the home where the child lived. This is no longer enough. The child must also qualify as the parent's dependent—which eliminates this status for some parents.

EXAMPLE: Virginia is a divorced mother of Tom, a 21-year-old, who lives at home and works part-time. Because Tom is over 19 and not a full-time student, he can't be Virginia's qualifying child. Because he earns too much money he can't be her qualifying relative, either. Since he doesn't qualify as Virginia's dependent, she can't file as head of household and must file as single.

Head of Household Status for Married People

Even if you're married, you can qualify for head of household status if:

- you don't file a joint return with your spouse
- your spouse was not a member of your household (physically living there) during the last six months of the year, and
- a qualifying child lived in your home for over half the year and you paid more than half the cost of maintaining the home.

If you don't want to file a joint return with your spouse, head of household status will be better than filing as single because you get a larger standard deduction and the tax brackets are more favorable. If you meet the requirements, you don't need your spouse's permission to file as head of household.

Widow or widower with dependent children status

You may be able to file as a qualifying widow or widower for the two years following the year your spouse died. To do this, you must meet all four of the following tests:

- You were entitled to file a joint return with your spouse for the year he or she died. It doesn't matter whether you actually filed a joint return.

- You didn't remarry in the two years following the year your spouse died.

- You have a child, stepchild, or adopted child for whom you can claim a dependency exemption.

- You paid more than half the cost of maintaining a household that was the principal home for you and the child, for the whole year.

People with this filing status receive the same treatment as married couples filing jointly. So, if you qualify, you should choose this filing status.

Taking All the Tax Exemptions You Deserve

Congress believes that a certain amount of income should not be subject to income tax at all—so it created tax exemptions. A tax exemption is similar to a tax deduction in that it's a sum of money you're allowed to deduct from your income to arrive at your taxable income.

Not everyone can take advantage of tax exemptions, however. Both the personal and dependent exemptions come with income restrictions and phaseouts (see "Phaseout of exemptions for high-income taxpayers," below).

On the other hand, many taxpayers mistakenly pass up valuable tax exemptions, not realizing that they qualify for them. For example, you may be entitled to additional dependency exemptions if you support your elderly parents, other relatives, or even people not related to you who live in your household. If you provide more than half the support for anyone you haven't claimed as a dependent in the past, make sure you read and understand these rules.

All exemptions are worth the same amount of money—$3,500 in 2008 (the amount is adjusted for inflation each year). For example, if you qualify for three exemptions, you'll be entitled to deduct $10,500 in 2008. As with tax deductions, the amount of taxes an exemption will save you depends on your tax bracket. In the 28% tax bracket, each $3,500 will save you $980 in federal income taxes; if you're in the 10% bracket, it will save you only $350.

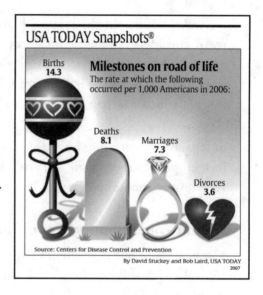

USA TODAY Snapshots®

Milestones on road of life
The rate at which the following occurred per 1,000 Americans in 2006:

Births 14.3

Deaths 8.1

Marriages 7.3

Divorces 3.6

Source: Centers for Disease Control and Prevention

By David Stuckey and Bob Laird, USA TODAY 2007

There are two types of exemptions: personal exemptions for yourself and your spouse (if any) and exemptions for your dependents (typically, your children), but in some cases other relatives as well, such as a parent or sibling. Each type of exemption is worth the same amount of money, but different rules apply to each.

Personal exemption for yourself

You're entitled to one personal exemption for yourself, as long as no one else is entitled to claim you as a dependent. Even if the other taxpayer doesn't actually claim you as a dependent, the very fact that that person could have claimed you bars you from taking an exemption.

Personal exemption for your spouse

Exemptions for spouses depend on how you file.

Joint return. If, like most married couples, you file a joint return, you can claim two personal exemptions—one for yourself and one for your spouse.

Separate return. If you're married and file a separate return, you can claim the exemption for your spouse only if your spouse had no gross income, is not filing a return, and wasn't another taxpayer's dependent (even if the other taxpayer doesn't actually claim your spouse as a dependent).

Head of household filing status. If you qualify for this status because you're considered unmarried for tax purposes (see "Head of Household Status for Married People," above), you can still claim an exemption for your spouse if he or she had no gross income, is not filing a return, and was not another taxpayer's dependent.

Divorced or separated spouse. If you obtained a final decree of divorce or separate maintenance by the end of the year, you can't take your former spouse's exemption. This rule applies even if you provided all of your former spouse's support.

Dependent exemptions for children

You may claim one dependent exemption for each child who is what the IRS calls a "qualifying child." This is where the rules can get tricky. A qualifying child is:

- **related to you**—your son, daughter, stepchild, adopted child, foster child, brother, sister, stepbrother, stepsister, or a descendant of any of them (for example, your grandchild, niece, or nephew).

- **under age 19 (or a student under 24)**—the child must be under age 19 at the end of the tax year, or under age 24 if a full-time student for at least five months of the year, or any age if permanently and totally disabled at any time during the year.

- **not self-supporting**—did not pay for over half of his or her own support during the year.

- **lives with you**—either for more than half of the year or falls within special rules for children of parents who are divorced, separated, or living apart (see below). (Temporary absences for things like schooling, medical treatment, vacations, business, or military service don't count.)

- a U.S. citizen or resident—a U.S. citizen, U.S. national, or resident of the United States, Canada, or Mexico for some part of the year.

Most qualifying children are the biological, adopted, or stepchildren of the taxpayers who claim them as dependents, but this doesn't have to be the case. For example, a brother, sister, or grandchild can be your qualifying child if he or she is under 19, lives with you over half the year, provides less than half of his or her own support, and is a U.S. citizen or resident. Moreover, a qualifying child can be as old as 23 if he or she is enrolled in school full-time.

Dependent Children Must Have Social Security Numbers

To obtain an exemption for a dependent child, you must list the child's Social Security number on your tax return. No number, no exemption. This rule is intended to prevent people from claiming exemptions for children who don't really exist. You may obtain a Social Security number for your child by filling out Social Security Form SS-5 and filing it with your local Social Security office or by mail. See the Social Security Administration website at www.ssa.gov for details. It takes about two weeks to get a Social Security number. If you do not have a required SSN by the filing due date, you can file IRS Form 4868, *Application for Automatic Extension of Time to File U.S. Individual Income Tax Return*. If you or your spouse is expecting a child, apply for a Social Security number at the hospital when you apply for your baby's birth certificate. The state agency that issues birth certificates will share your child's information with the Social Security Administration and it will mail the Social Security card to you.

Who supports a qualifying child? Before the law changed in 2005, you had to provide over half of a child's support to claim a dependent

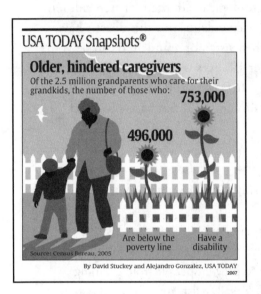

USA TODAY Snapshots®

Older, hindered caregivers
Of the 2.5 million grandparents who care for their grandkids, the number of those who:

753,000

496,000

Are below the poverty line

Have a disability

Source: Census Bureau, 2005

By David Stuckey and Alejandro Gonzalez, USA TODAY 2007

exemption. But now all that's required is that the child not provide over half of his or her own support. Thus, as long as a child lives with you for more than half the year, you qualify for the exemptions even if the child is financially supported primarily by someone other than you—for example, a former spouse. See "Dependent exemptions for qualifying relatives," below, for a discussion of the ins and outs of the support test for the dependent exemption.

Relatives only. You'll qualify for a dependent exemption only if your child or other dependent is a relative—whether by blood, marriage, or adoption; or a foster child. You can't get a credit for a child who is not related to you, even if you support that child. However, you can still get an exemption if the person meets the requirements to be your qualifying relative (see the next section).

Divorced or separated parents. If you're divorced or separated, the dependent exemption ordinarily goes to the parent with whom the child lived for the longest time during the year; or, if the time was equal, to the parent with the highest adjusted gross income. This means that a noncustodial parent will not get the exemption, even if he or she pays for the bulk of the child support. However, the parents can agree that the noncustodial parent should get the exemption, or a divorce decree or child support order may require it.

No personal exemption for dependent children. A child who can be claimed as a dependent by a parent or anyone else is not entitled to a personal exemption. This matters, of course, only if the child has income he or she must pay tax on.

When Not to Claim a Dependent Exemption

If your child attends college, you may be better off not claiming the child as a dependent. This is because of the Hope tax credit, which is worth up to $1,800 per year, and the Lifetime Learning credit, which is worth up to $2,000 per year (in 2008). Since a credit is a dollar-for-dollar reduction in your taxes, it can be worth more than an exemption. For example, if you're in the 28% bracket, a $3,500 dependent exemption will save you $980 in federal income taxes. A $1,800 Hope credit saves $1,800 in taxes. A $2,000 Lifetime Learning credit saves $2,000.

Unfortunately, you can't claim these credits if your adjusted gross income is $116,000 or more (if you file a joint return), or $58,000 or more (if you're single) in 2008. In this event, you could be better off if your child claims the credit and uses it to reduce his or her own taxes (but that won't work if you claim the child as a dependent). It's not necessary that the child pay for education expenses from his or her own money to get the credits—or at least part of the credits—since the credit amount is limited to the child's tax liability for the year. If a child doesn't earn much, there won't be much of a credit.

EXAMPLE: Jarvis and Kaia are married, file jointly, and have an AGI of $120,000. Their daughter, Jana, is in her sophomore year at the local university. Jana earned $25,000 from a job. Jarvis and Kaia paid $4,300 tuition and related fees for Jana in 2008. The couple can't claim the Hope or Lifetime Learning credits because they earn too much money. They decide not to claim Jana as their dependent and allow her to claim the Hope credit. Jana's Hope credit can be as much as $1,800, but no more than her tax liability for the year. Her taxes due for the year were $2,128, so she gets the full $1,800 credit. Jarvis and Kaia lost their $3,500 dependent exemption for Jana, but this would have saved them only $980 in taxes in their 28% tax bracket.

See Chapter 3 for a detailed discussion of the Hope tax credit and Lifetime Learning credit.

Dependent exemptions for qualifying relatives

You can also claim a dependent exemption for a person the IRS calls a qualifying relative—for example, a parent or grandparent you support.

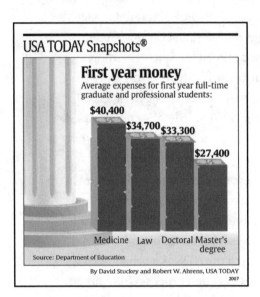

USA TODAY Snapshots®

First year money
Average expenses for first year full-time graduate and professional students:

$40,400
$34,700
$33,300
$27,400

Medicine   Law   Doctoral   Master's degree

Source: Department of Education

By David Stuckey and Robert W. Ahrens, USA TODAY
2007

Believe it or not, that person doesn't have to be related to you by blood or marriage; and a child who is not your qualifying child can still be your qualifying relative.

These rules are confusing, but worth knowing. If you contribute toward the support of a parent or other relative (or even a nonrelative in some cases), you could be entitled to claim a dependent exemption for that person. Even if you haven't taken a dependency exemption for the person in the past, in some cases paying just a few dollars more to support the person during the year could entitle you to a valuable exemption.

To be your qualifying relative, a person must pass three tests:

Member of household or relationship test. First of all, the person must either be related to you or live with you as a member of your household. "Related" means the person is either:

- your child, stepchild, eligible foster child, or a descendant of any of them (for example, your grandchild) (a legally adopted child is considered your child)
- your brother, sister, half brother, half sister, stepbrother, or stepsister
- your father, mother, grandparent, or other direct ancestor, but not foster parent

- your stepfather or stepmother
- a son or daughter of your brother or sister
- a brother or sister of your father or mother, or
- your son-in-law, daughter-in-law, father-in-law, mother-in-law, brother-in-law, or sister-in-law.

If any of these relationships were established by marriage, they don't count if the marriage was later ended by death or divorce.

Confusingly, a person who is not related to you by blood or marriage can still be your qualifying relative for purposes of the dependency exemption. Such a nonrelative must be a member of your household—that is, live with you full time except for temporary absences for things like schooling, medical treatment, vacations, business, or military service. However, this person doesn't help you qualify for head of household filing status.

Gross income test. The person's taxable income must be very low—no more than the dependent exemption, which is $3,500 in 2008. No need to count nontaxable income, such as Social Security payments (unless the person earns too much money) or tax-free interest from municipal bonds. Tax-free student scholarships also aren't included in income. (See Chapter 2 for a detailed discussion of the types of income that are tax free.)

Support test. Finally, you must pay for over half the person's support during the year (unless there is a multiple support agreement as discussed below). This differs from the qualifying child test, which requires only that the child not provide more than half of his or her support, but doesn't require that the person claiming the exemption pay for more than half of such support.

Supporting someone else's child. As a general rule, a person can't be a qualifying relative if he or she is already someone else's qualifying child—for example, the child's parent. However, there is an important exception. A child can be a qualifying relative if the child's parent (or other person for whom the child is defined as a qualifying child) is not required to file an income tax return, or files a return only to get a refund of income tax withheld.

EXAMPLE: Alfred lives with his girlfriend Bonnie and her ten-year-old daughter Cordelia. Alfred provides all the financial support for their little household. Bonnie doesn't work and has no income. Alfred may claim a dependency exemption for Bonnie, and also for Cordelia, since her mother wasn't required to file a tax return.

Your Nonqualifying Child Can Be Your Qualifying Relative

A child who doesn't meet the test to be your qualifying child can still be your qualifying relative, which lets you claim a dependent exemption for the child. Take, for example, the case of the "boomerang child"—who's already grown up, but comes back to live with mom and dad. It's unlikely you could claim your boomeranger as a "qualifying child," because after age 23, the child would have to be totally and permanently disabled for this to work (not even being a full-time student counts). But a child of any age can be a qualifying relative if the support and gross income tests are met.

EXAMPLE: Sarita quits her job and returns home to live with her parents. She is 25 years old, so she is too old to be her parent's qualifying child. However, she meets the requirements to be their qualifying relative: Her total taxable income for the year is only $3,000, and her parents pay for almost all her support. Sarita's parents can claim a dependent exemption for her.

Are you really "supporting" those dependents?

When you're dealing with an older child or other person who has income, it can be hard to figure out (or prove) whether you actually provide over half that person's support. The support tests differ depending on whether a qualifying child or qualifying relative is involved. But for either test, you must first determine the total support provided for the person from all sources.

Total support includes amounts spent to provide food, lodging, clothing, education, medical and dental care, child care, recreation, transportation, payments to nursing homes, and similar necessities. Things you might not consider necessities may also be included, such as education, music and dance lessons, summer camp, wedding expenses, birthday expenses, toys, vacations, and entertainment such as movies and concerts. However, money used to pay taxes doesn't count as support.

Qualifying relative. You must provide more than half a person's support for that person to be a qualifying relative. You do this by comparing the amount you spent on the person's support with the entire amount of support he or she received from all sources. This includes support the person paid for with his or her own money, even if the person used tax-exempt income like Social Security. However, a person's own funds are not support unless they're actually spent for support. Money kept unspent in the bank or elsewhere doesn't count.

EXAMPLE: Your mother received $2,400 in Social Security benefits and $300 in interest. She paid $2,000 for lodging and $400 for recreation. She put $300 in a savings account. Even though your mother received a total of $2,700, she spent only $2,400 for her own support. If you spent more than $2,400 for her support and no other support was received, you've provided more than half of her support.

When you figure how much you spent for a person's support, include the fair market value of any property you give the person—for example, food and clothing. If you provide a person with a place to live, you are considered to provide support equal to the fair rental value of the lodging. Fair rental value includes a reasonable allowance for the use of furniture and appliances, and for heat and other utilities that you pay for.

EXAMPLE: Grace lives with her daughter, Mary, her daughter's husband, Frank, and their two children. Grace gets Social Security benefits of $2,400, which she spends on clothing, transportation, and recreation. Grace has no other income. Frank and Mary's total food expense for the household is $5,200. They pay Grace's medical and drug expenses of

$1,200. The fair rental value of the lodging provided to Grace is $1,800 a year, based on the cost of similar rooming facilities. They figure Grace's total support as follows:

Fair rental value of lodging	$1,800
Clothing, transportation, and recreation	2,400
Medical expenses	1,200
Share of food (1/5 of $5,200)	1,040
Total support	$6,440

The support Frank and Mary provide ($1,800 lodging + $1,200 medical expenses + $1,040 food = $4,040) is more than half of Grace's $6,440 total support. Grace, therefore, is a qualifying relative of Frank and Mary and they may claim a dependent exemption for her on their tax return.

If you're contributing to the support of a parent or other person you want to claim as a qualifying relative, you need to keep track of how much money you and they spend on their living expenses. Keep copies of bills, receipts, cancelled checks, and credit card statements. Your goal is to pay at least 51% of the person's total support for the year. If toward the end of the year you are at or below 51%, ask the person to stop spending his or her own money on as many support items as possible until the following year.

Qualifying child. You don't need to be able to prove that you provide more than half of the support for a qualifying child. All you need is proof that the child didn't pay for more than half of his or her own support.

As is the case with qualifying relatives, only money actually spent by a qualifying child on his or her support counts. Moreover, a child doesn't have to spend any money on his or her own support. Money a child keeps in the bank isn't counted, whether a child earns it from a job, or gets it as a gift or from investments. As a general rule, it makes no difference where a child gets the money he or she spends on support. It can be from a job (even if a parent is the employer), cash from parents or other relatives, school loans or other loans, or Social Security benefits. However, a scholarship received by a child who is a full-time student is not taken into account in determining whether the child provided more than half of his or her own support.

USA TODAY Snapshots®

Two-parent homes decline

Percentage of children younger than 18 who lived with two parents:

Source: National Fatherhood Initiative

By David Stuckey and Marcy E. Mullins, USA TODAY
2007

EXAMPLE: Jason is an 18-year-old college freshman at Podunk U. This year, he took out a $5,000 school loan to help pay his tuition, and he earned $5,000 from a part-time job, which he spent on his living expenses. Jason's grandfather gave him $5,000, but he spent only $1,000 of it. Jason's total contribution to his support for the year was $11,000. Jason's total expenses for the year included $20,000 for college tuition and another $5,000 for room and board and other living expenses. Because $11,000 is less than 50% of $25,000, Jason did not pay for over half of his own support during the year.

In close cases, remember that money you give a child does not count as support by you, but things you buy for the child do. For example, if you give your child $10,000 cash as a gift, it will not count as support you paid for even if the child later spends it for his support. But if you personally pay $10,000 of your child's college tuition, it will count as support you provided.

With lots of supporters, who gets the exemption?

Sometimes no person provides more than half of the support for a qualifying child or qualifying relative. Instead, two or more people, each of whom would be able to take the exemption but for the support test, together provide more than half of the person's support.

> EXAMPLE: Wilma is an 80-year-old widow with four children. Each of the children pays for 20% of Wilma's support, with Wilma paying the remaining 20%. Wilma meets the requirements for a qualifying relative, but none of her children pays for over 50% of her support, so none of them satisfies the support test for a dependent exemption for a qualifying relative.

So the question is: Who gets to claim the tax exemption? The people providing the support can decide who gets the exemption, but that person must provide over 10% of the support. Each of the others must sign a statement agreeing not to claim the exemption for that year. The person who claims the exemption must keep these signed statements as records. A multiple support declaration identifying each of the others who agreed not to claim the exemption must be attached to the claimant's tax return. IRS Form 2120, *Multiple Support Declaration*, can be used for this purpose. Each year a different member of the group can claim the exemption by changing the agreement.

> EXAMPLE: Wilma's children agree that Bob, her eldest son, should claim the dependent exemption for Wilma because he's in the highest tax bracket. They complete and sign IRS Form 2120, which Bob files with his tax return.

Phaseout of exemptions for high-income taxpayers

As your adjusted gross income grows over a certain point, your personal and dependent exemptions are gradually phased out until they're eliminated entirely. The following chart shows the phaseout income ceilings.

Phaseout of Exemptions for High-Income Taxpayers—2008		
Filing Status	Beginning of Phaseout	Exemption Fully Phased Out
Married, filing jointly	$239,950	$362,450
Head of household	$199,950	$322,450
Single (not head of household)	$159,950	$282,450
Married, filing separately	$119,975	$181,225

Calculating how much a phaseout of your exemptions will actually cost you has gotten a bit more complicated, because they're actually phasing out the personal exemption phaseout! It was cut by one-third for tax years 2006 and 2007, by two-thirds for 2008 and 2009, and will be eliminated entirely in 2010. However, the phaseout will be reinstated in its pristine form starting in 2011, unless Congress acts to eliminate it permanently. These scheduled changes are shown in the following chart.

Year	Phaseout
2006–2007	66.67%
2008–2009	33.33%
2010	0%
2011 and later	100%

You begin the phaseout calculation by reducing the dollar amount of your exemptions by 2% for each $2,500, or part of $2,500 ($1,250 if you are married filing separately), by which your AGI exceeds the amount shown in the first chart above for your filing status. You then reduce this amount by two-thirds (through 2009).

If you're in the phaseout range, but not too far above it, you can try to cut your AGI. For example, increase your contributions to your retirement accounts, such as a 401(k) or IRA. If you own losing stocks, you can sell them and deduct up to $3,000 of your losses from your AGI. See Chapter 1 for a detailed discussion of AGI.

Another strategy for high-income taxpayers is to ensure that a child fails the support test for the dependent exemption. This way, the child may not be claimed as a dependent by the parents, but may instead claim his or her own personal exemption, which is the same amount as the dependent exemption. The parents lose nothing because they couldn't have gotten a dependent exemption anyway (or would have lost most of it) because their income was too high. The child gets the full exemption instead. This would mean that in 2008, the child could deduct $3,500 from his or her income. The child will also be allowed the full standard deduction for singles ($5,450 in 2008). If the child is in college, he or she may also be able to claim the Hope or Lifetime Learning credits (see Chapter 3). ●

Help Beyond This Book

There are many resources available to supplement and explain more fully the tax information covered in this book. Many are free; others are reasonably priced. The more expensive tax publications for professionals are often available at public libraries or law libraries. And, a lot of tax information is available on the Internet.

Information From the IRS

The IRS has made a huge effort to inform the public about the tax law, creating hundreds of informative publications, an excellent website, and a telephone answering service. However, unlike the regulations and rulings issued by the IRS, these secondary sources of information are for informational purposes only. They are not official IRS pronouncements, and the IRS is not legally bound by them.

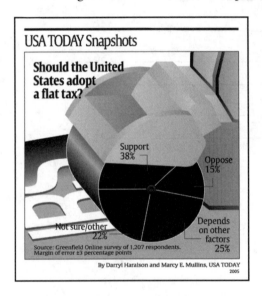

USA TODAY Snapshots

Should the United States adopt a flat tax?

Support 38%

Oppose 15%

Depends on other factors 25%

Not sure/other 22%

Source: Greenfield Online survey of 1,207 respondents. Margin of error ±3 percentage points

By Darryl Haralson and Marcy E. Mullins, USA TODAY 2005

Reading IRS publications is a good way to obtain information on IRS procedures and to get the agency's view of the tax law. But keep in mind that these publications present only the IRS's interpretation of the law, which may be one-sided and even contrary to court rulings. That's why you shouldn't rely exclusively on IRS publications for information.

IRS website

The IRS has one of the best Internet websites of any federal government agency. Among other things, almost every IRS form and informational publication can be downloaded from its site. The Internet address is www.irs.gov.

IRS booklets

The IRS publishes over 350 free booklets explaining the tax code, called IRS publications ("pubs," for short). Many of these publications are referenced in this book. Some are relatively easy to understand, others are incomprehensible or misleading. As with all IRS publications, they present only the IRS's interpretation of the tax laws—which may or may not be upheld by the federal courts.

You can download all of the booklets from the IRS website at www.irs.gov. You can also obtain free copies by calling 800-TAX-FORM (800-829-3676) or by contacting your local IRS office or sending an order form to the IRS.

IRS telephone information

The IRS offers a series of prerecorded tapes of information on various tax topics on a toll-free telephone service called TELETAX (800-829-4477). See IRS Publication 910 for a list of topics.

You can talk to an IRS representative on the telephone by calling 800-829-1040. (It's difficult to get though to someone from January through May.) Be sure to double-check anything an IRS representative tells you over the phone—the IRS is notorious for giving misleading or outright wrong answers to taxpayers' questions, and the agency will not stand behind oral advice that turns out to be incorrect.

Other Online Tax Resources

In addition to the IRS website, hundreds of privately created websites provide tax information and advice. Some of this information is good; some is execrable. A comprehensive collection of Web links about all aspects of taxation can be found at www.taxsites.com. Other useful Web pages that link to a wide variety of tax information can be found at:

- www.willyancey.com/tax_internet.htm
- www.abanet.org (at the bottom of the home page, click "Topics A-Z," and look for "Tax Tips," and "Taxation Section")

- www.natptax.com (click "Federal Tax Information," then "Tax Links")
- www.el.com/elinks/taxes.

Other useful tax-related websites include:

- www.accountantsworld.com
- www.unclefed.com
- www.smbiz.com
- www.smartmoney.com (click "Personal Finance," then "Tax Guide")
- www.taxguru.net.

Nolo's Website

Nolo's website, www.nolo.com, is full of free information for small businesses and the self-employed. The site contains helpful articles, information about new legislation, book excerpts, and an online store. The site also includes a legal encyclopedia (the "Nolopedia") with specific information for businesspeople, as well as a legal research center you can use to find state and federal statutes, including the Internal Revenue Code.

Tax Publications

A number of books (like this one) attempt to make the tax law comprehensible to the average person. The best known are the paperback tax preparation books published every year. Two of the best are:

- *The Ernst and Young Tax Guide* (Vanguard Press), and
- *J.K. Lasser's Your Income Tax* (Wiley).

J.K. Lasser publishes many other useful tax guides. You can find a list of these publications at www.wiley.com (search for "Lasser").

Tax guides designed for college courses can also be extremely helpful. Two good guides to all aspects of income taxes that are updated each year are:

- *Prentice Hall's Federal Taxation Comprehensive* (Prentice Hall), and
- *CCH Federal Taxation Comprehensive Topics* (CCH).

Nolo also publishes several books that deal with tax issues:

- *Stand Up to the IRS*, by Frederick W. Daily, explains how to handle an IRS audit.

- *Tax Savvy for Small Business*, by Frederick W. Daily, provides an overview of the entire subject of taxation, geared to the small business owner.

- *Working With Independent Contractors*, by Stephen Fishman, shows small businesses how to hire independent contractors without running afoul of the IRS or other government agencies.

- *Working for Yourself: Law & Taxes for Independent Contractors, Freelancers & Consultants*, by Stephen Fishman, covers the whole gamut of legal issues facing the one-person business.

- *Every Landlord's Tax Deduction Guide*, by Stephen Fishman provides detailed guidance on tax deductions for small residential landlords.

- *IRAs, 401(k)s & Other Retirement Plans: Taking Your Money Out*, by Twila Slesnick and John C. Suttle, covers the tax implications of withdrawing funds from retirement accounts.

- *What Every Inventor Needs to Know About Business & Taxes*, by Stephen Fishman, covers tax aspects of inventing.

Tax software

Today, millions of taxpayers use tax preparation software to complete their own income tax returns. The best-known programs are *TurboTax* and *TaxCut*. These programs contain most IRS tax forms, publications, and other tax guidance. Each has a helpful website at www.turbotax .com and www.taxcut.com, respectively.

Myth: e-Filing Your Taxes Makes It More Likely You'll Be Audited

Reality: Taxpayers have an equal chance of being audited whether they file a paper or electronic return, says Robert Marvin, a spokesman for the IRS.

In fact, e-filing could reduce your chance of an audit. Those who use tax software to prepare and file their returns tend to make fewer errors than paper filers, the IRS says. Paper filers are more likely to omit information, too. And when you leave stuff out of your return, you're more likely to draw scrutiny from the IRS.

 "10 financial myths," by Sandra Block, Kathy Chu, Christine Dugas, and John Waggoner, April 18, 2008.

Consulting a Tax Professional

Hundreds of thousands of tax professionals (tax pros) in the United States are ready and eager to help you—for a price. A tax pro can answer your questions, help you make key tax decisions, prepare your tax returns, and help you deal with the IRS if you get into tax trouble.

Types of tax pros

There are several different types of tax pros. They differ widely in training, experience, and cost:

- **Tax preparers.** As the name implies, tax preparers prepare tax returns. The largest tax preparation firm is H&R Block, but many mom-and-pop operations open for business in storefront offices during tax time. In most states, anybody can be a tax preparer; no licensing is required.

- **Enrolled agents.** Enrolled agents (EAs) are tax advisers and preparers who are licensed by the IRS. They must have at least five years of experience or pass a difficult IRS test. They can represent taxpayers before the IRS, and in administrative proceedings, circuit court, and, possibly tax court, if they pass the appropriate tests. Enrolled agents are the least expensive of the true tax pros, but are reliable for tax return preparation and more routine tax matters.

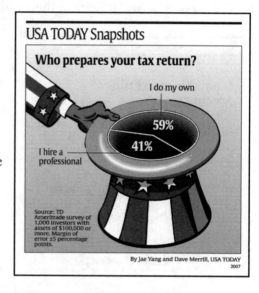

USA TODAY Snapshots

Who prepares your tax return?

I do my own **59%**

I hire a professional **41%**

Source: TD Ameritrade survey of 1,000 investors with assets of $100,000 or more. Margin of error ±5 percentage points.

By Jae Yang and Dave Merrill, USA TODAY 2007

- **Certified public accountants.** Certified public accountants (CPAs) are licensed and regulated by each state. They undergo lengthy training and must pass a comprehensive exam. CPAs represent the high end of the tax pro spectrum. In addition to preparing tax returns, they perform sophisticated accounting and tax work. CPAs are found in large national firms or in small local outfits. The large national firms are used primarily by large businesses. Some states also license public accountants. These are competent, but are not as highly regarded as CPAs.

- **Tax attorneys.** Tax attorneys are lawyers who specialize in tax matters. The only time you'll ever need a tax attorney is if you get into serious trouble with the IRS or another tax agency and need legal representation before the IRS or in court. Some tax attorneys also give tax advice, but they're usually too expensive for most individuals. You're probably better off hiring a CPA if you need specialized tax help.

Finding a tax pro

The best way to find a tax pro is to obtain referrals from a friend or business associate. If none of these sources can give you a suitable lead, try contacting the National Association of Enrolled Agents or one of its state affiliates. You can find a listing of affiliates at the NAEA website at www.naea.org. Local CPA societies can give you referrals to local CPAs. You can also find tax pros in the telephone book under "Accountants, Tax Return." Local bar associations can refer you to a tax attorney. Be aware that CPA societies and local bar associations refer from a list on a rotating basis, so you shouldn't construe a referral as a recommendation or certification of competence.

USA TODAY Snapshots®

It pays to be a certified accountant

Accountants who are certified earn 27% more than those who are not. Average salaries for accountants with and without certification:

No certification	$79,217
Certified public accountant	$98,600
Certified management accountant	$102,429
Both CMA and CPA	$107,120

Source: Institute of Management Accountants 2006 Annual Salary survey

By Jae Yang and Adrienne Lewis, USA TODAY 2007

Be picky about the person you choose. Talk with at least three tax pros before hiring one. You want a tax pro who takes the time to listen to you, answers your questions fully and in plain English, seems knowledgeable, and makes you feel comfortable. ●

Index

Get the Latest in the Law

Nolo's Legal Updater
We'll send you an email whenever a new edition of your book is published! Sign up at **www.nolo.com/legalupdater**.

Updates at Nolo.com
Check **www.nolo.com/update** to find recent changes in the law that affect the current edition of your book.

Nolo Customer Service
To make sure that this edition of the book is the most recent one, call us at **800-728-3555** and ask one of our friendly customer service representatives (7:00 am to 6:00 pm PST, weekdays only). Or find out at **www.nolo.com**.

Complete the Registration & Comment Card ...
... and we'll do the work for you! Just indicate your preferences below:

Registration & Comment Card

NAME _____ DATE _____

ADDRESS _____

CITY _____ STATE _____ ZIP _____

PHONE _____ EMAIL _____

COMMENTS _____

WAS THIS BOOK EASY TO USE?   (VERY EASY)   5   4   3   2   1   (VERY DIFFICULT)

☐ Yes, you can quote me in future Nolo promotional materials. *Please include phone number above.*

☐ Yes, send me **Nolo's Legal Updater** via email when a new edition of this book is available.

Yes, I want to sign up for the following email newsletters:

    ☐ **NoloBriefs** (monthly)
    ☐ **Nolo's Special Offer** (monthly)
    ☐ **Nolo's BizBriefs** (monthly)
    ☐ **Every Landlord's Quarterly** (four times a year)

☐ Yes, you can give my contact info to carefully selected partners whose products may be of interest to me.

Send to: **Nolo** 950 Parker Street Berkeley, CA 94710-9867,
Fax: (800) 645-0895, or include all of the above
information in an email to regcard@nolo.com with
the subject line "US-LOTX1."

US-LOTX1